TRUE STORIES OF NL.. ...
TO CANADA DURING THE OLD FRENCH AND
INDIAN WARS
BY
Charlotte Alice Baker

TRUE STORIES OF NEW ENGLAND CAPTIVES CARRIED TO CANADA DURING THE OLD FRENCH AND INDIAN WARS

Published by Firework Press

New York City, NY

First published 1897

Copyright © Firework Press, 2015

All rights reserved

ABOUT FIREWORK PRESS

<u>Firework Press</u> prints and publishes the greatest books about American history ever written, including seminal works written by our nation's most influential figures.

TO

THE MEMORY OF THOSE NUNS AND PRIESTS WHO SHELTERED AND PROTECTED OUR CAPTIVES IN CANADA AND TO THEIR SUCCESSORS BY WHOM I HAVE BEEN KINDLY HELPED IN MY WORK THESE NARRATIVES ARE AFFECTIONATELY DEDICATED

PREFACE

As often as I have read in the annals of the early settlers of New England the pathetic words, "Carried captive to Canada whence they came not back," I have longed to know the fate of the captives. The wish has become a purpose, and I have taken upon myself a mission to open the door for their return.

It is just fifty years since that indefatigable Antiquary, Mr. Samuel G. Drake, published at Boston his "Tragedies of the Wilderness." I offer these narratives as a modest sequel to the work of my illustrious predecessor.   c. a. b.

Cambridge, Mass. March, 1897.

CHRISTINE OTIS.A ROMANCE OF REAL LIFE ON THE FRONTIER AS TOLD IN THE RECORDS.INTRODUCTION.

The magnificent obelisks of Central America lay crumbling to decay in the thickets of Yucatan. The mines of the Mound Builder were deserted and silent. The eagle screamed undisturbed in the homes of the Cliff Dweller.

A race who possessed no traditions of these old civilizations held the soil of North America, when, from Greenland poured down a horde of those Norse pirates, whose name from time immemorial had been a terror to every land. The story of the first meeting of the white man and the red man on our shores is an interesting one. Let us read it from the sagas of the Northmen. They will be apt to tell it flatteringly to themselves.

In the year of our Lord 999, Leif the Lucky, son of Eric the Red, spent the winter in Vinland,—wherever that may be,— whether Nantucket, Narragansett, or Nova Scotia, we have as yet no ken. "Leif was a mickle man and stout, most noble to see; a wise man, and moderate in all things."

Apparently he had no encounter with the natives. Whether his mickleness, or his moderation and wisdom, had anything to do with this, the chronicler saith not. Now there was great talk about Leif's Vinland voyage, and Thorvald, his brother, thought the land had been too little explored. Then said Leif to Thorvald, "Thou shalt go with my ship, brother, if thou wilt to Vinland."

So in 1002, Thorvald and his men came to Vinland, to Leif's booths, and dwelt in peace there that winter. In the summer they sent the long boat along to the westward to explore. On the island they found a corn-shed of wood. More works of men they found not, and they went back to Leif's booths in the fall. "After that they coasted into the mouths of firths that were nearest to them. . . . . .and to a headland that

stretched out, and they saw upon the sands within the headland three heights. They went thither, and saw there three skin boats and three men under each. Then they divided the people, and laid hands on them all except one, that got off with his boat. They killed these eight, and then went back to the headland, and saw in the firth some heights, and thought they were dwellings. Then came from the firth innumerable skin boats and made towards them." Thorvald said, "We will set up our battle shields, and guard ourselves as best we can, but fight but little. So they did, and the Skraelings shot at them for a while, but they fled, each as fast as he could." Thorvald was killed.

Karlsefni came next, "And this agreement made he with his seamen: that they should have even handed all that they should get in the way of goods. They bore out to sea. . . . . .and came to Leif's booths hale and whole. . . . . .After the first winter came the summer,. . . . . .then they saw appear the Skraelings, and there came from out the wood a great number of men. At the roaring of Karlsefni's bulls the Skraelings were frightened and ran off with their bundles. These were furs and sable skins, and skin wares of all kinds.

Karlsefni had the doors of the booths guarded. Then the Skraelings took down their bags, and opened them and offered them for sale, and wanted weapons for them. But Karlsefni forbade them to sell weapons. He took this plan: he bade the women bring out their dairy stuff, and no sooner had they seen that, than they would have that and nothing more. Now this was the way the Skraelings traded: they bore off their wares in their stomachs; but Karlsefni and his companions had their bags and their skin wares, and so they parted. . . . . .Karlsefni then had posts driven strongly about his booths, and made all complete."

"Next winter the Skraelings came again, and were more than before, and they had the same wares. Then Karlsefni said to the women, 'Now bring forth the same food that was most liked before, and no other.' And when they saw it, they cast their bundles in over the fence. But one of them being killed by one of Karlsefni's men, they all fled in haste, and left their garments and wares behind. ' Now,' said Karlsefni, ' I think they will come for the third time in anger, and with many men.' It was done as Karlsefni had said, ...there was a battle and many of the Skraelings fell."

The whole story of the dealings of the white man with the red man is here in a nutshell. Thorvald goes ashore with his company. "Here it is fair," he cries, "and here would I like to raise my dwelling," but seeing upon the sands three boats, and three men under each, "this iron-armed and stalwart crew,"—thirty broad-breasted Norsemen, lay hands upon the helpless nine and kill them. One escapes to tell the tale.

A fight ensues, and Thorvald pays the penalty of his misdeeds. The savage has felt the power of the white man's weapons. He covets them. He comes the next year to Karlsefni with sable skins. . . . . .and wants weapons in exchange. Karlsefni wisely refuses. The women bring out the dairy stuff, and the simple savages trade. "They bear off their wares in their stomachs! " But Karlsefni had their bags, and their precious skin wares. So they part. The booths are palisaded. Winter brings the hungry savage once more to the white man's door. With reckless generosity he throws his bundles in over the palisade. Supplied with food in return, he is going peacefully away, when, for mere pastime, he is felled to the earth—killed by one of Karlsefni's men. His followers flee. They come back. There is a battle and many of them fall.

Here we might rest the ease of the red man versus the white man. But the evidence is cumulative against the latter. Columbus has left us an account of his reception by the "Indians," as he names them. Native and Spaniard were an equal surprise to each other. The savage thought that the ships of the strangers were huge birds, that had borne these wonderful beings down from heaven on their great, white wings. They were "friendly and gentle" to the new comers. Columbus gave them colored caps, beads and hawks bells, in exchange for twenty-pound balls of cotton yarn, great numbers of tame parrots and tapioca cakes. He coasted about the island in the ship's boat, and some of the natives swam after him, while others ran along on the shore, tempting him with fruits and fresh water to land. He speaks of them always as decorous, temperate, peaceful, honest, generous and hospitable. "They are very simple and honest," he says, "and exceedingly liberal with all that they have, none of them refusing anything he may possess, when asked for it, but on the contrary inviting us to ask them. They exhibit great love towards all others in preference to themselves; they also give objects of great value for trifles, and content themselves with little or nothing in return   A sailor received for a leather strap as much gold as was worth three
golden nobles, they bartered like idiots, cotton and gold, for fragments of bows, glasses, bottles and jars; which I forbade, as being unjust, and myself gave them many beautiful and acceptable articles,   taking nothing from them in return. . . . ..They practice no kind of idolatry, but have a firm belief that all strength, and all power and all good things are in heaven, and that I had descended thence. . . . ..Nor are they slow or stupid, but of very clear understanding. . . . . ..I took some Indians by force from the first island I came to. . . . ..These men are still travelling with me, and they continue to entertain the idea that I have descended from heaven, and on our arrival at any new place they cry out to the other Indians, 'Come and look upon beings of a celestial race,' upon which men, women and children . . . . ..would come out in throngs to see us,—some bringing food, others drink, with astonishing affection and kindness."

On every voyage Columbus carried back to Spain, men, women and children taken by force from their homes. Worse than that, he farmed out these poor children of the forest to the indolent Spanish colonists of Hayti, and they died by hundreds from ill treatment and overwork. Worst of all, to satisfy Spanish avarice, he sent great numbers of them to be sold as slaves in Spain for the benefit of that kingdom.

In 1498, Sebastian Cabot carried to King Henry the Seventh three savages as trophies of his discoveries in North America.

France had her share of the spoils. In 1524, John Verrazano, in his ship the Dolphin, reached the shore of Carolina. Fires were burning along the coast and the savages crowded to the beach making signs of welcome. The French were in want of water and tried to land, but the surf was too high. A sailor, carrying bells and other trifles, leaped overboard from the boat. His courage failed and he threw the trinkets towards the natives. The waves tossed him back upon the shore, and the Indians, snatching him from the sea, dragged him towards a great fire. The sailor shrieked with fear. His comrades in the boat gazed with horror, expecting to see him roasted and eaten before their eyes. But after tenderly warming and drying him they led him back to the shore, and stood aloof while he swam off to his friends. Shall I tell you how this kindness was repaid? Coasting north, a party of them landed. The natives fled to the woods. Only two women and half a dozen children remained, hiding terrified in the grass. These civilized Frenchmen carried off one of the babies and would have taken the younger woman, who was handsome, but her outcries made them leave her behind. There is no clue to the fate of Verrazano; it may be true, as Ramusio affirms, that on a later voyage he was killed and eaten by the savages.

Ten years later, Jacques Cartier sailed into the mouth of the St. Lawrence and bore away for France to tell the King he had discovered the northwest passage to Cathay. He carried with him two young Indians "lured into his clutches," says Mr. Parkman, "by an act of villainous treachery." I suppose "the greasy potentate," whose sons they were, loved his boys as well as any father loves his children, but the wild Indian was no more than a wild turkey to the European explorer, and both were constantly carried over as samples of the natural products of the New World. Cartier brought back the boys the next year to guide him up the river. He went up as far as Montreal, and coming back to Quebec his crew were smitten with scurvy. There he might easily have been cut off by the savages, but "they proved his salvation." He learned from them a cure for the distemper, and his crew were restored to health. "When the winter of misery had worn away," he seized Donnacona and his chiefs, to carry them back to the French court. Air. Parkman tells the story: "He lured them to the fort and led them into an ambuscade of sailors, who, seizing the astonished guests, hurried them on board the ship. This treachery accomplished, the voyagers proceeded to plant the emblem of Christianity. The cross was raised, the fleur-de-lis hung upon it, and spreading their sails they steered for home." Cartier came back once more, and told the natives that their chief, Donnacona, was dead, and the others were living like lords in France;—which information must have been very gratifying to them, under the circumstances!

In 1602, Gosnold visited the Massachusetts coast. The Indians traded with him valuable furs and "their fairest collars" of copper for the merest trifles. "We became great friends," says one of the party. "They helped cut and carry our sassafras, and some lay aboard our ship. . . . . . .They are exceeding courteous and gentle of disposition," . . . . "quick-eyed, and steadfast in their looks, fearless of others' harms, as intending none themselves. Some of the meaner sort, given to filching, which the very name of savages, not weighing their ignorance in good or evil, may easily excuse."

In 1605, Weymouth entered the Penobscot river. He gave the savages "brandy, which they tasted, but would not drink.". . . . . . .He had two of them at supper in his cabin, and present at prayer time. "They behaved very civilly, neither laughing nor talking all the time, and at supper fed not like men of rude education; neither would they eat or drink more than seemed to content nature." They carefully returned pewter dishes lent them to carry peas ashore to their women. As Weymouth "could not entice three others aboard," whom he wished to kidnap, he "consulted with his crew how to catch them ashore." Then they carried peas ashore, "which meat they loved" and a box of trifles for barter. "I opened the box," says an actor in this tragedy, "and showed them trifles to exchange, thinking thereby to have banished fear from the other and drawn him to return. But when we could not, we used little delay, but suddenly laid hands on them, and it was as much as five or six of us could do to get them into the light gig, for they were strong, and so naked as by far our best hold was by the long hair on their heads; and we would have been very loath to have done them any hurt, which of necessity we had been constrained to have done if we had attempted them in a multitude, which we must and would, rather than have wanted them, being a matter of great importance for the full accomplishment of our voyage." The chronicler after praising the country, thus concludes his relation: "Although at the time we surprised them they made their best resistance, ...yet, after perceiving by their kind usage we intended them no harm, they have never since seemed discontented with us, but very tractable, loving, and willing by their best means, to satisfy us in anything we demand of them. . . . . . .Neither have they at any time been at the least discord among themselves, insomuch as we have not seen them angry, but merry and so kind, as, if you give anything to one of them, he will distribute part to every one of the rest."

Mr. Higginson tells us that Weymouth's Indians were the objects of great wonder in England, and crowds of people followed them in the streets. It is thought that Shakespeare referred to them in "The Tempest" a few years later. Trineulo there wishing to take the monster Caliban to England, says: "Not a holiday fool there but would give a piece of silver. . . . . . .When they will not give a do it to relieve a lame beggar, they will lay out ten to see a dead Indian."

John Smith's disasters in Virginia were due to the disorderly conduct of his men towards the natives.

It is true that an Indian arrow was "shot into the throat" of one of Hudson's crew, but the chronicler who tells the tale, says they found "loving people" on their first landing; and the disgraceful debauch in the cabin of the "Half Moon," does not speak well for the conduct of the Dutch on that occasion.

John Smith narrates how Captain Hunt "betrayed" twenty savages from Plymouth, and seven from Cape Cod "aboard his ship, and most dishonestly and inhumanly, for the kind usage of me, and all my men, carried them with him to Maligo (Malaga) and there, for a little private gain, sold these silly savages for rials of eight." An old woman of ninety afterward told Edward Winslow, with tears and groans, that her three sons, her only dependence, were among the number.

The unscrupulousness of Morton's followers at Merrymount, who cheated, abused, and stole from the Indians, and sold them liquor and weapons, came near being the destruction of the Pilgrims.

It is an unwelcome task, while commemorating our ancestry who suffered death or a cruel captivity at the hands of the savage, to say a word in extenuation. I am no hero-worshipper. I find more shrewdness than saintliness in Massasoit's friendship. It was for him a choice of evils. I see nothing of statesmanship or valor to admire in Philip. No more do I think there is any basis for a wholesale denunciation of his race. We have seen how from Maine to Cuba the explorer was the aggressor. In later colonial times it was a poor schooling we gave the red man, and he did credit to our teaching. We know little of the savage before his contamination by the white man. Revenge belongs to the childhood of nations as well as to that of individuals. To love our enemies,—to do good to them that despitefully use us, is a hard feat even for an adult Christian civilization. If, as John Robinson wished, we had converted some before we had killed any, we should make a better show in history. That was a grim satire of old Ninigret, who told Mr. Mayhew, when he wanted to preach to his people, that he "had better go and make the English good first." We should not shrink from tracing effects to their causes. The Indian trader from Karlsefni to Richard Waldron, (I may say to the frontier agent of to-day,) was dishonest. He sold rum to the savage, and then fined him for getting drunk. Was it truth the Indian uttered, or a bitter jest on the diluted quality of the liquor, when he testified before the court that he "had paid £100 for a drink from Mr. Purchas his well?" The fine was not always crossed out when it was paid till the exasperated savage crossed it out with one blow of his hatchet, for which he had paid ten times its worth in furs. The Government was not always responsible, though the "Walking Purchase" and the murder of Miantonomoh are rank offences. Usually the frontier settlement suffered for the sins of individuals. There is no more striking illustration of this fact than the story of

CHRISTINE OTIS.

In 1623 some London fishmongers set up their stages on the Piscataqua river.

Passaconaway, the sagacious sachem of the Pennacooks, desirous of an ally against his troublesome neighbors, the Tarratines, urged more English to come. He gave them deeds of land in exchange for coats, shirts and kettles. The natives continued peaceable,—the whites fished, planted and traded unmolested. Feeling death approaching, old Passaconaway made a great feast, and thus addressed his chieftains: "Listen to your father. The white men are the sons of the morning. The Great Spirit is their father. Never war with them. If you light the fires His breath will turn the flames upon you and destroy you." Knowles, a tributary chief, whose tribe occupied the region round about the settlers on the Piscataqua, felt similar presentiments. Sending for the principal white men, he asked them to mark out and record in their books a grant of a few hundred acres for his people. The old sachem's son Wannaloncet, and Blind Will, successor to Knowles, determined to heed Passaconaway's advice, and keep peace with the whites, and the Pennacooks remained neutral through Philip's war. At that time Cocheco, now Dover, New Hampshire, was the main trading post with the Indians of all that region. Major Richard Waldron was the most prominent man of Cocheco. He held many offices of trust under the Government, and a command in Philip's war. He was naturally severe; was a successful Indian trader, and had the reputation of being a dishonest one. It was said that he did not cancel their accounts when they had paid him, and that in buying beaver he reckoned his fist as weighing a pound. Though

Philip's war began later in the Eastern country, it raged there with terrible ferocity, "where," says Mr. Palfrey, "from the rough character of the English settlers, it may well be believed that the natives were not without provocation." Troops were ordered out by the General Court of Massachusetts to subdue the eastern Indians, but the snow lay four feet on a level in December, and military operations were impossible. The Indians, pinched with famine from the severity of the winter, and dependent upon the frontier settlements for food, sued for peace through Major Waldron, promising to give up their captives without ransom, and to be quiet in the future. In July, 1676, Waldron, on behalf of the whites, signed a treaty with them at Cocheco. After Philip's death some of his followers fled to the Pennacooks. They were taken and put in Dover jail. Escaping, they incited some of the Maine Indians to renew their depredations. Two companies were sent to the East under Captains Sill and Hathorne. They reached Dover on the 6th of September. There they found four hundred Indians, part of them Pennacooks who had taken no part in the war; others who had been party to the treaty a few months before, and the rest, southern Indians, who, fleeing to the eastward after Philip's death, had been received into the tribes there. Why they were at Dover we are not told, but evidently with no hostile intent, as their women and children were with them.

The belligerent captains would have annihilated them at once, as their orders were to seize all Indians concerned in the murder of Englishmen, or who had violated the treaty. Waldron proposed a stratagem instead. Inviting the Indians to a sham fight the next day, having drawn the Indians' fire, the English soldiers surrounded and disarmed them. Wannaloncet and the Pennacooks were set free. The rest were sent to Boston, where seven or eight of the well-known murderers were hung, and the rest sold as slaves abroad. It is said that Major Waldron was opposed to the seizure, but regarded it as a military necessity. It is true that he might have been censured by his government if he had refused to obey its orders, but a strictly honorable man would rather have left his ease to the judgment of posterity, or have thrown up his commission, than to have committed so gross a breach of hospitality and faith. The Pennacooks looked upon his conduct as treachery. It was a time of peace. They had never broken faith with him. They were, as it were, surety for the good behavior of Philip's Indians and the rest. They never forgave him.

Thirteen years passed. Some of those who had been sold into slavery came back. The emissaries of Castine whispered vengeance. The opportunity for retaliation came to the Pennacooks, and a plot was laid for the destruction of Dover. In June, 1689, the Dover people began to be suspicious that the Indians were unfriendly. Larger numbers seemed to be gathering in the neighborhood than usually came to trade. Strange faces were noticed among them, and now and then they were seen eyeing the defenses. More than one friendly squaw hinted of danger to the settlers' wives who had been kind to them, but they were not heeded. "Go plant your pumpkins," cried Waldron to those who told him their fears, "I know the red skins better than you, and I will let you know soon enough if there are any signs of an outbreak."

Waldron, Richard Otis, John Heard, Peter Coffin and his son Tristram had each a garrison house at Dover at that time. Into these their neighbors who felt uneasy, retired to sleep. On the morning of the 27th of June, a young man rushed to Waldron's house and told him that the town was full of Indians, and that the people were thoroughly frightened. "I know the Indians well," replied Waldron with some asperity, "and I tell you there is no danger." That very morning, however, the following letter from Major Henchman of Chelmsford was received by Gov. Bradstreet at Boston:

June 23, 1689.

Honored Sir:—This day two Indians came from Pennacook, viz., Job Marainasquand and Peter Muckamug, who report that damage will undoubtedly be done within a few days at Piscataqua, and that Major Waldron in particular is threatened. The Indians can give a more particular account to your Honor. They say if damage be done, the blame shall not be on them, having given a faithful account of what they hear, and are upon that report moved to leave their habitation and cover at Pennacook. I am constrained from a sense of my duty, and from love to my countrymen, to give the information as above, so with my humble service to your Honor, and prayers for the safety of an endangered people,

I am your humble serv't,

Thos. Henchman.

A messenger was at once dispatched to Cocheco with a letter from the Governor and Council " To Major Richard Waldron, and Mr. Peter Coffin, or either of them. These with all possible speed."

The Governor's letter is dated June 27th, 1689. It informs Major Waldron of the receipt of Major Henchman's letter and tells him that "one Hawkins is the principal designer" of the intended mischief. That it is particularly designed against Waldron and Coffin, and that they are to be betrayed "on a pretention of trade." The Governor warns them to take "care of their own safeguard "and to report "what information they may receive of the Indians' motions." Unfortunately the messenger was detained at Salisbury ferry and reached Dover only after the tragedy was over.

Mesandowit, an Indian chief, took supper at Waldron"s house that night, as he had often before. During supper he said, half jestingly, "Suppose strange Indians come now, Brother Waldron ?" "I have but to raise my finger," replied Waldron, boastfully, " and a hundred soldiers will be at my command." Later in the evening two squaws applied at each garrison house for leave to sleep on the hearth before the kitchen fire. As this was no unusual request, it was readily granted, and they were shown how to open the doors in case they might want to go out during the night. Tristram Coffin alone refused to admit them. As Waldron was barring his doors for the night, one of the squaws quartered with him said to him, " White father big wampum ; much Indian come." Still unsuspicious, he retired to dream of the morrow's gains.

Just before dawn, at that hour when night is darkest and sleep is heaviest, the treacherous squaws rose softly in all the houses, and opening the doors, gave a long, low whistle. A dog at Heard's garrison answered with a furious barking, which awoke Elder Wentworth. He hurried down stairs. The savages were just entering. Pushing the oaken door back against them, the old man of seventy-three threw himself on his back and held it against them till help came. Bullets crashed through the door above his head, but the heroic old Puritan did not flinch and the garrison was saved. Placing a guard at Waldron's door, the waspish horde swarmed into his room. He sprang from his bed, and though over eighty years old, he drove them at the point of his sword, through three or four rooms. As he turned back for other weapons, they followed him and dealt him a blow with a hatchet, which stunned and prostrated him. With horrid threats, they ordered his family to get supper for them. When they were surfeited, they placed the old man in his arm-chair on the table and tortured him. They gashed him with their knives, screaming derisively, "Now we cross out our accounts." They cut off his finger joints and threw them in his face, asking with fiendish glee, "How much will your fist weigh now, Father Waldron ? " Finally as he fell fainting from his chair, they held his own sword under him, and death came to his relief. His daughter and his little grandchild, Sarah Gerrish, were taken captive, his son-in-law killed, his house pillaged and burned. The houses of Peter Coffin and his son were also destroyed.

Richard Otis, the blacksmith of Dover, occupied the next garrison house to Waldron's. He was of good family, and had removed from Boston to Dover in 1656. At the time of the attack he was well on in years, had married sons, and was living with his third wife, Grizel Warren, a young woman of less than half his years. She had borne him two children. Hannah, the elder, was about two; but the delight of her old father's heart, was his three months old baby, Margaret, fair as a summer daisy. Otis was shot dead as he was rising up in bed, or had reached the window, seeking the cause of the alarm. The savages killed his little daughter Hannah, by dashing her head against the chamber stairs. His wife and baby were dragged from their beds, and with more of his family, hurried with the other captives to the woods to begin the doleful march to Canada.

Meantime, all unconscious of these horrors, the Widow Heard and her sons, with her daughter and son-in-law, were returning from a day's trading at Portsmouth. The soft air of the summer night was heavy with the scent of the sweet brier; the frog croaked hoarsely from his solitary pool; an owl, scared from his hunting, flitted screeching to the woods. No other sound was heard save the plash of their oars as they rowed up the placid river, when suddenly on the midnight stillness, burst forth the awful war-whoop. Faster they plied their oars, not daring to think of the possible fate of kindred left safe in the garrison at morn. Silently passing a body of the enemy, they landed near Waldron's garrison. Seeing a light in a chamber window and supposing it put there as a signal of refuge to the English, they demanded entrance at the gate. No answer being returned, they shook and pounded the palisades, in agonized tones reproaching their friends within for not opening to them. At last one of the young men looked through a crack of the gate, and saw to his horror an Indian with his gun guarding Waldron's door. Despair seized them at the sight. Mrs. Heard sank fainting, and declaring she could go no further, ordered her children to leave her. After much entreaty, feeling that all would be sacrificed if they remained, they left her and proceeded to their own garrison. On the way they met one of Otis's sons, who told them that his father was killed. John Ham and his wife, Mrs. Heard's daughter, rowed rapidly down the river again, to give the alarm at Portsmouth. Meantime Mrs. Heard had revived a little, and dragged herself to the garden, hiding there among the barberry bushes. With the approach of daylight, she fled to a thicket at some distance from the house. A savage who had watched her, came twice to her hiding place, pointed his pistol at her and ran back with loud yells to the house, leaving her in safety. She recognized him as a young Indian, whom at the time of the seizure by Waldron, she had hidden in her own house and aided to escape. Thanking God for her preservation, she remained in her covert, till the enemy had retired with their captives. Then stealing along by the river, she crossed it on a boom, and reaching Gerrish's garrison, learned of the brave defence of her own house by Elder Wentworth, and of the safety of its inmates.

At eight o'clock in the morning, John Ham and his wife, spent with fatigue and anxiety, reached Portsmouth. A letter was at once written by Richard Waldron, Jr., still ignorant of his father's fate, to the Governor and Council in Boston, giving the facts so far as related by Ham. This letter was enclosed in the following :

" *To the Hon. Maj. Robert Pike of Salisbury—Haste post Haste:—*

Portsmouth, 28th June, 1689. *Honored Sir:*—We herewith send you an account of the Indians surprising Cocheco this morning which we pray you immediately to post away to the Honorable, the Governor and Council at Boston, and forward our present assistance, wherein the whole country is immediately concerned.

We are Sir your most humble servants,

Richard Martyn.
William Vaughn.
Richard Waldron,
Jr. Samuel Wentworth.
Benj. Hull.

This dispatch was received at noon by Maj. Pike, who immediately forwarded it to Boston with the following :

"*To the much Honored Syman Bradstreet, Esq., Governor, and the Honorable Council now sitting at Boston, these present with all speed—Haste, post Haste*" :—

Salisbury, 28th June, (about noon) 1689. *Much Honored:*—After due respect, these are only to give your honours the sad accounts of the last night's providence at Cocheco, as by the enclosed, the particulars whereof are awful. The only wise God, who is the keeper that neither slumbereth nor sleepeth is pleased to permit what is done. Possibly it may be either better or worse than this account renders it. As soon as I get more intelligence, I shall, God willing, speed it to your honours, praying for speedy order or advice in so solemn a case. I have dispatched the intelligence to other towns with advice to look to yurselves. I shall not be wanting to serve in what I may. Should have waited on your honours now, had I been well. Shall not now come except by you commanded, till this bustle be abated. That the only wise God may direct all your weighty affairs, is the prayer of your honours' most humble servant,

Robert Pike."

The post went spurring into Boston at midnight with Pike's dispatches, and the next noon an answer was returned to Portsmouth as follows:

"To Messrs. Richard Martyn, William Vaughan, Richard Waldron,

Boston, 29th June, 1689.

Gentlemen:—The sad account given by yurselves of the awful hand of God in permitting the heathen to make such desolations upon Cocheco and destruction of the inhabitants thereof. . . . . .arrived the last night about twelve o'clock. Notice thereof was immediately despatched to our out towns, and so they may provide for their security. . . . . .The narrative you give. . . . . . .was laid before the whole Convention this morning, who are concerned for you as friends and neighbors, and look at the whole to be involved in this unhappy conjuncture and trouble given by the heathen and are very ready to yield you all assistance as they may be capable and do think it necessary that (if it be not done already) you shall fall into some form. . . . . .for the exercise of government so far as may be necessary for your safety. . . . . .this Convention not thinking to meet under their present circumstances to exert any authority within your Province. Praying God to direct in all the arduous affairs the poor people of this country have at present to engage in, and to rebuke all our enemies desireing you would give us advice from time to time of the occurences with you.

Your humble servant,

Isaac Addington, Sec'y.

Per order of Convention."

Aid was at once sent to Cocheco, and the progress of events there may be seen from the following letter, dated

"Capt. Gerrish's Garrison House,

Cocheco, 5th July, 1689.

May it please your Honors:—On Wednesday evening Major Appleton with between forty and fifty men (most of Ipswich) arrived here accompanied by Major Pike, and yesterday morning with wt additional force we could make, marcht into the woods upon track of the enemy abt twelve miles to make what Discovery they could, but returned in ye evening without any further discovery save ye dead body of one of the captive men, they carried hence nor since at last

has any of the enemy been seen hereabout. . . . . .Doubtless the main body are withdrawn to a considerable distance.

Your most humble servants,

William Vaughan.

Richard Waldron."

While these things were transpiring, the hellish crew and their hapless prisoners were marching towards Canada. On the morning of the attack, a party of Cocheco men started out in pursuit, but, as usual, the enemy had divided their forces. The Cocheco party overtook some of them near Conway, and succeeded in recovering some, among them three of Otis's daughters. When the rest of the family reached Canada, we do not know. On their arrival, baby Margaret was at once taken from her savage captors by the priests, baptized anew, and under the name of Christine, given to the nuns of Montreal to be reared in the faith of the Romish church. When she was four years old, her mother was baptized into that church, with the name of Mary Madeleine, and the next October, married Mr. Philip Robitaille, "a French gentleman of Montreal in the service of Monsieur Maricom." It is probable that the little girl spent most of her childhood with the good nuns of Montreal, in the very heart of that religious community founded by Maisonneuve and his followers. She would have been fifteen years old when the Deerfield captives were carried to Montreal. As in her coarse serge gown, she passed with the nuns in and out of the old cathedral, good Mr. Williams may have seen her, and groaned in spirit at the sight. She must have been a girl of strong character, for she absolutely refused to take the veil, though persistently urged to it by priest and nun. As the next safest thing for the interests of the church, they married her at sixteen to a Frenchman of Montreal, named Le Beau. The following, translated from the parish records of Montreal, bears the autographs of the newly wedded pair, and of the bride's friend, Marie Joseph Sayer :

"On the 14th day of June, of the year 1707, after publishing one ban, and dispensing with the other two by permission from M. François Vachon de Belmont, Grand Vicar of Monseigneur, the Bishop of Quebec, I, the undersigned priest, officiating as curate of the parish of Ville-Marie, having obtained the mutual consent of Louis Le Bau, aged twenty-nine years, son of Jean Le Bau and Etiennette Loré, inhabitants of the parish of Boucherville in this Diocese, of the one part, and of Christinne Otesse, aged eighteen years, daughter of the defunct Richard hautesse and Marie Madeleine la garenne of the town of Douvres, in old England, now living in this parish, of the other part,—having married them according to the rites of our Holy Mother Church, in presence of the said Jean Bau, father of the bridegroom, of the Sieur Dominiqua Thaumur Surgeon, of Philippe Robitail Master cooper, father-in-law of the said bride. The aforesaid Jean Bau and Robitail have declared that they could not sign this certificate according to the ordinance."

Christine's husband may have entertained her with the story of Thomas Baker, an English youth, one of the Deerfield captives, who had tried to run away from Montreal that summer, and having been caught by the Indians, would have been burned at the stake, had he not escaped from his tormentors, and fled to the house of a Frenchman, who ransomed him.

The Governor had ordered him put in irons and closely imprisoned for four months, "and served him right," Le Beau may have said. *"Pauvre garçon,"* perhaps Christine sighed, for the story of Baker's adventures may have set her thinking of her own captivity, and she may have wished that she could go back to New England once more, and see the spot where she was born. These longings were probably dispelled, and Christine reconciled to her lot, by the births of her own three children. We hear no more of her until the arrival of Major Stoddard at Montreal.

Mr. Sheldon had returned in 1707, from his last expedition for the redemption of the captives, but many more English were still held in Canada, among them Eunice Williams, the eldest daughter of the minister of Deerfield. Accordingly in November, 1713, commissioners were again sent by Gov. Dudley to Canada to negotiate the redemption of Eunice and the other New England captives. At the head of the commission, was Captain John Stoddard of Northampton, son of the minister of that place. Mr. Williams accompanied him. Martin Kellogg, one of the Deerfield captives, who had finally escaped with Baker from Montreal, went as interpreter. There were three other attendants, of whom one was Baker himself. Both Kellogg and he had become noted characters since their flight from Montreal. He was Captain Thomas Baker now. The year before he had gone up the Connecticut river with a scouting party, crossed over to the Pemigewasset, and at its confluence with one of its tributaries—since called Baker's river,—he had killed the famous sachem, Wattanummon, without the loss of a man. Taking as much of the Sachem's beaver as the party could carry, he burned the rest and went down the Merrimac to Dunstable, and thence to Boston. The Council Records of the 8th of May, give his report of his proceedings and his application for scalp money. He produced but one scalp but prayed " for a further allowance for more killed than they could recover their scalps as reported by the enemy themselves." After some delay the General Court, willing to encourage and reward such bravery and enterprise as Baker had shown, allowed him and his company twenty pounds, " for one enemy Indian besides that which they scalped, which seems very probable to be slain." On the 16th of February, 1714, the commissioners reached Quebec. We have the record of their negotiations with the governor of Canada. De Vaudreuil assures them that all the captives are at liberty to go home; the more, the better, for him and his country; and his blessing shall go with them. He gives the ambassadors permission to mingle unrestrained with the English, and to have free speech with those in religious houses. Learning that the priests and some of the laity are terrifying and threatening the prisoners against returning, the commissioners complain to the Governor, who replies that he " can as easily alter the course of the waters as prevent the priests' endeavors." Finally, under the pretext that the captives have been naturalized by the King, he refuses to let any return except those under age. Discouraged by this unexpected obstacle, and in order to be nearer the captives, the Commissioners return to Montreal, arriving there on the 3rd of March, 1714.

Christine's husband had died a few months before. The young widow had doubtless heard of the presence of the ambassadors in the city, as they passed through to Quebec, and all her old longing for release returned upon her. While the naturalization question is pending, Mr. Williams, whose heart is occupied with Eunice's affairs, demands that" men and women shall not be entangled by the marriages they may have contracted, nor parents by children born to them in captivity." Christine sees here her chance. We may assume that she seeks an interview with the commissioners and tells them her wishes. Brave Captain Baker, a bachelor of thirty-two, is smitten with the charms of the youthful widow. He undertakes her cause. The Governor cunningly concedes that French women may return with their English husbands,—that English women shall not be compelled to stay by their French husbands,—but about the children he " will take time to consider." Christine now reciprocating the passion of her lover becomes doubly anxious to return. The Intendant and the Governor violently oppose her. By order of the former, the property of her deceased husband is sold, and the money is withheld from her. The priests bring their authority to bear upon her. " If you persist in going," they say, " you shall not have your children; they must be nurtured in the bosom of the Holy church." Her mother by turns coaxes, chides and tries to frighten her from her resolution. " What can you do in New England? " she says to her. " There are no bake shops there. You know nothing about making bread or butter, or managing as they do there." All this Christine confides to her lover, who kisses away her tears and calms her fears. If she will but trust to him, and go with him, he tells her, his mother shall teach her all she need to know, and his government will see to it that her children are restored to her. In the midst of his wooing, Captain Baker is sent back to Boston by Stoddard to report progress, and demand instructions. He was too good a soldier not to obey orders, though he would, doubtless, have preferred to make a short cut through the difficulties, by running oft the prisoners and taking the risk of re-capture. In his absence Christine secretly conveys her personal effects on board a barque bound for Quebec, intending to follow, and put herself under the protection of Stoddard and his party who have returned thither and are trying to collect the captives there. The Intendant orders Christine's goods ashore, and forbids her to leave Montreal. In vain the Commissioners protest. " She is a prisoner of the former war," replies the Intendant, " and cannot be claimed by the English under the present Articles of Peace." But " Love laughs at locksmiths," and when Captain Baker returns from his embassy and tells her that the good brigantine Leopard is probably then lying at Quebec, and that she must go with him, now or never, she does not hesitate. We have no record of her flitting, except the pithy sentence in Stoddard's Journal announcing Capt. Baker's return from New England, "bringing with him one English prisoner from Montreal." We cannot doubt that this one is Christine.

The anger of the Intendant, when he learned of her disobedience and escape, may be better imagined than described. De Vaudreuil used his most politic endeavors to get possession of her again, promising if she might be returned to Montreal, he would send her under escort by land to New England. Stoddard knowing the value of " A bird in the hand," refused to give her up. The Governor finally threatened if she went, to give her children to the Ursuline sisters and never let her see them again. But her lover triumphed, and she embarked with him for Boston, where they arrived on the 21 st of September, 1714.

On the Brookfield land records, Dec. 9th, of the same year, there is a grant of " upland and meadow " to "Margarett Otice, alias Le Bue, one that was a prisoner in Canada and lately came from thence, provided she returns not to live in Canada, but tarries in this province and marries to Captain Thomas Baker." Christine tarried and married. The advent of Captain Baker, with his foreign wife and her strange speech, and her Romish observances, must have made quite a sensation among the straight-laced Puritans of Northampton. Good Parson Stoddard took her at once in hand, however, and she became a Protestant, being rebaptized by him with her original name of Margaret. The birth of her first child by Thomas Baker, stands to-day on the

Northampton records as follows: "June 5, 1716, Christine Baker, daughter to Thomas and Margaret."

About 1717, Christine removed with her husband to Brook-field, Mass. Shortly afterwards her half-brother, Philip Robitaille, came from Montreal to visit her and worked a year on her farm. It was probably when he returned to Canada, that she undertook a journey thither, in the hope of getting possession of her children, but the Governor had kept his word, and she was deprived of them forever. In 1719, Captain Baker was the first Representative to the General Court from Brookfield. In 1727, he was tried at Springfield for blasphemy, on the following charge: " There being a discourse of God's having in His providence put in Joseph Jennings, Esq., of Brookfield, a Justice of the peace," Captain Baker said, ' If I had been with the Almighty, I would have taught Him better.' The verdict of the jury was " Not guilty." The same year Christine received a long and earnest letter from Monsieur Seguenot, the Seminary priest, who had been her former confessor at Montreal, urging her to return to Canada and to the Romish church. The letter being of course in French, and " written in a crabbed and scarcely legible hand," her husband advised her " to have it copied in order to get some person to answer it," in order to convince the priest of the folly of any further attempts to convert her. The letter came to the notice of an influential lady of Boston, who showed it to Governor Burnet and urged him to answer it for Christine, which he did.

"My dear Christine," the priest begins, "whom I may call my spiritual daughter, since I esteemed and directed you as such whilst   you had the happiness of making one of the family of Jesus, Maria, Joseph, Joachim and Anne,. . . . . .and that you, as well as Madame Robitail your mother, (whose confessor I have become,. . . . . .) were of the Number of about Two Hundred Women of the best fashion of Ville Marie, who then made up the mystical Body of that holy Association. I own also that all our Members of the Seminary, as well as all Mount Real, were edified with your Carriage, you being sober, and living as a true Christian and good Catholic having no remains of the unhappy Leaven of the irreligion and errors of the English out of which M. Mériel had brought you as well as your Mother, taking you out of the deep darkness of Heresy to bring you into the Light of the only true Church and the only Spouse of Jesus Christ."

"The Catholic Church is the only mystical Ark of Noah in which Salvation is found. All those who are gone out of it, and will not return to it, will unhappily perish, not in a deluge of Waters, but in the Eternal Flames of the last Judgment. . . . . .Who has so far bewitched and blinded you as to make you leave the Light and Truth, to carry you amongst the English where there is nothing but Darkness and Irreligion?" The priest goes on to appeal to her conscience, and to her love for her children in Canada, as incentives to her return. " Dear Christine," he says, " poor stray Sheep, come back to your Heavenly Father,". . . . . .own yourself guilty. . . . . .to have forsaken the Lord, the only Spring of the healing Waters of Grace, to run after private Cisterns which cannot give them to you. . . . . .hearken to the stings of your Conscience. . . . . .Read the two Letters I send you concerning the happy and Christian Death of your Daughter;   weigh with care the particular Circumstances by which she owns herself infinitely indebted to the Mercy of God, and the watchfulness of her Grandmother for having withstood her Voyage to New England, and not suffered her to follow you thither. Consider with what inward peace she received all her Sacraments and with what tranquility she Died in the Bosom of the Church. I had been her Confessor for many Years before her Marriage, and going to Quebec where she lived with her Husband peaceably and to the Edification of all the Town. Oh! happy Death! my dear Christine, would you Die like her as predestinated; come in all haste, and abjure your Apostasy and live as a true Christian and Catholick else fear and be perswaded that your Death will be unhappy and attended with madness and despair as that of Calvin was, and also that of Luther. . . . . . .Once more, dear Christine, return to this Land where you have received your Baptism and which I may say has given you Life. Prevail with your Husband to resolve on the same undertaking. The Holy church will on your abjuring your Errors receive you with open Arms, as well as Mr. Robitail and his Wife, your Mother. You shall not want Bread here, and if your Husband will have Land, we shall find him some in the island of Montreal. But if he doth not desire any, and hath a Trade, he shall not want for Work. But what is most essential is that you shall be here both of you enabled to work out your Salvation, which you cannot do where you are, since there you are not in the Mystical Ark of Noah, which is the Catholic church, in which your Daughter was bred and in which She died. . . . . .I await your answer to my letter, and am, dear Christine, entirely yours in Jesus and Marie.

SEGUENOT,

Priest of the Seminary at Ville-Marie, you know me very well. At Ville-Marie, the 5th of June, 1727·"

Gov. Burnet begins his reply as follows:

Boston, Jan. 8, 1728-9.

Madam :—I am very sensible of the Disadvantages I lie under in not being able to address myself to you under as endearing a Title as that which Mr. Seguenot takes to himself. But I don't doubt but your good sense will put you on your guard against such flattering expressions which are commonly made use of for want of good

Arguments." ..."Mr. Seguenot has proved nothing of what he should have done in that very place of his Letter where he seems resolved to muster up all his strength to overpower us. But because he has scattered several things up and down in his letter which might startle you, I will take the pains to go through it, from one end to the other, to make you feel the weakness and false reasoning of it."

The Governor then proceeds with calmness to refute the priest's assertions and expose his .specious arguments. He shows Christine how Christ gives "visible marks" by which his true followers may be known. "By this shall ye know that ye are my disciples if ye have love one to another," "which," says Governor Burnet, "can never agree to a persecuting church, as the

Roman is." He points her to Paul's description of false Christians in the Epistle to Timothy, "Of this sort are they which creep into houses and lead captive silly women; " and asks, "Would not anybody say that the Apostle points directly to those Confessors who pretend to direct the Consciences of the Ignorant and chiefly of Women in the Church of Rome? "

Alluding to the priest's offer of lands and work to Captain Baker, the Governor says, "It is hoped that Mr. Seguenot does this out of ignorance. But for Persons that know what it is to live in a free Country, to go and throw themselves headlong into the Clutches of an absolute Government, it cannot be imagined that they can do such a thing, unless they have lost their Senses." He concludes by telling her to send this letter to Canada and let it be answered, that she may see both sides, and "Fix on what is best for the salvation of your soul and the Happiness of your Life, which is the hearty desire, Madam of your unknown but humble servant." The Governor's letter, which was in French, together with that of the priest, was afterwards translated and printed in Boston.

By the sale of their Brookfield property to a speculator in 1732, Captain Baker and his wife became impoverished. They lived for awhile at Mendon, Mass., where we find Christine connected with the church,—and were for a short time at Newport, R. I., and finally removed to Dover, N. H. In the latter part of the year 1734, Baker's health gave out entirely, and the next year his wife applied to the Legislature for leave to keep a tavern for the support of her family.

"The humble petition of Christina Baker, the wife of Copt. Thomas Baker, of Dover, showeth: That your petitioner in her childhood was captured by the Indians in the town of Dover, aforesaid, (where she was born) and carried to Canada, and there bro't up in the Roman superstition and Idolitry. And was there married and well settled and had three children; and after the Death of her Husband she had a very Great Inclination to see her own country, and with great Difficulty obtained permission to Return, leaving all her substance and her children, for by no means could she obtain leave for them; and since your petitioner has been married to Capt. Baker, she did undertake the hazzard and fatieug of a Journey to Canada again, in hopes, by the interest of Friends, to get her children; but all in vain ! so that her losses are trebbled on her. First, the loss of her house, well fitted and furnished, and the lands belonging to it; second, the loss of considerable part of her New England substance in her last journey to Canada, and thirdly, the Loss of her children. Yet still she hath this comfort since her return, that she is alsoo returned into the Bossum of the Protestent church ; for such she most heartily thanks Almighty God. And now your petitioner, having a large family to support, and by the chances and Changes of fortune here, is Reduced to very low circumstances, and her husband past his Labour. Your petitioner ladely made her case known to several Gents in the Government of the Massachusetts, who out of a charitable Disposition did supply yo'r Petitioner with something to set her in a way to subsist her family; and also advis'd to keep a house of Entertainment, and the General assembly of that Government.................made her a present of 500 acres of land in the Province of Maine, and put it under the care of Coll. William Pepperell, Esq., for the use of your

Petitioner (exclusive of her husband's having anything to do with it.) Now your Petitioner by the help she hath had has bot a lot of land and Built a house on it on the contry Rhoade from Dover Meeting House to Cocheco Boome; and have Bedding and other necessaros fit for a Public House for Entertainment of Travellers, &c."

The former taverner, not keeping an orderly house, had been refused a continuance of his license by the Selectmen. Christine having submitted her plan to their approval, had applied to the Courts for a license. The judges, probably for political reasons, refused it to her, and renewed the license to the former inn-keeper.

The Legislature on hearing Christine's petition voted that her " prayer be granted,"—and she kept her house of entertainment at Dover for many years. Her husband died of "the lethargy" at Roxbury in 1753, while on a visit to some cousins there. Her mother, Madame Robitaille, died in Canada at the age of ninety, being bedridden the last years of her life.

Christine or Margaret Otis Baker closed her eventful life on Feb. 23, 1773, leaving a large posterity. "She lived," says her obituary, "in good reputation, being a pattern of industry, prudence and economy. She bore a tedious illness with much patience, and met death with calmness."

ESTHER WHEELWRIGHT.

In the first part of the decade immediately preceding the landing of the Pilgrims, two lads from the middle class of society, entered Sydney College at the University of Cambridge. Of these, the elder, John Wheelwright, was born on the Lincolnshire fens, not far from old Boston. His fellow student, Oliver Cromwell, first saw the light at Huntingdon.

While we have no record that either of these youths distinguished himself in his college studies, we have no scant testimony to the excellence of both in athletic sports. Cotton Mather says, that he had heard that "when Wheelwright was a young spark at the University, he was noted for a more than ordinary stroke at wrestling." Cromwell's biographer declares, that at Cambridge he was far "more famous for football, cudgelling and wrestling than for study."

Judge Bell, in his memoir of Wheelwright, quotes the Lord Protector himself, as being reported to have said, "I remember the time when I was more afraid of meeting Wheelwright at football, than I have been since of meeting an army in the field, for I was infallibly sure of being tripped up by him."

It was hardly to be expected that these pugnacious young athletes would have no convictions, or would prudently refrain from expressing their sentiments on subjects, that were at that time rending the political and religious world. As vicar of the little hamlet of Bilsby in Lincolnshire, John Wheelwright became recognized as a Puritan leader. Silenced for non-conformity, about 1633, Wheelwright naturally followed many of his Lincolnshire friends and neighbors to America, landing in Boston, May 26, 1636. Here he was warmly welcomed by his wife's[1] brother, William Hutchinson, and by Rev. John Cotton, to whose preaching in St. Botolph's church in old Boston, he had often listened.

Soon admitted to the church in Boston, the brilliant young Puritan divine became such a favorite with the people, that many wished him to be settled with Pastor Wilson and Mr. Cotton, as second teacher of the church in Boston. Cotton favored the plan, but Wilson and Winthrop opposed it, on the ground that Wheelwright, to a certain extent, shared the religious opinions of his sister-in-law, Anne Hutchinson. It was therefore decided, that Wheelwright should have charge of a new church to be gathered in what is now Quincy.

From this time on, the great Antinomian controversy waged fiercely. In March, 1637, John Wheelwright preached his famous Fast Day Sermon, that led to his arraignment by the General Court, to answer to the charge of sedition and contempt. In the strife that followed, Wheelwright showed that he had not forgotten that " more than ordinary stroke at wrestling," for which the youth had been famous.

At length the Synod, assembled at Newtown, August 30, 1637, declared, that eighty-two errors of doctrine were rampant, and making sad havoc among the Puritan flocks. This was the view halloo, for which the General Court was waiting, to set about hunting down the heretical wolves,—and soon they were in at the death.

In November, Wheelwright was disfranchised, and banished, with orders to settle his affairs, and be gone from the Patent, within fourteen days. To the added condition, that he should not preach again during his stay in Massachusetts, Wheelwright gave a scornful refusal.

It was a bitter winter. Beyond the Merrimac, the snow lay three feet on a level, from the 4th of November till the 5th of March.

The place of Wheelwright's sojourn during that dreary winter cannot be definitely stated, but as early as April, he had bought of the Indians the land at Squamscot Falls, now the site of Exeter, N. H. He was soon joined by several of his Massachusetts friends and parishioners. The land was cleared, a church gathered, wise regulations for self-government agreed upon, and all seemed prosperous, when the claim of Massachusetts to the region of the Piscataqua, " and the desire of some of the Exeter people to come under the jurisdiction of the Bay Colony, made it prudent for Wheelwright and his flock to seek a new home."

In 1641, some of the Exeter congregation got permission from Thomas Gorges, nephew of Sir Ferdinand, and Deputy-Governor of the province of Maine, to occupy the land between the Ogunquit and Kennebunk Rivers, from the sea, eight miles inland, and two years later, " Mr. John Wheelwright, minister of God's word, and others, " are granted absolute power, to sett forth any lott or bounds unto any man
that shall come to inhabit.".............

Thus the towns of Exeter, N. H., and Wells, Maine, were both founded by the Antinomian exile and his friends. As a pioneer in two frontier settlements, the athletic training of our Puritan preacher must have stood him in good stead. The historian of Wells, in speaking of the connection of the Rev. John Wheelwright with that town adds, " He left sons whose energies were instrumental in building it up, and giving it an influential position in the public councils;— men whose services were of immense benefit in those early days, when souls were exposed to the most severe tests of a true citizenship."

Samuel, son of the Reverend John Wheelwright, filled successively all offices of trust in the gift of his townsmen.

"In 1677 he was the representative of York and Wells. In 1681 he was one of the Provincial Council, and later he became Judge of Probate and of the Court of Common Pleas."

Picture the Wells of two hundred years ago. On a plateau, perhaps a mile back from the ocean, a narrow clearing, bounded on three sides by a vast and gloomy wilderness. A stony highway following the trend of the ridge. On one side of the road, a row of houses scattered far apart. Opposite, the rocky slopes descending, subdued by incessant toil, bear a scanty harvest of maize. Below, wide reaches of marsh, threaded by winding creeks, the haunt of countless wild fowl. The desert beach, and the sullen sea beyond. To York, the nearest settlement, a day's journey by the shore if the tide was right; if not, by any way that a man or horse could take.

With few exceptions, if we may credit its historian, the people of Wells, up to about the year 1700, were poor,— materially, intellectually and morally. Their houses were mostly of logs, daubed with clay. They had few personal comforts or conveniences. Their beds were of the cattail rushes, which they gathered from the marsh. Knives and forks, teacups and saucers, silver spoons, chairs, carpets and looking glasses, were luxuries almost unknown. Their food was of the simplest. They had milk, but no butter, and no tea nor coffee. Corn and such fish as they could catch, were the chief of their diet. The house of the richest man in Wells is thus described by the town historian: "The kitchen is also the sitting room and parlor. Looking around, we discover a table, a pewter pot, a hanger, a little mortar, a dripping pan and a skillet. No crockery, tin nor glass ware. No knives, forks, nor spoons,—not a chair to sit in. The house contains two other rooms, in each of which is a bed, a blanket and a chest."

This was the home of Edmund Littlefield, his wife, and six children between the ages of six and twenty. We cannot wonder at this condition of affairs, when we remember that the labors of the people were often interrupted by Indian attacks. Rather let us admire the unflagging energy and undaunted courage, with which, in the face of hardship and danger, they steadfastly held on to their territory. Poor and ignorant they may have been,—not of the highest morality according to our standard; but no peril could drive these brave settlers from their frontier post. Every hour their lives were in jeopardy. Again and again their fields were devastated, their houses burned, their neighbors butchered or carried into captivity, but not once was the little settlement wholly deserted.

From 1688 to the peace of Ryswick, [1697] a series of unprovoked and unjustifiable attacks was made upon our frontier, by the French, under the pretext of protecting the Eastern Indians, from encroachments by the English. To divert the Abenaquis, to prevent their being approached by the English with proffers of friendship, to keep the English to the west of the Piscataqua, and thereby to secure Maine as a part of Acadia, was the motive of these attacks. The instructions to Villebon on his appointment as Governor of Acadia, were to make the Abenaquis live by war against the English, and himself to set them a laudable example.

Admit that the blow struck at Pemaquid[1] in 1689, and at Casco in 1690, were the legitimate fruit of the pillage at Pentagoet in 1688,—no such justification can be offered for the butcheries at Kittery, Berwick, York and Oyster River.

In this border warfare, religious fanaticism was the strongest weapon of the French. If the Abenaki chieftain flagged, and seemed willing to listen to overtures of peace from the English, the exhortations of the mission priests of the Kennebeck and Penobscot, fanned the flame of war afresh. The scene at Father Thury's mission on the departure of these war parties was one of great religious excitement. The warriors crowded the chapel, seeking confession and absolution, as if going to certain death, and when these savage crusaders, hideous in fresh war paint, set out from the mission, headed by their priest, their women and children threw themselves upon their knees before the altar, and relieving each other by detachments, counted their beads continually from daybreak till nightfall, beseeching Jesus, the Saints and the Blessed Virgin, for protection and victory in the holy war. The infant towns of Eastern New England received a baptism of blood at the hands of the Abenaki converts, which was sanctioned and encouraged by their mission priests.

The French archives contain abundant authority for these statements, in the correspondence of those concerned, in the instructions of the government, and in the reports of officials.

We of to-day are not responsible for the unpleasant facts of history. They must be met without excuse or denial, without prejudice or passion. The evidence that the mission priests of the Abenakis were active promoters of the strife can no more be refuted, than the testimony against the Puritan ministry for their part in the persecution of the Quakers, and the horrors of the Witchcraft delusion.

The names of the Fathers Thury and Bigot are as truly and painfully connected with the tragedies of Pemaquid and Oyster River, as those of Cotton Mather and Pastor Wilson with the whipping, mutilating and killing of Quakers, and the hanging of witches. It was an age of intolerance. We may not judge the past by the standards of the present.

During the period I have mentioned, Maine had passed under the jurisdiction of Massachusetts, but though every English settlement to the east of Wells had been laid waste, (the survivors fleeing to Wells for refuge,) the authorities at Boston seem to have shown an indifference to the needs of that place. There were, however, valiant men in Wells, keenly alive to the perils of the hour, and ever on the alert to save the town, and defend the province. Conspicuous among them were Lieut. Joseph Storer and Capt. John Wheelwright. In the annals of New England there are no nobler names.

John Wheelwright was the son of Samuel, and grandson of the pugilistic Puritan, Rev. John Wheelwright. By his prudence, his energy, his fidelity, his bravery and his patriotism, he earned the distinction, of being "the bulwark of Massachusetts for defence against Indian assaults."

Letters abound in our archives, signed by Storer and Wheelwright, and other faithful sentinels on this outpost, entreating that they may not be left to perish, but that soldiers and ammunition may be sent to their relief, with money and provision for their support.

By their foresight, some houses were palisaded, and Storer and others built garrison houses as early as 1689. As these garrison houses are a feature fast disappearing from the face of New England, I may be pardoned for describing them. They were two stories in height, the upper story projecting a foot or two beyond the lower, small port holes being sometimes made in the floor of the projection, through which those within might fire down, or pour boiling water upon an enemy attempting to force an entrance through the door or windows below. There were also portholes in other parts of the house. Other garrison houses were built of hewn timbers, eight or ten inches square, laid horizontally, one over the other. The doors were of heavy plank, and often there were port holes for windows. Some of these houses had flankers, or watch towers, at two diagonal corners, from which one could see every part of the building. The principal garrison houses of the town were palisaded, and like the so-called "Old Indian House" in Deerfield, served as a refuge for the neighbors in any alarm;—and as quarters for the soldiers, sent for their protection. Storer's was the largest garrison house in Wells. For his heroic defence of Storer's house in 1692, Captain Convers was made Commander-in-Chief of all the forces in Maine.

In the midst of these troublous times, in the very year of the building of Storer's fort, John Wheelwright married Mary Snell and took her home to the little one story house, built by his grandfather, the Puritan preacher. It was probably palisaded at this time. Peace being nominally restored by the treaty of Ryswick, the people of Wells returned to their farms and went courageously to work; but peace was of short duration. By his acceptance of the throne of Spain for his grandson in 1700, the French king broke the solemn engagement made to William of England, in the two Treaties of Partition. His subsequent recognition of James Edward, the Pretender, as king of England, was a gross infringement of the treaty of Ryswick.

On the nth of June, 1702, Joseph Dudley returned to Boston as Governor of Massachusetts Bay. Within ten days after his arrival, he was formally notified of England's declaration of war against France. Fearing trouble from the Indians at the Eastward, he with a party of friends, went at once to Pemaquid, and received from the sachems of that region, promises of peace. Satisfied with this assurance, he returned to congratulate the General Court on the success of his journey, and to reiterate his demand for the restoration of the fort at Pemaquid.

The following extract from a letter of John Wheelwright to the Governor, dated Aug. 4, 1702, shows that the former had no faith in the words of the savages.

"Sir,—I understand that the Indians at the Eastward vearey redily Professed Great fidelity to yourself, and the English nation, with Great Promis of Peace and friendship, which Promises so long as it may stand with theire own Interest, I believe they may keep, and no longer, their teachers Instructing them that there is no faith to be kept with Hereticks, such as they account us to be, themselves allso being naturaley deseatful......... I having Experienced so mutch of their horable deseatfulness in the Last war, upon many treaties of Peace, so that I cannot but apprehend ourselves that live in these remote parts of the countrey, and being frontires, to be in Great Danger, and considering that war was Proclaimed with the French...... who may send out an army against us............ this town being the nearest to the Enemy, our Inhabitants doth therefore Pray, that your Excelency would assist us with sum men twenty or thirtie, or so many as your Excellency in Wisdom may think fit."

Wheelwright goes on to ask for the "Liberty of a Garrison [house] Informing your Excellency that if I must remove into the middle of the town, I must leave that Little Estate I have to maintain my Family with, and Carey a large Family where I have but little to maintain them withall."

Six or seven of their eleven children had already been born to John Wheelwright and Mary Snell, and the little one story house at the Town's End, being in an exposed and isolated situation, and now too small for his increasing family, Wheelwright asked the consent and help of the government to build a substantial garrison house, not only for the safety of his own family, but as a refuge in case of attack, for his nearest neighbors.

Storer and Wheelwright, being the leading men of the town, were licensed as retailers of beer and strong liquors, and their houses served as ordinaries or taverns for the public. "In those days," sighs the historian of Wells, "public houses were not always nurseries of virtue." It is a hint of the morals of the times, that both Storer and Wheelwright were "indicted for keeping Keeles and bowls at their houses contrary to law.'' Perhaps the ordinary was not an unmixed evil. Ministers and judges put up here, in their journeys from place to place, bringing the latest news from other parts. Courts were held here. Here the town officers met to deliberate, and the men of the village gathered here for. social chat and pastime. Commissioners, referees and executors met in the "foreroom" of the ordinary, to lay out roads, decide disputes, and settle estates. Rum was a necessity of life in those days, and the flip and toddy, mixed by John Wheelwright on such occasions, was scored against the town, the man, or the estate, whose business was there transacted. To the boys, who had neither books, nor games, nor school, the ordinary was amusing, and I have not a doubt, that little Esther Wheelwright stole away now and then from her busy mother, to look on at the games. We may fancy her with her closely cropped head, her Puritan cap and homespun frock, clapping her baby hands and shouting in glee at a ten strike with the bowls and keels, made by some gaunt frontiersman.

Early in June, 1703, Dudley was notified by the Governor of New York, that the French and Indians were preparing for an attack on Deerfield. Whereupon Dudley invited the Abenaqui sachems to a conference at Casco. Thither he repaired with a splendid retinue on the 20th of June, and there to meet him, came all the famous sachems of the time. For the Norridgewocks there was that loup-garou Hopehood, excelling all other savages in cruelty,— and Moxus the braggart, and Adiawando, for the Pennacooks, and Wattanummon, for the Pequawkets, and Bomazeen, the crafty, for the Kennebecks, and Wanungunt, for the Penobscots. The Governor tells them that commissioned by his victorious Queen, he has come as to friends and brothers, to reconcile all differences since the last treaty. After a solemn pause, their Interpreter replies:

"Brother,—the clouds fly and darken, yet we still sing the songs of peace. As high as the sun is above the earth, so far are our thoughts from war, or from making the least breach between us."

After an interchange of gifts, both parties cast more stones on the mounds heaped up at a former treaty and called the Two Brothers, to signify fraternal love existing between the English and Abenakis. At this memorable council, Captain Samuel, a savage of great renown, who was most officious in trying to lull the fears of the English, said: "Several missionaries have come among us, sent by the French Fryars to break the peace between the English and us, yet their words have made no impression on us. We are as firm as the mountains and will so continue as long as the sun and moon endure."

Parting volleys were fired on both sides, and Dudley retired, believing that present danger was averted from Deerfield and the whole frontier. His satisfaction with this remarkable love feast, must have been somewhat lessened by the presence of Mesambowit and Wexar for the Androscoggins, who though "seemingly affable and kind, came with two hundred and fifty men in sixty five canoes, well-armed and gaudily painted,"—by the late arrival of Wattanummon, who purposely lingered, as was afterwards said, expecting a re-enforcement of two hundred French and Indians, with whom they were to fall upon the English,—and by the discovery at the parting salute, that the guns of the savages were charged with ball.

Not two months had passed since the treaty of Casco, when one midsummer day, six or seven bands of French and Indians fell upon the scattered settlements. Charlevoix says calmly, "They committed some trifling ravages, and killed about three hundred men, but the essential point was to engage the Abenakis, in such a manner, that to retract would be impossible."

Wells, Winter Harbor, Spurwink, Cape Porpoise, Searboro, Saco, Perpooduck and Casco were attacked. "At Hampton," says the chronicler, "they slew four besides the Widow Mussey, a remarkable speaking Quaker and much lamented by that sect."

At Haverhill, in February, Joseph Bradley's garrison house was attacked. Goodwife Bradley, " perceiving the misery that was attending her, and having boiling soap on the fire, scalded one of them to death." She was carried captive for the second time. Her husband attended Ensign Sheldon, on his second expedition to Canada, and Goody Bradley and James Adams of Wells were two of the forty-four captives redeemed on that expedition.

The merciless fusillade on our frontier began Aug. 10, 1703, at Wells in the east and virtually ended Feb. 29, 1703-4, at Deerfield in the west. Thenceforth the lines of the lives of the captives of both towns, often cross each other.

Wells, having successfully resisted the assault of 1692, became the special object of savage fury. Anticipating victory at that time, Cotton Mather says: "They fell to dividing persons and plunder ....Such a gentleman should serve such an one, and his wife be maid of honor to such a squaw, and Mr. Wheelwright, instead of being the worthy Counsellor he now is, was to be the servant of such a netop." The capture of Wheelwright was a much coveted prize.

The tragedy which began at Wells at nine o'clock on the morning of Aug. 10, 1703, ended in the capture or death of thirty-nine of the inhabitants. Wheelwright's house being at the eastern end of the village, was probably one of the first attacked. His little daughter Esther, then seven years old, was captured. The intrepid Storer was also bereft. His daughter Mary, aged eighteen, was among the captives. One longs to know what followed. Was there pursuit ? Whither were the captives hurried, and how did it fare with them on the retreat? Alas! no echo from the past replies. We may assume that Mary Storer and Esther Wheelwright were kindly treated by their savage captors, who knew the value of their prize, and doubtless expected a large sum for the ransom of the two girls.

In gloom and despair, the meagre harvest was gathered that autumn by the survivors at Wells.

Drearily the winter settled down,—joylessly came planting time again, and a second harvest was garnered, before the veil of silence and suspense, that hung over the fate of the captives was lifted. Then came a letter from Samuel Hill, dated Canada, Oct. 4, 1704, with assurances of the safety of his family, and that of his brother Ebenezer. Meantime Deerfield had been sacked, and in the December, following Hill's letter, Ensign Sheldon of that town set out for Canada. The hearts of all the New England captives there were cheered by the news of his arrival. On the 29th of March, 1705, while in Quebec, he received from his son's wife, Hannah Chapin of Springfield, then a captive in Montreal, a letter enclosing the following, from James Adams, a Wells captive:

" I pray giue my Kind loue to Landlord Shelden, and tel Him that i am sorry for all his los. I doe, in these few lins showe youe, that god has shone yo grat Kindness and marcy. In carrying youre Daighter Hanna and Mary in partickeler, through so grat a jorney far beiend my expectation, noing How Lame they was; the Rest of yore children are with the Indians,—Rememberrance hues near cabect, Hannah also Liues with the french, Jn in the sam house i doe."

In reply to his daughter's letter Mr. Sheldon says: "My desire is that Mr. Addames and you, wod doe al you can with your mistres that my children mite by redemed from the indanes."

Shortly after this, on the 2nd of April, 1705, the captive Samuel Hill, was sent on parole to Boston, as Interpreter with De Vaudreuil's reply to Dudley's proposal for exchange of prisoners, which proposal John Sheldon had carried to Canada. Hill visited his friends in Wells, while on this embassy, and was probably the bearer of the following letter from his brother Ebenezer:
"Quebec March 1705.
Cousin Pendleton Fletcher of Saco, Mary Sayer, brother Joseph's daughter, and Mary Storer of Wells, with our other friends and neighbors here, are all well. Myself, wife and child are well. Pray that God may keep, and in due time deliver us.
                                Your loving brother and sister,
Ebenezer and Abiah Hill."

Never was the sea so blue,—never did the waves leap so gaily to the shore,—never was the sky so fair, or the air so soft, or the scent of the pines so sweet, as when the news of that letter spread from door to door at Wells. For nearly two years they had mourned their loved ones as dead, when the glad tidings comes that "Cousin Fletcher and Mary Sayer and brother Joseph's daughter and Mary Storer and other friends and neighbors as if named, are well." All was joy in Storer's garrison. In Wheelwright's, not joy, but hope revived, and yearning more intense, and resolve strengthened, to find and rescue Esther if alive.

But where was Esther? Clearly the Hills and James Adams were ignorant of her fate,—but how did this child elude the sharp eyes of John Sheldon, and the vigilance of De Vaudreuil?

Far away in the .depths of the forest, to the head waters of the Kennebec, the Abenaki wolf had swiftly fled with the bleating lamb thus snatched from the fold. There, in one of the Abenaki villages of Father Bigot's mission, Esther lived in the wigwam of her tawny master, an object of wonder to his children, of jealousy, perhaps, to his fierce squaw.

The days lengthen into weeks,—the weeks to months, and these to years, when one day as he is making his arduous round from village to village, baptizing, catechizing, confessing his converts, Father Bigot sees a little girl, whose pale face, shrinking manners and tattered garments, show her to be of different race from the bold, dusky, naked rabble around her. He calls her to him. He speaks to her, perhaps, an English word. She does not answer. She has lost her childhood's speech. He sends for her savage master, and learns that she is Wheelwright's child. "'The English rose is drooping," says the priest, "the forest life is too hard for her." He will "transplant her to Canada, where she will thrive better under the nurture of the gentle nuns." "The little white flower must not be plucked up," says the Indian, "let her grow up among the pine trees, to deck by and by, the wigwam of some young brave." On each return of the priest to the village, this discussion is renewed, but neither promise nor threat can move the sullen savage.

The lot of the little captive is easier from that day. The Indian knows it is in the power of his Great Father the French Governor, to take the child from him, and he tries by kindness to win her to stay. The priest spares no pains to teach her, and the intelligent child quickly responds to his efforts. Soon she can say her *credo* and her catechism in French, as well as in Abenaki. Only she finds it hard that even Father Bigot does not seem to understand her when she talks about her mother, and her brothers and sisters. And if she asks when her father will come for her, her master is angry and the priest frowns. Meantime De Vaudreuil is informed by Father Bigot of the hiding place of the child, and in some way or other, the news reaches Boston, that Esther Wheelwright, long since given up by her parents as dead, is alive.

On the 23rd of April, 1708, Lieut. Josiah Littlefield of Wells, while on his way to York, was captured and carried captive to Canada, arriving at Montreal on the 3rd of June. Soon after, he writes as follows:

''Dear and loving children, my kind love ....to you all,   and to my brother and sister ....and to all my friends att Wells   I have liberty granted to me to rite to my friends, and to the governor, and for my redemtion and for Wheelrite's child to be redeemed, by two Indens prisoners. . . . . .with the English ....and 1 have been with the Governor this morning, and hee have promised, that if our governor will send them, that wee shall be redeemed, for the governor have sent a man to redeem Wheilerites child, and do looke for him in now every day with the child to Moriel where I am, and I would pray Whilrite to be very brief in the matter, that we may come home before winter, for we must come by Albany, and I have allso acquainted our gofnear Dedly with the same."

In a postscript to another letter, written at the same time, Littlefield writes:

"Mary Storar is well and Rachel Storer is well, and Storar is well and Mary Austin of York is well. I pray you charge Wheelright to be mindful   consearning our redemption."

We need no assurance, that a demand was at once made by Dudley, upon the French Governor, for the release of Esther Wheelwright. After much trouble, Father Bigot succeeds in buying the English rose from the Abenaqui sachem. In. the autumn of 1708, he transplants her to Quebec, where she is kindly welcomed by the Governor and his wife, who received her into their own household. From the squalor and rags of the wigwam on the Kennebec, to the luxury of the Château Saint Louis, what a contrast!—What are the thoughts of the twelve years old girl? Have the five years of forest life blotted out her remembrance of the little house at the town's end at Wells? She has learned to love Père Bigot as her kindest friend and father. To priest and child alike, the parting must have been painful. Does she console herself with the belief that she is now to be restored to home and friends, or is she dazzled and pleased by her surroundings?

No effort seems to have been made by De Vaudreuil to restore Esther to her parents. Madame la Marquise, his wife, having received an appointment as assistant-governess to the royal children at the French Court, decides to place her eldest daughter, Louise, with Esther in the boarding school of the Ursuline Convent.

"The 18th of January, 1709, says the Register of the Convent, "Madame la Marquise brought us a little English girl, as a pupil. She is to pay 40 *écus.*"

The names of Louise de Vaudreuil and Esther Wheelwright stand side by side on the list of pupils at the *pension* of the Ursulines at Quebec. Thanks to Father Bigot, shortly after entering the school, Esther took her first communion "with angelic fervor." Beloved by the sisters, and happy in her convent home, Esther expressed a strong desire to become a nun. "But," says the annalist of the Ursulines, "the Marquis who considered himself pledged to restore her to her family, would not hear a word to this, and took her home

with his daughter to the château." A political prisoner of such importance, could not be permitted to immure herself in a convent. Graceful, amiable, modest, Esther won all hearts at the château, as before at the convent,—but her life for the next two years must have been restless and unhappy. It was a time of much negotiation between the two governments, concerning a general exchange of prisoners. During this business, Esther accompanied De Vaudreuil to Three Rivers and Montreal. At Three Rivers she stayed with the Ursulines, and at Montreal, in the cloisters of the Hôtel-Dieu. On Saturday, Oct. 3, 1711, while at Montreal, she was godmother at the baptism of Dorothée de Noyon, infant daughter of Abigail Stebbins, a Deerfield captive, and signed her name in a handsome handwriting in the parish register, with Father Meriel, and the son of the Baron of Longueil.

In June, 1712, the French Governor proposed that our captives be brought from Canada into or near Deerfield, and French prisoners sent home from thence. Two of the French in our hands, absolutely refusing to return to Canada, young Samuel Williams set out from Deerfield with the others on the 10th of July, returning to Boston in September, with nine New England captives.

The absence of Madame de Vaudreuil in Europe, making it inconvenient for the Governor to keep Esther with him at the château, he yielded at last to her entreaties to be allowed to go back to her Ursuline mothers. Fostered by the atmosphere of the convent, a religious exaltation took possession of her soul.—"One thought alone," says the annalist, "occupied her mind,—the preservation of her faith and the salvation of her soul." On the second of October, 1712, on the festival of Saint Ursula, she began her novitiate as an Ursuline nun. On the third of January, 1713, she took the white veil. The joy of Father Bigot in seeing his *protégée* arrayed as the "bride of Jesus" knew no bounds. He insisted on defraying the expenses of the- occasion, and preached to the multitude assembled to witness the ceremony, a sermon glowing with feeling and eloquence. From the text, "Thy hand shall lead me and thy right hand shall hold me," the priest shows Esther the hand of Providence in every event of her life.

"Dear sister," he says, "in these words the Psalmist seems to me to have expressed as in a picture the story of your life. . . . .Hell! Profane world!—in vain do you array your strongest batteries against God's elect. . . . . His right hand shall hold them   By what marvels of God's goodness do you find yourself to-day, my sister, happily transplanted from a sterile and ingrate land, where you would have been the slave of the demon of heresy, to a land of blessing and promise, where you are about to enjoy the sweet freedom of the children of God."

The priest admonishes the nuns, that they should be inspired with the more tenderness for this young stranger, from the fact that their Immortal Bridegroom went so far to seek her.

Turning again to Esther he cries, "Are you not, my dear Sister another little Esther to whom a harsh captivity is about to open the door to the throne, not of a powerful Ahasuerus,—but of the Master of Ahasuerus—the Lord of Lords and King of Kings. To Him and for Him, she is led in triumph, and if this triumph seems to you to have nothing of the magnificence of a marriage festival,—if instead of joyful acclamations and the harmony of musical instruments, nothing is heard but the confused and fierce yells of savage warriors, none the less is it a triumph for her the last scene of which is represented to-day, when she stands about to be clad in the livery of the Divine Bridegroom." He depicts with pathos the sorrow of Esther's childhood, "snatched from all that was dearest to you, following your savage masters with unequal footsteps, by paths difficult beyond the conception of all who have not experienced them as you and I have my dear Sister." He repeats to her the sorrowful circumstances m which he found her, in order to prove to her that in all her perils, privations and sufferings, she had been uplifted and led by the hand of God.

Alluding to her reluctance to leave the convent at the Governor's command, and to the year of absence so full of doubt, suspense, anxiety and grief to her, he bursts into this invocation: "Oh my God! to whom nothing is unknown, that transpires in this vast universe, wilt Thou be insensible only to the sorrowful adventures of a young stranger, so worthy of Thy care and who seems destined for such great things?— Didst Thou seek her in the very midst of heresy, and stir up so great a tumult to carry her away from her native land, only to see her snatched from Thee now? Hast Thou led her into this country, only to let her taste a happiness she may never attain? Hast Thou shown her the inestimable prize, only to make her regret its loss more bitterly? No! no! dear sister,—You cannot escape from the hand of your God. All obstacles are removed. Nothing stands in the way of your happiness. So long as you were not of an age to dispose of yourself, Providence suspended the natural tenderness of your father and mother, and abated the eagerness of their first pursuit of their child.

Now that the law makes you mistress of yourself, they can no longer oppose the choice you have made of a holy religion, and a condition of life which they disapprove, only because they know not its excellence or its sanctity."

In April following the Treaty of Utrecht, Captain John Schuyler arrived in Canada as ambassador for a general exchange of prisoners. Later in the year, Reverend John Williams and Captain John Stoddard were in Canada on a similar errand.

By all these envoys, a special demand was made for the release of Eunice Williams, and doubtless for Wheelwright's daughter; and Esther received pressing letters from her family urging her return. This is the first record of letters to Esther from her family, but her resolution to become a nun was unshaken by them. However, lest stronger temptation should assail the young novice, and at her most urgent entreaties, it was thought best to shorten her term of probation, the circumstances being considered by all, sufficiently extraordinary to warrant this exception to their rules,—the only one of the kind ever made by the Ursulines of Quebec. Whether the Governor wholly approved of this proceeding, or whether in this instance, the state succumbed to the church, we have no means of knowing.

On the morning of the 12th of April, 1714, the Marquis de Vaudreuil with his brilliant suite,— the Bishop of Canada and the dignitaries of the church, in all the splendor of their priestly vestments,—with all the beauty and fashion of Quebec, assembled in the church of the Ursulines, which was decorated as if for the grandest festival. There Esther Wheelwright was invested with the black robe and veil of their order, by the Sisters of Saint Ursula, and the young New England captive, known thereafter as Mother Esther Marie Joseph of the Infant Jesus, serenely turned her face away forever from her childhood's home and friends.

A quarter of a century passes before the curtain rises again on Esther Wheelwright.

It is just one hundred years since the Ursuline, Marie de l'Incarnation, and her sister nuns landing at Quebec from a little boat "deeply laden with salted codfish, on which uncooked, they had subsisted for a fortnight,............   fell prostrate, and kissed the sacred soil of Canada."

Just a hundred years, too, since the Puritan exile, John Wheelwright formed with his companions at Exeter, that remarkable Combination for self-government.

It is the year of our Lord, 1739. For a year by prayer and penance extraordinary, the Ursulines of Quebec, have been preparing themselves with rapturous devotion to celebrate worthily the centennial anniversary of their foundation.

At midnight the cathedral bells, echoed by a gayer peal from the convent, announce to the city of Quebec, that a festival day is at hand. The altars of the Ursuline church are magnificently decked. The freshly gilded altar screen reflects the light from hundreds of wax tapers blazing in silver candlesticks. From four in the morning till noon, mass is celebrated uninterruptedly. Processions of priests, in vestments stiff with gold, and lace from the looms of Europe, come and go chanting the Te Deum.

As the day declines, the plaintive voices of the nuns, singing their vesper hymns, steal softly from behind the *grille.*

In the little house at the town's end in Wells, in the dim candle light, an old man, and his old wife sit alone together. The click of her knitting needles is in sweet accord with the scratch of his quill, while he writes as follows:

"I commend my soul to God my Creator, hoping for Pardon of all my Sins, and everlasting salvation through the alone merits of Jesus Christ."

He makes his wife, Mary, sole Executrix of his will, and bequeaths to her lands, mills, his household goods, his cattle of all kinds, his negro and mulatto servants, and a share of his money. Then his thoughts dwell on the little child, long ago so cruelly torn from him:

"I give and bequeath to my daughter Esther Wheelwright, if living in Canada, whom I have not heard of for this many years, and hath been absent for more than 30 yeares, if it should please God that She return to this country and settle here, then my will is that my four sons viz: John, Samuel, Jeremiah and Nathaniel each of them pay her Twenty Live pounds, it being in the Whole One Hundred Pounds, within six months after her Return and Settlement."

Captain John Wheelwright died Aug. 13, 1745.

On the 16th of November, 1750, his widow who survived him ten years, disposed by will of her temporal estate.

She bequeaths to her four sons, "each 5£ in old tenor bills, or the value thereof in lawful money."

To her daughters Mary Moody and Sarah Jeffords, all her "wearing Apparell," including her "Gold Necklace, Rings and Buttons to be equally divided between them," and to Sarah Jefferds in addition, a "negro boy named Asher."

Of her "Real and Personal Estate, within Doors or without," one fourth is bequeathed to each of her two daughters aforesaid, one fourth to her "three beloved Grand-daughters," children of her "deceased daughter Hannah Plaisted," and one fourth to her "four beloved Granddaughters," children of her "deceased Daughter Elizabeth Newmarch."

In the division of her property, her "Negro servant Woman named Pegg, shall be Divided to such of my Aforesaid Daughters or Granddaughters which she shall choose to live with after my Decease". . . .and "furthermore Provided my. . . . . .Beloved Daughter Esther Wheelwright, who has been many years in Canada, is yet living and should by the wonder working Providence of God be Returned to her Native Land, and tarry and dwell in it, I give and bequeath unto her, one Fifth part of my Estate which I have already by this Instrument will^d should be divided to and among my afores Daughters and Granddaughters, to be paid by them in Proportion to their Respective Share in the above mentioned Division unto her my Said Daughter Esther Wheelwright, within one year after my Decease Anything above written in this Instrument to the Contrary notwithstanding."

It would seem from the wills of Captain John Wheelwright and his wife, that the testators did not know that their daughter had bound herself by irrevocable vows to a monastic life. The History of the town of Wells, published in 1875, confirms this opinion. Its author, alluding to the refusal of some New England captives to return from their captivity, says, "Esther Wheelwright was one of the number. . . . Whether she acquired any more intimate than the natural relationships of life, does not appear from any tradition or written relics of the day. . . . . .She wrote to her father from her captivity. He lived in the hope that she would come back, and provided for her in his will, in the event she should return from her wandering after his death. . . . . . . .the fate of all humanity may have overtaken her before that time.". . . . .On the contrary, the annalist of the Ursulines states, that "Immediately after Esther's profession as a nun, word was sent to her family, who far from being offended with this step of the young girl, sent her a messenger from Boston, charged with letters and gifts." These statements, both made by respectable authority, are irreconcilable. Careful study forces me to the conclusion, that the annalist of the convent records actual events, of which at the date of the publication of the history of Wells, not even a tradition remained to Wheelwright's descendants in New England.

Imagine the stir at the convent, when in January, 1754, a young gentleman from Boston presented himself at the door, announcing himself as the nephew of Mother Esther of the Infant Jesus, and demanding an interview with his beloved aunt. The flutter of the *Tourière,* the hesitation of the Mother Superior, the hurried consultation of all in authority,— may be better imagined than described. After some delay, the Bishop kindly granted entrance to Major Wheelwright, "hoping that it might result in his conversion."

How one longs to know what this aunt and nephew, meeting then for the first time, had to say to each other,—in what language they talked,—what questions were asked by the captive of fifty years.

All we know is, that at his departure, the young man gave to his aunt a miniature portrait of her mother, and presented the Community with some "fine linen, a beautiful silver flagon, and a knife, fork and spoon, of the same material."

At the moment of Major Wheelwright's return to New England, young Major Washington was making his report to Governor Dinwiddie, of the refusal of the French to abandon their fort at the headwaters of the Ohio. The tardy attempt of the English in the following February, to build a fort at the fork of the Ohio, brought on a skirmish between Washington and the French commander, which, says Mr. Parkman, "began the war that set the world on fire."

The siege of Quebec began on the 12th of July, 1759. The cannonade of the 13th and 14th, proved that the convent must be vacated. Eight of the sisters got leave to remain in charge. Though there is no positive proof, we have a right to believe that Esther of the Infant Jesus, was one of the eight. With the fervor of a devotee, she had the force and the fearlessness of the Wheelwrights. She was sixty-three years old, and the fifth on the list of choir nuns.

At sunset of the 15th, [July 25, 1759, N· S.] the rest of the Ursulines, bidding a reluctant farewell to the courageous little band, sped swiftly down to the meadows of the Saint Charles, to seek shelter in the convent attached to the General Hospital. The sisters of the Hôtel-Dieu were there before them. The Hospital, being out of reach of the projectiles, was the refuge of hundreds of people, fleeing in fright from the ruins of the Lower Town.

Imagine the consternation and anguish of the next few weeks. The nuns at the Hospital were busy night and day, with the care of the maimed and dying of both armies. At intervals, the quick stroke of the convent bells calling them to their devotions, gave them their only rest. Above their prayers rose the groans of the wounded, the scream of shot and shell, the roar of flames and the crash of falling buildings. In the gray of the morning of the sixtieth day of the ever memorable siege, the straggling file of red-coated soldiers, clambered up the rocky steeps, and formed in line of battle on the Plains of Abraham. When the shadows of night gathered on that gory field, the Seven Years War in America was virtually ended, and the question whether France or England was to be master of this continent was forever settled.

On the morning after the battle, the gallant Montcalm breathed his last. The day was one of dire distress.

Venturing from the narrow cellar of the monastery, where they had stayed out the siege, Esther Wheelwright and her companions gazed upon a desolate scene. In peril of then lives, and with great labor and fatigue, they had saved most of their windows. Their cells were demolished, their chimneys battered and tumbling, their roofs charred and riddled.

Confusion reigned everywhere. No workman could be found to make a coffin for Montcalm. Finally old Michel, factotum and general overseer at the Convent, the tears streaming down his face, nailed together a rough box from the *debris* of the bombardment. In this rude casket, at nine o'clock that evening, the Marquis de Montcalm was carried to his rest.

Silence and gloom brooded over the city. "Not a drum was heard, nor a funeral note." No gun was fired—not a bell tolled. Men and women, wandering dazed among the ruins, fell into line with the little procession that bore the dead soldier from the house of the surgeon Arnoux to his burial in the chapel of the Ursulines. Two little girls stealing unnoticed into the church, stood by his grave, while by the flare of torches, the body of the hero was lowered into a hole in front of the altar, made by the bursting of a shell. The service for the dead was chanted by three priests. The quivering voices of Esther Wheelwright and her sister nuns were heard in response, then sobs, repressed through all the horrors of the siege, burst forth, "for" says the annalist, "it seemed as if the last hope of the colony was buried."

General Murray, who was left in command of the English troops in Canada, repaired the Ursuline convent, and quartered there a part of his wounded men. Esther Wheelwright and her companions cheerfully assumed the duties of Hospital nuns, and the soldiers proved themselves truly grateful for the Christian charity thus shown them. Among the troops, was a Scotch regiment. The good nuns were so distressed at seeing the strangers in a costume so ill-suited to a Canadian winter, that they fell to knitting long stockings to cover the bare legs of the kilted Highlanders.

On the 8th of September, 1760, the Capitulation was signed at Montreal. It secured to the Canadians the free enjoyment of the Catholic religion and to the Communities of nuns, their constitutions and privileges. The 15th of the following December, Sister Esther Wheelwright of the Infant Jesus, was elected Superior of the Ursulines. Thus, strangely enough, at the moment of the establishment of the English Supremacy in Canada, the first (and last), English Superior of the Ursulines of Quebec, was elected. Her election is a proof of her robust health at this time, and of the confidence placed in her by the Community. That she was worthy of the trust, appears in all her acts.

After the fall of Quebec, rations were issued by the conquerors for the subsistence of the people. The summer before Esther's election, on the withdrawal of the soldiers from the convent,

General Murray had ordered that no more provisions should be furnished to the nuns, except for ready money. Such representations had been made to the General by Esther's predecessor in office, that the order was countermanded. In the spring after Esther's election, a bill of $1352.6, was rendered by the commissary for provisions furnished the Community from Oct. 4, 1759, to May 25, 1761.

Mother Esther wrote at once to General Murray, stating the inability of the nuns to pay the debt thus contracted; at the same time putting at the disposal of the government certain of the Community's lands. "Nevertheless." she adds, "we hope that upon the representations which you will kindly make in our behalf, his Majesty will not refuse to absolve us from this debt. In our confidence in your goodness, of which you have hitherto given us the most convincing proofs, we assure you of our sincere gratitude, and of the respect with which I have the honor to be, &c., &c, &c." She might have hinted, that the shelter and care given to the wounded English ought to count for something towards the payment of the debt. In the interval of suspense, while Murray wrote for instructions to England, Esther wrote to the Mother Community in Paris: "We shall try to do without everything, for, for some years we shall have to heap up the interest on our French possessions, to pay the King of England whom we owe thirteen hundred and fifty-two dollars."

From the Capitulation at Montreal to the Peace of Paris, the lot of the French Canadians was hard. A sorrowful suspense, as to whether Canada would be restored to France, agitated all hearts. In 1761, Esther writes to the Superior at Paris, "It has just been announced to us that peace is made, and that this poor country is restored to the French. I hope it may be true."

The non-arrival of letters from France, caused much anxiety. In October, writing again to Paris, she says, "Everybody of position is surprised not to hear a word by way of England, though many laymen have received letters. I can hardly believe, however, that some are intercepted, more than others."

A later letter runs thus: "We shall very soon be in a condition not to be able to dress ourselves according to the rules. Since the war, we are especially in need of bombazine for our veils. Indeed the need is so pressing-, that soon we shall not be able to appear decently, having nothing but rags to cover our heads. We cannot buy these things of the English. They don't yet know how to *coiffer* the nuns. I think, my dear mother, you might send us a few pieces of bombazine by some of our Canadians, who must return to their poor country. M. de Rouville who was the bearer of your letters, would have considered it a pleasure to bring some bombazine to us, and could have done so without much trouble. There is plenty of food, but everything is very dear, and silver is very scarce, never having been much current in Canada."

A courteous letter from General Murray to Mother Esther is extant, dated Jan. 2nd, 1764, thanking her for a "Happy New Year" she had sent him, and wishing her many in return. After Murray's return to England, the Mother Superior and sisters send him gifts of their own beautiful handiwork, which he acknowledges with graceful compliments and more than civil expressions of esteem and friendship.

The first days of April, 1764, were spent by Mother Esther of the Infant Jesus, in profound retreat, to prepare herself for the festivities of her Golden Jubilee, (the fiftieth anniversary of her espousals as the bride of Christ,) which occurred on the twelfth of April, 1764.

Nothing was omitted in the celebration of Esther's fiftieth year of religious profession as an Ursuline nun, to convince her of the love and appreciation of the Community. The chapel was beautifully lighted and decorated. After the public renewal of her vows in the presence of the Bishop and a multitude of people, mass was celebrated with fine organ music, and much singing of motets. A sermon on the happiness of a religious life followed. At the close of the mass, the nuns, each with a lighted taper in her hand, sang the *Te Deum,* accompanied by a flute and violin. The day was given up to recreation and congratulation. In the Refectory, there was feasting and joyful conversation. The great hall was gay with flowers and gifts, and the children of the *pension,* with song and dance, brought their offerings to their beloved Mother Superior. Late in the afternoon, a benediction service was held, and the day ended with jubilant music of drum and fife.

In her girlhood, Esther had embroidered much for the altars. Seeing at this time the great admiration of the English for embroidery on birch bark, she encouraged this kind of work among the nuns, and gave herself up to it with incredible industry.

In May, 1761, writing to the Procurator of the Ursulines in Paris, she says, "It is true that notwithstanding our misfortunes one need not lack the necessities of life, if one had plenty of money, but we have only what we earn by our birch bark work. As long as this is the fashion, the money we earn by it is a great help towards our support. We sell it at a high price to the English gentlemen, yet they seem to consider it a privilege to buy, so eager are they for our work. It is really impossible for us notwithstanding our industry,
to supply the demand."........."I should like to know," she continues, alluding to their indebtedness to the government, "exactly what will be left, after paying Captain Barbutt. According to what you will do me the honor to write me on this point, we shall pay some debts here,—for we are not lacking in debts, and some pretty large ones. Nobody but myself, however, knows about them, and I am in no hurry to acquaint the Community with the fact, for fear of distressing them." This extract shows her self-reliance, and her tender consideration for her sister nuns, in sparing them anxieties which weighed heavily on her own heart.

Too constant use of her eyes, brought on in her declining years, weakness of sight and disease. When she could no
longer embroider exquisitely, she busied herself with mending the underclothing of the Community, showing the same skill and delicacy in darning and patching that characterized her more beautiful handiwork.

For nearly seventy years, Esther Wheelwright fulfilled with fervor and fidelity, all the duties of a monastic life. No one was more scrupulous in the observance of all its rules. In the feebleness of age, as in the vigor of youth,—in summer's heat and winter's cold, she was always in her place. In learning to obey, she learned to command. As a teacher of young girls, she was very successful. Her happy disposition and sweet temper, made her example even more eloquent than her precepts. With her, forbearance and gentleness, with the most charming politeness, took the place of a stricter discipline, and never failed to win the love and obedience of her pupils. She was promoted to her responsible position as Superior, at the most critical epoch in the history of her adopted country. French in all her sympathies,—a Romanist of undoubted zeal,—yet, undaunted by embarassments to which a woman of less strength and breadth of character would have yielded, she so adapted herself to the exigencies of the situation as to win for herself, and the Community, the favor and respect of the conquerors.

In 1766, the rules of her Order not allowing her re-election for a third successive term, she was discharged, but again reelected in 1769. She was then seventy-two years of age,— but her mind and heart never grew old.

In 1771, writing to the Mother Superior of Paris, she says, 'I, beg you to accept the assurance of our most tender attachment. I wish I could give you some proof of it, other than by words, but we cannot even find a way to send you those trifles from this country, which we used to take pleasure in sending you. In our prayers, you always have a large share. Pray for me that God in his infinite mercy may grant me a happy death." In October, 1772, it was feared that Mother Esther would not live till the December elections. She rallied, however, and on the 15th was honorably discharged from the superiorship, only to be made Assistant Superior, and six years later Zelatrix.

At S o'clock in the evening of the 28th of October, 1780, Esther Wheelwright died, at the age of eighty-four years and eight months. "She died as she had lived," says the annalist, "in continual aspirations towards Heaven, repeating unceasingly some verses of the Psalms

Her ancestors were noble, but her heart was nobler still, and the memory of her virtues will be forever dear to this House. . . . . .From 1712 to 1780, she was one of its finest ornaments and firmest supports."

The name of Wheelwright is still reverenced by the Ursulines of Quebec. At the convent to-day, they tell you with pride of the gifts bestowed on them by Esther's cousin and fellow captive, Mary Sayer.

The silver flagon presented by Major Wheelwright is still in use in their Infirmary, and the miniature of Esther Wheelwright's mother, a blonde with hazel eyes and an oval face, is sacredly preserved. Retouched by the addition of a veil and drapery, and enclosed in a richly embossed frame, containing also four relics of the Saints, it is now reverently cherished as a Madonna.

I have been permitted to stand in the inner chapel of the Ursulines at Quebec, above the spot where the mortal part of Esther Wheelwright lies buried.

My fondest ambition in writing this story is that in some hour of recreation, it may be read to the novices by the Mother Assistant, who entering the convent fifty years ago, found there as a nun, the little girl who saw the burial of Montcalm, and later was an inmate of the convent, during the last seven years of Esther Wheelwright's life.

'See "Story of a York Family."

STORY OF A YORK FAMILY.

One midsummer day in the year 1588, the duke of Medina Sidonia looked in at the Plym's mouth as he sailed by with the Invincible Armada to conquer England, and said to himself in good Spanish, "When I shall have finished the business I have in hand, I will build me a lordly pleasure house on yonder height and there I will take mine ease."

Sir Francis Drake looked up from the game of skittles he was playing on the Hoe at Plymouth, and curling his moustache, as was his custom when angry, he said to his companion, "I'll finish the game when I shall have clipped the wings of yonder brave bird." Whether Drake returned to finish his game history does not tell us. We are also left to infer that the Don's plaisance remained a castle in the air.

Seventeen years later, on another midsummer day, somebody roused the Governor of Plymouth from his siesta, with the exciting news that George Weymouth had come into port with five Indians, whom he had kidnapped on the Kennebec river, in his otherwise fruitless voyage to New England.

Sir Ferdinando Gorges, at that time Governor of Plymouth, was living there the listless life of a garrison officer. Into the gubernatorial mansion on the Hoe he took three of Weymouth's Indians, had them taught English and kept them three years. Did anybody ever compute the influence of these "three little Indian boys" on our history? They told him about the "stately islands," "safe harbors" and "great rivers" of their native land, and inspired him to plant a colony there. "This accident," says Sir Ferdinando, "was the means under God of putting on foot and giving life to all our plantations."

Being a man of wealth, rank and influence, he easily secured the cooperation of Sir John Popham, Lord Chief Justice of England. How the Popham colony, planted by the Plymouth Company in August, 1607, on Company, thanks to a milder clime, survived,—how Capt, John Smith, "a fugitive slave," as Mr. Palfrey happily calls him, after founding the Old Dominion, sailed up and down the New England coast, printed lavish praise of its resources, and made a map of all its capes, inlets, islands and harbors, to which Prince Charles gave the familiar names they bear today,—how Gorges, not doubting that God would effect that which man despaired of, was a part of every scheme of colonization:—all this is known to every careful reader of our history.

It was doubtless under the auspices of Gorges that the first English settlement at Agamenticus was made, and when in 1635, the charter of New England was surrendered to the crown and its territory parcelled out among the patentees, Gorges received the territory between the Merrimac and the Kennebec, extending one hundred and twenty miles inland. With this province of Maine, the Crown conferred upon him almost unlimited power and privilege.

Mr. Bancroft says of Sir Ferdinando, "The friend and cotemporary of Raleigh, he adhered to schemes in America for almost half a century. . . . . . and was still bent on colonization, at an age when other men are but preparing to die with decorum. . . . . . Like another Romulus, this septuagenarian royalist. . . . . and veteran soldier resolved to perpetuate his name," and in 1642 the ancient Agamenticus became the city "Gorgeana," "As good a city," says Bancroft, "as seals and parchment, a nominal mayor and alderman, a chancery court and a court leet, sergeant rolls and white rods can make of a town of less than 300 inhabitants."

In the King's patent to Gorges it had been expressly stipulated that Episcopacy should be the established religion of his province.

In 1643 John Wheelwright, removing from Exeter to escape the bigotry of the Bay settlements, betook himself to a tract adjoining Agamenticus, which he bought of Gorges, to which he gave the name of Wells.

The same year Plymouth and the Bay Colony made a league with Connecticut and New Haven for mutual protection.

"Those of Sir Ferdinando Gorges his province. . . . . were not received or called into the Confederation," writes Winthrop, "because they ran a different course from us, both in their ministry and civil administration, for they had lately made Accominticus (a poor village) a corporation, and had made a taylor the mayor, and had entertained one Hull, an excommunicated person, and very contentious, for their minister." Whatever may have been the faults and follies of Sir Ferdinando we cannot help admiring his persistence—his life-long devotion to the great idea of colonizing New England.

In the civil wars Sir Ferdinando fought with the cavaliers and died before the execution of the King. The population of the ancient city was increased by the accession of a contingent of Scotch prisoners taken by Cromwell in his famous victory over Charles II, at Dunbar in 1650. These were shipped overseas to be sold as apprentices for a term of years, and naturally found a home in the plantation of the royalist Gorges. Scotland Parish is to-day a thriving and interesting locality of the old town, and the names of McIntyre, Junkins and Donald still survive there.

Old York is now New York. Many of its old-time houses have been drummed out by the so-called march of improvement. The straggling cottages of the fishermen have disappeared from the landscape. The winding cowpath along the cliff, through bayberry bushes and sweet-briar roses, has been supplanted by the smooth-clipped lawns of costly seashore estates, packed in too close proximity to one another along the water front. The rugged face of the cliff, over which the woodbine and beach pea used to scramble, is now disfigured by the unsightly waste pipes of modern improvement that wriggle like so many foul serpents to bury themselves beneath the ocean. Pretentious hotels and livery stables obtrude themselves upon the moorlands, where the "fresh Rhodora" used to spread its "leafless bloom."

College youths in yachting costume and city belles with tennis rackets, flirt harmlessly on the beach at bathing time, and in the late afternoon, the brilliant parasols of the gay butterflies of fashion flutter far afield, and prancing steeds with glistening trappings curvet over the rocky roads under the guidance of liveried coachmen. On Sunday, a crowd in silk attire, with gilded prayerbooks, wends its way to a little church whose golden cross towers aggressively above the rock-bound coast.

"Behold!" cries the Puritan antiquary, "the fulfilment of Sir Ferdinando's dream." Then he turns away to the river bank, where to this day may be seen the veritable streets of the "Ancient city" as laid out by Thomas Gorges, its first

mayor. Pursuing his history, he reads that at Sir Ferdinando's death the people of Gorgeana wrote repeatedly to his heirs for instructions, but receiving no answer they, with Wells and Piscataqua, formed themselves into a body politic for self-government.

In 1652, Massachusetts assumed control of the settlement, the city charter was annulled and Gorgeana, degraded from her commanding position as the first incorporated city in America, joined the rank and file of New England towns under the name of York.

The alarm of Philip's war in 1675, extending to the eastward, the distressed inhabitants built garrison houses against Indian attack. Two, known as the Junkins garrison and the McIntyre garrison, were standing on a hilltop in Scotland Parish of Old York as late as 1875. Of the former not a vestige now remains, except a panel that forms a cupboard door in Frary house.

The first blow struck by the enemy in the old French and Indian war fell upon the eastern towns. At the instigation of the Jesuit priests, Wells, York, Berwick, Kittery and others received their baptism of blood at the hands of the French and Indians, even before Deerfield, Hatfield, Northampton and Springfield.

On the same page in the parish records of Canadian towns and villages, I have often found the deaths, marriages and baptisms of hapless captives, carried from the border towns of Maine and Massachusetts. This is why I tell the story of a York family.

Edward Rishworth, or Rushworth as the name is known in England, the friend and son-in-law of John Wheelwright, and his companion in exile, was one of the grantees to whom Thomas Gorges, nephew of Sir Ferdinando, gave authority to lay out and assign lots at Wells.

In the history of both Wells and York, his intellectual ability is prominent. He was one of the commissioners of the newly made town of York and clerk of the court there the same year.

In the prolonged resistance of the Province of Maine to the jurisdiction of Massachusetts, Rishworth was prominent. His commanding intelligence and his personal influence in the province is shown in the humble petition of the leading men of Wells, in 1668, to be restored to the jurisdiction of Massachusetts, with apologies for their former disobedience, the petitioners assigning as the cause of their dereliction, the influence of Mr. Edward Rishworth, they "having been well affected with said Rishworth, and confiding in him."

Rishworth was appointed Recorder for the province, in October, 1651, and held the office continuously, except in 1668 and 9, for thirty-three years. In June, 1686, Rishworth wrote his last official line, being then an old man.

The name of his wife, Susannah, appears on a legal paper for the last time in 1675. So far, I have found but two children of Edward and Susannah Rishworth, daughters Mary and Susannah. Her grandfather Wheelwright, in his will dated Nov. 15, 1679, names "my son-in-law, Edward Rishworth," and "my grandchild, Mary White, daughter of ye said Rishworth." This proves that Mary Rishworth, then about eighteen, was, at this date, the wife of one White.

I assume that this White, and Rishworth's wife had both died before October, 1682, when, as he says, for "diver's good causes   and more espetially for yt tender love and affection which I beare unto my beloved daughter, Mary Say word, wife to John Say word," he conveyed all his property to his "son-in-law, John Say word," for £60, to be used in the payment of Rishworth's debts.

At the same time, Sayword gives his bond, "to pay unto father Rishworth. . . . . . . the just some of six pounds per Ann: to bee pay'd in good Mrchan'ble pay, boards, provisions, or such other goods as his ocations. . . . . . . shal require   to bee Delivered at Yorke at the house of sd John Say word which hee bought of ye sd Rishworth his father-in-law who. . . . . . . is to have ye free uss of ye lower Roume hee now liveth in. . . . . . . at his soole disposeing, as also to have his horse kept by sd John Say word, at. . . . . . . Sayword's charge. . . . . . . and yt is to bee understood. . . . . . . that sd John Sayword is to mayntain sd Rishworth. . . . . . . with comfortable dyet, so long as he sees good to live with him. . . . . . . And is to provide convenient fire wood for his Roume as his necessity shall require."

"An inventory of the Estate of Mr. Edward Rishworth, deceased," dated Feb. 13, 1689, [sic] gives us approximately, the date of his death. On Feb, 25, 1690-91 [sic], Mrs. Mary Hull took oath that it was "a true Inventory of the Estate of her deceased father, Edward Rishworth."

By these three legal papers, we learn that John Sayword, millwright of York, was living in October, 1682, as the husband of Rishworth's daughter Mary, and that on the death of her father, either in 1689 or 1690, [see ante] this daughter, as Mrs. Mary Hull, attests the truth of the inventory of her father's estate.

I, as yet, find no record of John Sayword's birth and parentage. He may have been the son of Henry Sayword, a prominent man in the annals of Wells and York. Millwright is a common appendage to the names of Maine men of that period, for men must eat and be sheltered. The mill pond in York, where John Sayword must have ground the grists and sawed the lumber for the country round about, is well known.

We have a grant from the town of York to John Sayword, dated Dec. 10, 1680, of three 20-acre lots of land with mill privilege and timber rights, conditioned on his building galleries and seats in the meeting house.

"First that the Said Sayword, shall build or cause to bee built at ye meeting house at York, three sufficient Gallerys, with three convenient seats in each Gallery and one beanch beside, in ye hyest Rowme in every gallery If the sd Conveniency of Rowme will bare it, the fronture seats, hee is to make with barresters, and two peyre of stayrs to go up into the gallerys, one for ye men and another for the wimine. Second: The sd John Sayword stands Ingagd, to seat the sd Meeting house below, with convenient Seates, too Seates to be barrestred below, one for men and ye other for wimine; and repayreing of ye defects yt are in the ould Seates, and by makeing and adding so many more new Seates, as shall be necessary for ye full and decent seateing of the whoole house. Which worke in making of Gallerys and seateing the lower part of the sayd house, is by John Sayword to bee done and finished at his own proper Charge, (nayles onely excepted) which the Town is Ingag'd to provide, very speedily, at or before the last of October next Insewing, Ann: Dom: 1681.

There is a deed signed by Sayword, March 24, 1684, and also by "Mary Sayword, the younger." As I cannot suppose this to be his daughter Mary, (then only thirteen) it must be his wife, *nee* Mary Rishworth, who on this occasion signs herself Mary "the younger," to distinguish herself from his mother Mary, which again inclines me to the belief that John Sayword was son of Henry, whose wife Mary long survived him. John Sayword probably died early in December,

1689 ; for on Christmas Day of that year, which was neither a holy day nor a holiday with the Puritans, Mrs. Mary Sayword appeared and took oath to the inventory of her husband's estate, which was valued at £85.

She was administratrix, and with Matthew Austin, gave a bond for £ 166, for the lawful administration of her husband's estate. How soon after Sayword's death his widow became the wife of one Hull, does not yet appear, but as we have seen, she, as Mary Hull, testified to the inventory of her father's estate, on Feb. 25, 1690-91 [see ante]. Her connection with Hull must have been brief, for at the time of the attack on York, Feb. 5, 1692, Mary Rishworth, then but thirty-two years old, was living-with her fourth husband, James Plaisted. Of Plaisted's ancestry or antecedents, or of the date of his marriage to the young widow Hull, I have so far found nothing.

Of the calamity at York, Feb. 5, 1692, Cotton Mather writes: "Great was the share that fell to the Family of Mr. Shubael Dummer. . . . . . . .He had been solicited, with many temptations to leave his Place when the Clouds grew Thick and Black in the Indian Hostilities, but he chose rather with a Paternal affection to stay. . . . . . . In a word, he was one that might by way of Eminency be called A Good Man. . . . . . . He was just going to take Horse at his own Door, upon a journey in the Service of God, when the Tygres that were making their Depredations upon the sheep of York, seized upon this their shepherd; and they shot him so that they left him Dead.". . . . . . .

His wife, Susannah Rishworth, sister of Mary Rishworth Plaisted, "they carried into captivity," continues Mather, "where through sorrows and hardships among those Dragons of the Desart, she also quickly Died; and his Church as many of them as were in that Captivity, endured this among other anguishes, that on the next Lord's Day, one of the Tawnies chose to exhibit himself unto them [A Devil as an Angel of Light!] in the Cloaths whereof they had stript the Dead Body of this their Father—Many were the tears that were Dropt throughout New England on this occasion."

Mather calls the York minister,

> "The Martyr'd *Pelican,* who Bled
>
> Rather than leave his charge unfed.
>
> A proper Bird of Paradise
>
> Shot,—and Flown thither in a trice."

James Plaisted's wife was taken, with her two children, Mary and Esther Sayword, aged respectively eleven and seven, and her baby boy. This is Mather's relation:

"Mary Plaisted, the wife of Mr. James Plaisted, was made a captive, about three weeks after her Delivery of a male Child. They then took her, with her Infant off her bed and forced her to travel in this, her weakness, the best part of a Day without any Respect of Pity. At Night the Cold ground, in the Open Air, was her Lodging; and for many a Day she had no Nourishment but a little water with a little Bear's Flesh, which rendered her so Feeble that she, with her Infant were not far from totally starved.—Upon her cries to God, there was at length some supply sent by her Master's taking a Moose, the Broth whereof recovered her. But she must now Travel many Days through Woods and Swamps and Rocks, and over Mountains, and Frost, and Snow, until she could stir no farther. Sitting down to Rest, she was not able to rise, till her Diabolical Master helped her up, which, when he did, he took her Child from her, and carried it unto a River, where, stripping it of the few Rags it had, he took it by the heels and against a Tree dash'd out its Brains, and then flung it into the River. So he returned unto the miserable mother, telling her she was now Eased of her Burden, and must walk faster than she did before! "

Was this infant the posthumous son of her third husband, Hull? He does not appear on the old York records among the children of James Plaisted.

A native poet has thus immortalized the attack on York:

> They marched for two and tweniy daies,
> All through the deepest snow;
> And on a dreadful winter morn,
>   They siruck the cruel blow.
>
> Hundreds were murthered in their beddes,
> Without shame or remorse;
> And soon, the floors and roads were strewed
>   With many a bleeding corse.
>
> The village soon began to blaze,
> To heighten misery's woe;
> But, O, I scarce can bear to tell,
>   The issue of that blow!
>
> They threw the infants on the fire;
> The men they did not spare;
> But killed all, which they could find
>   Though aged, or though fair.

Our next meeting with Mary Rishworth Plaisted is at her baptism in Montreal. The following is a free translation of the Parish record:

On the 8th of December, 1693, there was baptized *sous condition,* an English woman from New England, named in her own country, Marie, who born at York on the 8th of January O. S. 1660, of the marriage of Edouard Rishworth, and Suzanne Willwright, both Pro-testants of Lincoln in old England, and married last to Jacques Pleisted, Protestant of New England, was captured the 25th of Jan-uary O. S. of the year 1692 with two of her children, Marie Geneviève Sayer born the 4th of April O. S. 1681, and

Marie Joseph Sayer, born the 9th of March O. S. 1685,—by the savages of Acadia, and now lives in the service of Madame Catherine Gauchet, widow of M. Jean Baptiste Migeon, appointed by the King first lieutenant general of the bailiwick established by his Majesty in Montreal. Her name Marie, has been kept, and that of Madeleine added to it. Her god-father was M. Jean Baptiste Juchereau, lieutenant-general of the Royal bailiwick of Montreal, and her god-mother, Madame Madeleine Louise Juchereau.

Signed.

Mary Magdalen Pleistead signs the record in a good handwriting. So also do her god-parents, Juchereau and Madame, his wife, Catherine Gauchet, and finally Jean Frémont, Curé —all as clear as if written yesterday.

Two lists in our archives tell briefly the story of the final separation of Mary Rishworth Plaisted from these Sayword children, one is the "Names of English captives Redeemed from Quebec by Math'w Carey in Oct'br, 1695," which contains the name of "Mrs. Mary Plaisted York." Another sent at the same time, is of "Those Remaining still in the hands of the French of Canada," and bears the names of the two sisters:

In October, 1696, a year after Mary Plaisted's redemption, she was "Presented at the court at Wells, for not attending ye Publick worship of God upon ye Lord's Day."

The godless weaklings of our day might find palliating circumstances, without considering the hardships of her every day life, and the terrible experiences of her recent captivity. Nevertheless,

"Mr. James Plaisted, at the following court held at York, on the 6th of April, 1697, appearing in behalf of his wife, to answer her presentment for not frequenting ye Publick worship of God upon ye Lord's Day, she being under some bodily infirmity, hindering her own appearance, Is for her offence to pay 4s. 6d. fine, and to be admonished; ffees payd in court."

In April, 1696, "Lycence was granted to Mr. James Playstead to retayle bear, syder an victuals at his now dwelling house." This license was renewed from year to year.

January 20, 1707, there is this vote of the town, from which it appears that the conditional agreement between the town and John Sayword had not been faithfully kept, by one or both parties:

"Whereas, there is several differences between the Inhabitants of the town of York in the Province of Maine in the Massachusetts Government, and Mr. James Plaisted and Mary his now wife, the Relict of John Saword, all of said York, relating to work done by said John Sayword aforesaid, to York meeting house. . . . . A referee shall be chosen by the town and another by Plaisted and his wife, to hear, and determine, all Differences."

James and Mary Plaisted both sign an agreement on penalty of fifty dollars, to accept the result of the arbitration.

Later "Wm. Sawer," [Sayword] and "Wm. Goodsoe" state that they "have looked over the matter and cannot agree and have left it out to Daniel Emery of Kittery to make a final end of the controversy."

July 11, 1710, Capt. James Plaisted and his wife Mary, deed land together. Here, busied with the occupations of the yeomanry of the period in New England, active in church and state, respected and worthy citizens of old York, and in the prime of life, we will leave them and look for their two daughters, left behind in Canada.

Many summers ago, in an idle hour and with no purpose. I copied a few pages from the old town records of York. It was long before I had heard of James Plaisted and his wife Mary Rishworth. The quaint spelling and simple directness of the language interested me, but it seems to have been by what Cotton Mather would have called a Remarkable Providence, that this particular page of the record should have captivated me.

A humble romance seemed to unfold itself in this stepfather, willing to father his wife's children by a former marriage, though his own children, later born, are naturally put first in the record. Here is the story as it stands, written more than two hundred years ago on the old book:

James Plaisted, Bearths of His children. Lydia Plaisted was Borne the fouerth day of Janerwary in ye year 1696.

Olife Plaisted was Borne the first day of May in ye year 1698. Mary Sayward was Borne the fouerth April 1681. Susannah Sayward was Borne the ninth day of May 1683. Esther Sayward was Borne the seventh day of March 1685. Hannah Sayward was borne the twenty-one of June 1687. John Sayward was Borne second of Janerwary 1690.

The last was evidently a posthumous child, the only son, born shortly after the death of his father, John Sayward, and named for him.

We are now to follow the fortunes of Mary, the first born, and Esther, the third child of John Sayward and his wife, Mary Rishworth.

On the parish records of Notre Dame in Montreal, with the baptism of their mother is a note interlined, in a different handwriting, and apparently written long after. This note records the indisputable fact that on the same day and in the same church, her two daughters were also baptized. As it was the custom of the church to add the names of saints to the newly baptized, Mary, the elder, then about thirteen, received the added name of Geneviève. Esther, the younger, lost her New England name entirely and was re-baptized as Marie Joseph, she being then about eight years old.

In a list of the pupils of the nuns of the Congregation in 1693, the name of one of the Sayer sisters appears.

When we remember that the captives were in Canada during the most romantic period of the history of New France —that they saw daily those whose religious devotion has won them world-wide fame, truth seems stranger than fiction.

A profound impression must have been made upon the sensibilities of all the young captive girls when Jeanne Le Ber, the only daughter of the richest merchant in Montreal, renounced the world and abandoned her family, to devote herself to a religious life. Marie Genevieve Sayer was, no doubt, perfectly familiar with the face of the young devotee, and witnessed her voluntary incarceration in the cell which she had had built for her, behind the altar in the chapel of the

Congregation.

At five o'clock on the evening of Aug. 5, 1695, after vespers, M. Dollier de Casson, with all his clergy in splendid attire, went to the house of the Seigneur Le Ber, whence, chanting psalms and prayers, they marched in procession. Behind them came the young Jeanne Le Ber. She was robed in gray, with a black girdle. Her father, pale with weeping, accompanied her, followed by all their friends and relatives.

The people who thronged the streets, awe-struck at the unusual spectacle, could not restrain their sobs. To them the act about to be consummated, seemed like a living death to both father and child. On arriving at the chapel the recluse fell upon her knees, while M. Dollier blessed her little cell and spoke to her a few words of counsel.

Her heart-broken father, unable to bear the sight, fled weeping from the spot. But Jeanne Le Ber, with tearless eyes and steady hand, firmly closed the door upon herself forever.

Three years later, Mary Sayer must have been present at a happier scene, in the same little chapel at what we may consider the permanent establishment of the order of the Nuns of the Congregation in Montreal. The three years of anxiety, discussion and delay were ended. The rules of the order had been the day before, "solemnly accepted and signed by all the Community." Now, on the morning of the 25th of June, 1698, the religious world of Villemarie had assembled to witness the performance of "that article of the regulations which prescribed the simple vow of poverty, chastity, obedience and the teaching of little girls."

There were the most distinguished of the Sulpitian priests, conspicuously the zealous and scholarly Father Meriel. There was the Vicar-General, Dollier de Casson, "tall and portly, a soldier and a gentleman—albeit a priest. . . . . . . As pleasant a father as ever said *Bcncdicitc"* says Mr. Parkman. There was the great bishop, Saint-Vallier—dominant, a passionate extremist, believing in himself and impatient of contradiction—fulminating in those days as sharply against the "big sleeves" and "lownecked dresses" of Quebec damsels as the sternest Puritan of the period, in Boston.

Perhaps a shade of disapointment clouded the brow of the haughty prelate at his failure to force the cloister upon the ladies of the Congregation; perhaps also a corresponding elation on the face of Marguérite Bourgeois at the success of her passage at arms with that almost indomitable will.

Well might she have said, "Lord, now lettest thou thy servant depart in peace." However this may be, the hour was one of peace and joy for the Sisters, as one after the other, each pronounced her vows and received from the bishop the name of some noted saint or martyr, by which thereafter she was to be known.

The fact that the name of Marie des Anges does not appear in the list of those who took part in this solemn ceremony seems to prove that Marie Geneviève Sayer had not yet completed the two years of preparation necessary before assuming all the rights and duties of a convent life, but was still living under the direction of the *Maîtresse des No-vices.* She was then about eighteen, and must soon after have taken up the full duties and responsibilities of her office; for, although the name of her sister appears often on Montreal records, her own is seen no more after the baptism of her mother in 1693.

The years following her novitiate were busy ones for the nuns of Canada. Up and down the St. Lawrence, missions had been early founded by the Sisters of the Congregation. With incredible fatigue, but untiring zeal, Marguerite Bourgeois had gone back and forth between Montreal and Quebec, often in winter creeping prostrate over frozen streams or wading knee-deep in the icy water.

The Mission of the Mountain was removed to Sault au Recollet. Soeur Marie des Anges, (the captive Marie Geneviève Sayer) was there at the head of the Mission School for girls, and the Deerfield captive, Abigail Nims, among others was there under her care.

The missions at Quebec were, for many reasons, of special importance, and the choice of the New England captive for that place, shows the esteem in which Marie Geneviève Sayer was held by her sister nuns. Only those "distinguished by their merits, by their courage, prudence and ability," were appointed. Though the records thereafter are silent concerning her, it would be easy to read her story between the lines that record the labors of the successors of Marguerite Bourgeois between 1698 and 1717 at Quebec.

While looking for Deerfield captives at Quebec, the word *Angloisc* in the margin of the record, led me to the following,—only this and nothing more:

"The 28th of March, 1717, was buried in the Parish Church, Sister Marie des Anges, a mission sister of the Congregation, who died the same day, aged about 36 years. The burial was made by me, the undersigned priest, Vicar of the Parish, Canon of the Cathedral, in presence of M. Glandelet, Dean, and M. Des Maizerets, precentor of said Cathedral."

So, far from kith or kin, Mary Rishworth's eldest daughter slept her last sleep, after a short, eventful and useful life.

The policy of the Canadian government was to keep as many of our captives as possible, especially those of leading New England families, to make good Catholics of them, and finally to wed them either to the church or state.

Esther Sayward, whom we know in Canada as Marie Joseph Sayer, was educated by the nuns of the Congregation, and probably remained under their protection till her marriage. Naturalization was granted her in May, 1710.

On the 5th of January, 1712, in the parish church of Montreal, "in presence of many relatives and friends of the par-ties," she was married to the Seigneur Pierre de L'Estage, merchant, of Montreal. The fact that the three banns were dispensed with, hints that ambassadors from our government, concerning an exchange of prisoners, were then in Canada, and it was thought best speedily to clip the wings of this captive bird.

Marie Joseph, the first child of Pierre de L'Estage and Marie Joseph Sayer, was born October i, 1712. The child's godmother was "Marie hardin," who "could not sign the record, on account of her great age." This child died at the age of four. Jacques Pierre, the second child, was born and baptized Aug. 5, 1714. Its godparents were Jacques Le Ber, Seigneur de Senneville, and Madame Repentigny. In the record the father is called "Monsieur Pierre Lestage, Marchand

Bourgeois of this city and treasurer for the king." In 1715, he became the owner of the Seigniory of Berthier, opposite Sorel, on the north shore of the St. Lawrence.

To the kindness of Rev. Père Moreau, curé of Notre Dame des Monts, county of Terrebonne, antiquary, savant and author of the History of Berthier, I am indebted for the following:

"Pierre de Lestage built the first Catholic church of Berthier, about 1723, and obtained on Dec. 3, 1732, from Governor Beauharnois and the Intendant Hocquart, a great addition to his Seigniory because, as is said in the deed; 'he was worthy of it.' "

He also improved the highways, and built at Berthier a saw mill, a gristmill and a fine mansion for himself with a grand avenue leading thereto, which still exist. His friend M. Louis Lepage, Vicar-general of Quebec, and Seigneur of Terrebonne, having founded there the parish of St. Louis, built for it a stone church, to which he gave a chime of bells and invited his friend De L'Estage to be godfather at the ceremony of the blessing of the bells.

At eight o'clock in the morning of the 21st of December, 1743, at the age of sixty-three, the Sieur de L'Estage, husband of Marie Joseph Sayer, died in Montreal. The next day his body was carried to the church of Notre Dame, where a solemn mass was said. From there it was borne to the church of the Récollet fathers, and buried.

Father Moreau writes that "he left his wealth jointly to his widow, Marie Joseph Esther Sayer, to his sister living in Bayonne, France, and to a nephew of the same place."

The death of her husband and children was a severe blow to Madame de L'Estage. She naturally turned for sympathy and consolation to her beloved nuns, who had befriended her girlhood. Doubtless by their advice, she purchased a house adjoining the convent and adopted two girls whom she educated at the convent. They afterwards became nuns, and were known as Soeurs Sainte Basile and Sainte Pierre. The ladies of the convent having permitted Madame de L'Estage to cut a door between the two houses, she spent the recreation hours with her adopted children in the convent. One of these daughters died at the age of twenty-five, the other at eighty. Affliction and increasing age led her to sell the Seigniory of Berthier in February, 1765. for a life annuity of 1500 livres, which, with an annual income from her husband's estates in France, handsomely supplied her wants. Tenderly cared for by the Sisters of the Congregation, she as "perpetual pensioner," spent with them peacefully and happily the remainder of her days. The loving hands of those who so long had ministered to her needs, closed her eyes at the last. The date of her death is as yet unknown to me. She was buried near her beloved Sisters of the Congregation, under the chapel of St. Anne in the old church of Notre Dame, which stood in the middle of what is now Notre Dame St., opposite the present cathedral. There, all that was mortal of the New England captive, Marie Joseph Esther Sayer, rested, until about 1830, when all who had been buried under the old church, were removed to the Cemetery of the Cote St. Antoine.

Again exhumed before 1866, they now rest in the present Cemetery at Côte des Neiges,—the site of the former Cemetery of the Côte St. Antoine being now occupied by Domin-ion Square and its fine surroundings.

She gave to the convent most of her household goods, among them elegant candelabra and other articles of silver.

Some of her bequests escaped the successive conflagrations from which the Convent has suffered. Among other things, a chest of drawers, arm chairs, silver snuffers and tray, and some exquisite embroidery.

The Curé, who has been kindly interested in this little sketch, writes me as follows:

"Indeed with her mother and sister she was greatly tried at the time of their captivity, but it was the way God judged proper to lead her to a religion, which they thought afterwards to be the only one able to lead men to eternal happiness, and for them to a suitable establishment."

DIFFICULTIES AND DANGERS IN THE SETTLEMENT OF A FRONTIER TOWN. 1670.

"The Independent Church," says a recent writer, "prepared the way for the Independent States, and an Independent Nation." The most superficial reader of history, in this preeminently secular generation, cannot ignore the fact that "The corner-stone of New England was laid in the cause of religion," nor can he fail to note how often the accidents of man were the providence of God in the settlement of our country.

When, to protect themselves against the lawlessness of a few of their number who were shuffled into their company at London, our forefathers signed the famous Compact in the little cabin of their storm-racked vessel, they builded better than they knew. Magnificent as have been the consequences of that simple act, to establish a democracy in America was not the purpose whereunto the Mayflower was sent.

> "What sought they thus afar?
> They sought a faith's pure shrine."

Later, it was the religious zeal of "that worthy man of God," Mr. John White of Dorchester, England, and his fear lest the English fishermen on our inhospitable coast, might lack the spiritual food so necessary for the salvation of their souls, that dispatched Roger Conant to Cape Ann, sent John Endicott to Salem, installed John Winthrop as governor, with the charter of Massachusetts at the Bay, and settled William Pynchon at Roxbury.

Their pious care to make plentiful provision of godly ministers for their plantation, sent over Mr. Skelton, Mr. Higginson, and Mr. Smith, and brought Eunice Williams's ancestor, John Warham, a famous Puritan divine of Exeter, to Dorchester. Their devotion to religion and their willingness to suffer exile for freedom to worship God according to the dictates of their own consciences, brought Thomas Hooker and Samuel Stone, as pastor and teacher, to Cambridge. This, too, led John Cotton, when driven by threats of the infamous court of High Commission, from "the most stately parish church in England," St. Botolph's in Old Boston, to preach the gospel "within the mud walls, and under the thatched roof of the meeting-house in a rude New England hamlet," which, in honor of his arrival, took thenceforth the name of Boston.

The same religious fervor, made the fathers of Massachusetts determine that the rights of citizenship, and offices of public trust, should belong "only to Christian men, ascertained to be such by the best test which they know how to apply,"—and however unwise, impracticable and unjust it would seem, in our day, to make the franchise dependent upon church membership, yet the bribery and corruption witnessed in our elections, and the moral unfitness of many of our candidates, make us wish that "not birth, nor learning, nor skill in war, alone might confer political power," but that to these we might add some test of personal character, of moral worth and goodness.

We need to remember amid the dissensions that are agitating the religious world of to-day, that the Puritanism of the fathers, which to us seems the extreme of conservatism, was really the radicalism of their time.

It is a curious study to trace the struggle between the old and the new, that began at the beginning and must endure to the end of time, as it is connected with the settlement of our state, and through that, with the history of our nation.

However they may have desired "to transfer themselves to the fertile valley of the Connecticut, from the less productive soil upon which they had sat down," and whatever other motives they may have alleged for their migration, it is easy to see that the same desire for greater civil and religious freedom, that planted the first settlers at Plymouth Rock and Massachusetts Bay, led to the removal of William Pynchon and his Roxbury neighbors to Springfield, of John Warham and his Dorchester flock to Windsor, of the Water-town church, with Henry Smith as its pastor, to Weathers-field, and of Hooker and Stone, with their congregations, to Hartford.

Still later, the radicalism of the majority of the Hartford church on the subject of baptism, extending to the church at Weathersfield, led to the settlement of Hadley by a small minority of the more conservative brethren of both parishes, under the leadership of Governor Webster of Hartford and Mr. John Russell of Weathersfield.

Another lesson of peculiar significance to us, at the present period of our religious history, is given in the fact that amid all their differences, our forefathers never lost sight of the common aim and purpose of their emigration, namely, "the advancement of the kingdom of the Lord Jesus Christ, and the enjoyment of the liberties of the Gospel, in unity with peace," whereto they bear noble testimony in the preamble to the articles of Confederation, signed by the four colonies, in 1643.

It could not be supposed that men professing "the propagation of the Gospel to be above all their aim in settling this plantation," would be long indifferent to the spiritual welfare of the savages around them. The conversion of the na-tives was early an object of their solicitude, but the obstacles were such as might have appalled the most enthusiastic zealot; and not until 1644, was the work begun in earnest.

John Eliot, destined to become the Apostle to the Indians, on quitting the University at Cambridge, England, was assistant to Thomas Hooker, in a private school. Leaving his native country for the same motives that impelled other Puritans at that time, and arriving in 1631, at Boston, he there for a season supplied the pulpit of the absent pastor, and later was appointed teacher of the newly organized church at Roxbury. The missionary spirit, which prompted him to undertake the conversion of the Indians, was greatly aided by his natural fondness for philological studies, in which he is said to have excelled at college. Employing his leisure hours in endeavoring to master the language of the natives, at length, in the autumn of 1644, he preached in a wigwam on Nonantum hill, his first sermon in the Indian tongue. Some authority seemed to be given soon after to his under-taking, by an order from the General Court to the County Courts, "for the civilization of the Indians and their instruction in the worship of God."

The passage of such a decree was an easy task. What benevolence and fortitude, what faith, patience and courage were requisite to its execution, those who have read the life of Eliot know full well. From this time to the end of his long life, his labors for the Indians were unflagging. Having the good sense to see that they must be civilized before they could be christianized, he wished to collect them in compact settlements of their own. "I find it absolutely necessary," he says, "to carry on civility with religion." To quote his

own words, he "looked for some spot somewhat remote from the English, where the Word might be constantly taught, and government constantly exercised, means of good subsistence provided, encouragement for the industrious, means of instruction in letters, trades and labor."

About the year 1650, he found a suitable site at Natick, and the records of this period attest the pertinacity of his application to the General Court for the same, and its patient endeavors to satisfy his demands, without interfering with the rights of those to whom these adjacent lands had already been granted.

The inhabitants of Dedham having signified their willingness to further the plantation at Natick by a tender of two thousand acres of their land to the Indians, "provided they lay down all claims in that town elsewhere, and set no traps in enclosed lands," the Court approving, in October, 1652, empowered Capt. Eleazar Lusher of Dedham, and others, to lay out meet bounds for the Indian plantation at Natick.

From this time, for several years, the records are occupied with the settlement of Natick bounds. Petitions from Dedham for relief from "affronts offered them by the Indians," and counter petitions from Mr. Eliot, "in behalf of the poor natives," concerning the monopoly by the English of the best meadow and upland, and encroachments upon the Indian grant, show that the task of adjustment was a difficult one. In May, 1662, the Court, "Finding that the legal rights of Dedham cannot in justice be denied, yet such has been the encouragement of the Indians in the improvement thereof, the which added to their native right, which cannot in strict justice be utterly extinct, do therefore order that the Indians be not dispossessed of such lands as they are at present possessed of there, but that the same, with convenient accommodations for wood and timber and highways thereto, be set out and bounded by a committee appointed for that purpose, and that the damages thereby sustained by Dedham, together with charges sustained in suits about the same, be determined by the said committee, such allowance being made them out of Natick lands, or others yet lying in common, as they shall judge equal."

One of the committee appointed "being disabled by the providence of God," and the other utterly declining the work, the Court at its autumn session, "Being sensible of the great inconveniency that accrues to both English and Indians by the neglect of an issue to the controversy, elects others in their stead and orders that the work be issued within six weeks at the fartherest."

June 16, 1663—"For a final issue of the case between Dedham and Natick, the court judgeth it meet to grant Dedham 8000 acres of land in any convenient place or places, not exceeding two, where it can be found free from former grants, provided Dedham accept of this offer."

At a general meeting, Jan. 1, 1664, the town, as we learn from the Dedham records, "Having duly considered this proposition, their conclusion is about the 8000 acres, that the care of managing the same so as the town may have their ends answered, be left to the Selectmen now to be chosen," among whom were Ensign Daniel Fisher and Lieut. Joshua Fisher.

Sept. 21, 1664, John Fairbanks having informed the Selectmen that Goodman Prescott, "an auntient planter and publique spirited man of Lancaster," thinks it probable that a suitable tract of land is to be found at some distance from there, they depute Lieut. Fisher and Fairbanks to repair to Sudbury and Lancaster, and report upon their return. An item here occurring of "9s allowed Henry Wright for his horse for the journey to the Chestnut country, judging it well worth that," has reference to this expedition, and Nov. 6, 1664, the committee reported that the tract of land where of they had been informed, was "already entered upon by several farms, and altogether unable to supply them."

It is precisely at this point that the history of Deerfield begins. I follow the records:

"The Selectmen in further pursuance of this case concerning the 8000 acres above mentioned having heard of a considerable tract of good land that might be answerable to the town's expectation, about 10 or 12 miles from Hadley, ... think it meete in behalf of the towne to provide that the 8000 acres be chosen and laid out to satisfie that grant, and that with all convenient speed, before any other grantee enter upon it and prevent us."

Eight men or any four of them, "whereof Lieft. Joshua Fisher is to be one," were appointed, "empowered and entreated to repayer to the place mentioned, ... to choose and lay out the Land according to their best discretion," each man being promised "100 acres of land in full satisfaction for their paynes, ... onely to Lieft. Fisher such other satisfaction as shall be judged equal." Further progress in the work was prevented by the coming on of winter, during which some unwillingness seems to have been shown by the committee, to undertake the business on the terms offered by the Selectmen.

As appears from the record of March 20, 1665, the difficulty was amicably settled, when "Upon further consideration of effecting the layeing out the 8000 Acres, ... Lieft. Fisher declaring his disaceptance of w^t was aboue tendered him, ... and his peremptory demaund being 300 acres, it is consented vnto provided he allso drawe for the Towne a true and sufficient platt of that tract and Edw: Richards, Antho: Fisher, Junio^r, and Tymo: Dwight, accept of the payem^t formerly tendered, viz. 150 achers to each of them."

If Timothy Dwight be unable to attend to the business himself, he agrees to furnish Sergt. Richard Ellis with a horse for the journey. A report of this committee with reference to an accompanying plot, certified and figured as "layd *out by* Joshua Fisher, May, 1665," proves that the work was accomplished without much delay.

The principle of Squatter Sovereignty by which men naturally at first possess themselves of lands in a new settlement, is as naturally set aside by the first attempts at corporate government. The land was granted by the General Court in townships, without prescription as to the manner of its apportionment among the inhabitants, and though persons and property seem to have had some consideration in the distribution, no uniform rule was observed in the different towns.

Dedham, at this period, was occupied by two classes of inhabitants,—landed proprietors, and landless residents. All the lands of the township, at first held as common property, had been divided into 522 cow commons, a name based upon the number of cattle then running on the common pasture, and by a somewhat arbitrary rule, a certain number of these shares assigned to each proprietor, with the understanding that his rights in all future grants of land to the township of Dedham would be proportionate to his proprietorship there. In the actual division of the Pocumtuck grant, however, there are 523 cow commons, one more than in the Dedham property, a discrepancy as yet inexplicable.

After the allotment of the 750 acres promised to Lieut. Fisher and his three associates, for their assistance in laying out the grant, the remainder was to be divided into cow com-mons. The surveyors doubtless selected their tract on their first expedition, and their choice was made with great sagac-ity. It included about one hundred and fifty acres of the very best land in the north meadows, situated as we believe from a careful comparison of allotments, in the region now known as Pogue's Hole, the Neck and White Swamp.

It may be a satisfaction to property holders there, to note the advance in real estate since Dec. 10, 1665, when Timothy Dwight, on condition that a plantation is effectually settled at Pocumtuck, agrees to resign all claim to his share for *"5£ ; 2£* to be paid in money, and in corn and cattell," and Lieut. Fisher makes a similar offer of his rights, for *"£4.* in cash and £6 in corn and cattell," the only time, probably, when 300 acres of good land in Old Deerfield could have been bought for about fifty dollars.

In the records, the surveyors' lands are spoken of as "Farms," to distinguish them from the cow commons of the other proprietors. On Jan. 22, 1666, it was voted, "That each proprietor's land shall pay annually towards the maintenance of an Orthodox Minister there, 2s for each cow common, whether the owner live there or at Dedham; and all others that hold any part of the 8000 in proportion upon any other account besides cow commons, shall pay proportionately upon such lands as shall be laid out for the accommodation of teaching church officers there." The last clause refers to the Puritan custom of employing both a Pastor and a Teacher for the same church.

Any man unwilling or unable to pay his tax for the ministry, was empowered to sell his rights, at a price to be fixed by a majority of the proprietors, and in case no buyer could be found, the inhabitants of Pocumtuck were to take his rights at that price, or free him from the aforesaid tax.

The bounds of the grant having been laid out in May, 1665, the next thing to be done was the extinction of the Indian title by a nominal purchase of their lands. A nominal purchase, I say, because remembering how all the fertile river lands from Suffield to Northfield, were purchased from the Indians for a few great coats and some hundred fathoms of wampum, I cannot quite agree with Dr. Holland, who declares that "All the land occupied by the settlers was fairly purchased of the natives."

Mr. Judd, in alluding to the fact that Penn's bargain with the Indians has been rendered famous by the historian and poet, says "It would be difficult to tell why Penn's purchase is more worthy of renown than the purchase of Indian lands in Hadley by John Pynchon twenty years before." With less partiality than the former writer, he adds, "both bought as cheaply as they could."

Let us cast no imputation on the general justice of the policy of the early settlers of Massachusetts towards the Indians. Still it is noticeable that the very records of their purchases make complacent mention of the "Indian title in [not to] the land," and we must admit that it was usually a bargain in which might made right, the simple wants and characteristic lack of foresight of the red man being no match for the ambition and shrewdness of the civilized white. Major John Pynchon of Springfield, (Worshipful John) in his double capacity of magistrate and trader, dealt largely with the Connecticut River Indians and effected nearly every important purchase from them. The Sachems of the valley kept a running account at Pynchon's shop, buying from him wampum and other small merchandise of which they stood in need, and pledging their lands in payment.

He in turn transferred the Indian deeds to the white settlers, receiving from them money, corn, wheat and other standard articles of trade. The following items from Pynchon's account book is a small part of the debt of Umpachala, the Norwottuck Sachem, in payment of which he gave Pynchon a deed of the town of Hadley:

"1660, July 10, 2 coats, shag and wampum, 5£; Red shag cotton, knife, 7s. July 30 to September 14, wampum and 2 coats, 5£ 10s; a kettle, 1£ 5s; for your being drunk, 10s."

Thus for the vice of drunkenness which the untaught Pagan had learned from our Christian civilization, we forced him to forfeit his home, and yet we boast of the fairness of our dealings with him.

Major Pynchon, acting in behalf of the Dedham proprietors, obtained from the Pocumtuck Indians four deeds of land. Three of these are extant.

The first, dated February 24th, 1665, is signed with his mark by Chaque, Sachem of Pocumtuck, who for good "and valuable considerations," transfers a large portion of the territory of his tribe, to John Pynchon for Major Eleazar Lusher, Ensign Daniel Fisher, and other Englishmen of Dedham, agreeing to defend the same from any molestation from Indians, and resending the right

"Of fishing in the waters and rivers, and free liberty to hunt deer and other wild creatures, and to gather walnuts, chestnuts and other nuts and things on the commons."

The second, dated June 16th, 1667, is from Masseamet, owner of certain lands at Pocumtuck, who in conveying them agreed to "save them harmless from all manner of claims."

By the third, dated July 22d, 1667, Ahimunquat, alias Mesquinnitchall of Pocumtuck, and his brother, devise and sell both Weshatchowmesit and Tomholisick "with all the trees, waters, profits and commoditys whatsoever," to the same parties to hold and enjoy, and that forever. The prosecution of this business was the chief topic of interest at Dedham.

"June 6th, 1667, the Selectmen after consideration of the case respecting Pocompticke and the Information brought by those bretheren lately upon the place,. . . . . . doe desire and depute them. . . . . . . .to make reporte in publike the next Lecture day after Lecture. . . . . .Allso that the Towne be made acquainted with the disbursm^{ts} of the Worp^{fult} Capt Pinchion in purchasing the Indians Right at Pocompticke . . . . . . who haue declared that he haue allready layed out about 40£ and is yet in prosecution of compleating that worke, and by word and writeing haue exp'ssed his desire to be reimbursed, the payem^l he desire is money, wheate and porke and wee would desire the Towne to remember and gratifie his paynes."

October 2d, 1667, a rate was laid to pay Capt. Pynchon the sum disbursed for Pocumtuck land, wherein 4s was assessed upon each cow common, reckoning 14 acres or thereabouts to each common, and an equal assessment, acre for acre on the "farms" of the surveyors.

The list of proprietors at this time numbers sixty Dedham men.

The deeds, meanwhile, having been delivered to Eleazar Lusher, by whom they were deposited in Deacon Aldis's box,—at a general meeting of the proprietors, September 29th, 1669, *96£*, 10s were ordered raised to pay Capt. Pynchon, (the first assessment evidently not having been collected), by an assessment of 3s 4d on each cow common, the 750 acres constituting the farms of the surveyors being rated at 54 commons, showing thus an estimate of about 14 acres to a common.

This list contains the names of eighty-four proprietors, proving that the fever of speculation in Deerfield land was spreading in Dedham. Among several transfers of rights recorded, is the purchase of Anthony Fisher's 150 acres by Gov. Leverett, who sold it again to John Pynchon "for *£9* current money and several barrels of tar," in the manufacture of which Springfield was largely engaged. Permission was also granted in 1668, to Lieut. Fisher, to sell a part of his rights to John Stebbins of Northampton, ancestor of the Stebbins family of Deerfield.

On May 10th, 1670, a committee of the proprietors, assembled to fix a time for drawing lots and settling proprieties at Pocumtuck, order notice to be given of a meeting of the proprietors for that purpose, at the meeting house in Dedham at seven o'clock in the morning of the 23d instant.

"The proprietors by Grant or purchase," assembled according to appointment on the morning of May 23d, 1670. At this meeting

"It is agreed that an Artist be procured upon as moderate tearmes as may be that may laye out the Lotts at Pawcompticke to each propriato^r.". . . . . .

Three Hadley men, as being more familiar with the situation than the Dedham committee, were "desired to direct the artist in the work abovesaid, and empowered to order the situation of the Towne for the most conveaniencie   the whole Tract, and the quallities of each sort of Land, and other accomadacions considered. . . . . . It is allso agreed that no man shall laye out more than 20 Cow Commons rights together in one place.   Joh. Pincheon is entreated and empowered. . . . . . to take his time to visit the

Committee and artist and to giue them such advice. . . . . . as he shall Judge most Conduceable to the good of the plantation. . . . . . It is further agreed to proceed to drawe Lotts, and pᵣpare accordingly and that in every deuision of Lands of all sorts (except house Lotts) the length of the Lotts shall runne easterly and westerly, and the begining of layeing out Lotts shall allwayes be on the northerly side and make an end on the southerly side. . . . . . "

The meadow lands only, were allotted in this drawing, and a cow common represented three acres of land. The list of proprietors includes two women, and contains in all thirty-four names, among which are those of Samuel Hinsdell and Samson Frary.

During the summer succeeding this allotment, the com-mittee visited the grant, and laid out the "town plat," which they divided into the same number of commons and lots as the meadows, a common being smaller, as the area set apart for their homesteads was, of course, much less than that reserved for tillage.

May 14th, 1671, the drawing for house lots took place. On the 16th, the committee made a detailed report to the town of Dedham, of all their proceedings, and a most interesting document it is. It shows us the lots as they front east and west on the street, the meadow roads at the north and south, and a highway from the middle of the street, east and west to the mountain and river, nearly as we see them to-day. The lots were numbered in regular order, No. 1 being at the north end on the west side; but as the area of each man's house lot was proportioned to the number of cow commons of which he was proprietor, they varied in extent from one acre nine rods, to seven acres ten rods, and cannot be identified. Various circumstances lead to the conclusion, that lot No. 13, drawn by John Stebbins, was that now owned by Samuel Wells.

The first and second divisions of the meadows were defined as they still appear, though we no longer recognize a curious distinction, borrowed doubtless from their salt marshes around Dedham, which they made between the lower lands on the river, called by them "the meadows," and "the more higher sort of lands," called "Intervale or plow lands." The report also furnishes the clearest evidence, that the country surrounding the meadows, (the east and west mountains, from Long Hill south, and from Cheapside hills north), was densely wooded, which is contrary to tradition.

It must not be supposed that Deerfield was settled by a colony from Dedham, as Windsor had been from Dorchester. The thirty-four names appearing on the list of original proprietors of Pocumtuck, do not represent actual settlers.

Robert Hinsdell and his son Samuel, Samson Frary, John Farrington and Samuel Daniels, are the only Dedham men appearing among the thirty-four original proprietors of Pocumtuck, who ever became actual settlers in Deerfield. John Stebbins, a Northampton man also on the list, settled here. The other Dedham proprietors sold out their rights.

Robert Hinsdell, his son Samuel, and Samson Frary, were living in Hatfield just previous to the allotment of lands at Pocumtuck, May 23d, 1670, and very soon after that date, the two latter took up their abode in Deerfield. The report to which I have alluded, fixes these two men as the first settlers of Deerfield. In it, the street is described as extending "from Eagle Brook on the south to the banke or falling ridge of land at Samson Frary's cellar on the north;" and permission is given to Samuel Hinsdell "to enjoy a percell of land on which at present he is resident, considering his expense on the same."

The third settler, Godfrey Nims, came from Northampton to Deerfield in 1670, living there "in a sort of a house where he had dug a hole or cellar in the side hill," south of Colonel Wilson's. At the allotment of the homesteads in 1671, he built a house, on what lot is not known.

In 1672, the town of Hatfield, complaining that their north boundary was obstructed by the Pocumtuck line, it was accordingly established where it now is.

The same year Samuel Hinsdell petitioned the town of Dedham, to appoint a committee of suitable persons to regulate the affairs of the new settlement. No heed being paid to this request, the petitioners renewed it the next year, urging their distress by reason of their remoteness from other plantations. Either directly or indirectly, through Dedham, their prayer was heard by the General Court, which in 1673,

"In ans^r to the peticon of. . . . . . ., Samuel Hinsdell, Samson Frary &c, the Court. . . . . . . allow the petitioners the liberty of a Township and doe therefore grant them such an addition. . . . . . . to the 8000 acres formerly granted. . . . . . . as that the whole be. . . . . . . seven miles square, provided that an able & orthodox minister wthin three yeares be settled,. . . . . . . and doe appointt. . . . . . . Lef^l. Wm Allys, Thos Meakins, Sen & Sergent Isaack Graues, wth Lef^l Samuel Smith, M^r. Peeter Tylton, & Samuel Hinsdell. . . . . . . or any fower of them, to admit inhabitants, grant lands, & order all their prudentiall affaires till they shall be in a capacity, by meet persons from among themselues, to manage their owne affaires."

During the two succeeding years, this committee was not idle. There were claims to be satisfied, and disputes concerning land titles to be adjusted. Among other grants was one of "20 Akars of land and Allsoe a hoame lott, to Richard Weier and his heirs forever:—of a hoame lott, and Allsoe a twelve common Lott of 36 Akars to Sergeant Plimpton and his heirs forever:—and to Zebediah Williams a house lott of 4 Akars: " on condition of their residing thereon for the space of four years from their first occupation. To Mr. Samuel Mather, the Dedham church lot was awarded, "and an 8 common lotte more in the most convenient place— 48 Akars in all," on the same condition.

In 1673, at the early age of twenty-two, he began his labors as first minister of Deerfield. He had been graduated two years before at Harvard, and was a nephew of the distinguished Increase Mather, and cousin to the more learned Cotton Mather.

In the fall of 1674, Moses Crafts, "was licensed to keep an Ordinary at Pocumtuck,"—the word tavern or ale-house was offensive to our Puritan fathers,—"and to sell wines and strong liquors for one year, provided he keep good order in his house."

Inhabitants came in gradually, men began to "stub up" their home lots, and the infant town, now known by the name of Deerfield from the number of those animals in its woodlands, seemed in a fair way to a prosperous growth.

The savages still hunted, fished, and fowled, in the woods and waters of Pocumtuck, maintaining entire friendliness to-wards the settlers. Often Goodwife Stockwell, cumbered with much care about the minister's dinner, would be startled at her work, by the dusky shadow of an old squaw gliding in at her doorway to bring her a mat or a basket, expecting a few beans or a trifle in return; or the Indian hunter strode through the little village with a haunch of venison on his shoulder, to barter with Moses Crafts for tobacco or powder; or his young wife, with her bright-eyed pappoose at her back, peered wonderingly in at the door of the little log meetinghouse, while the young divine poured forth his soul in prayer; and listened with pleased attention as the Psalms, deaconed out by old Robert Hinsdale, were sung to the fine old tunes of York or Windsor.

So, side by side, in peace, stood the wigwam of the savage and the cabin of the settler, in this valley, till the torch kindled at Swanzey by that "prime incendiary, Philip," as the historians of the time call him, set the whole country in flames. Driven from his throne at Mount Hope, the self-styled king, with a few followers, fled for aid and comfort to the country of the Nipmucks, his subjects or allies.

A quaint writer says, with much gravity, that "about now, Philip began to need money, and having a coat made all of wampum, cut it in pieces and distributed it among the Nip-muck sachems;" whereupon Drake remarks, that the coat must have been bigger than Doctor Johnson's, mentioned by Boswell, the side pockets of which, were each large enough to contain a volume of his folio dictionary. Doubtless Phil-ip's wampum and his wrongs, were freely used as incentives to the war, but at this period the quarrel was not one of individuals or of tribes. It was a struggle of races for the **possession** of a continent; or rather, it was a war of the incarnated principles of barbarism resisting the encroachments of civilization, the last rally of Paganism against Christian-ity. Philip or no Philip, sooner or later, the contest was inevitable. In the Connecticut valley, the carnival of blood opened with the Sugar Loaf fight, in the autumn of 1675. The defection of the Pocumtuck Indians, with later events sadly familiar to all, followed in quick succession. The bloodthirsty savage lurking in the forest, sped his bullet with unerring aim to the heart of the settler, as he plied his axe for his winter's fire; or creeping stealthily to the cabin whose occupants were wont to greet him with kindness, he tore the child from its mothers arms as she lulled it to rest, and with one blow of his tomahawk, silenced its cries forever. "A distressing sense of instant danger," pervaded every breast. The churches everywhere were before the Lord with humiliation and prayer, and pious preachers admonished their flocks, that their sufferings were directly chargeable to their sins. From the very midst of the alarm, Parson Stoddard writing to Increase Mather, at Boston, urges the need of a reformation. "Many sins," he says, "are grown so in fash-ion, that it is a question whether they be sins," and begs him to call the Governor's attention especially to "that intolerable pride in clothes and hair, and the toleration of so many taverns, especially in Boston, and suffering home dwellers to be tippling therein." "It would be a dreadful token of the displeasure of God," he adds, "if these afflictions pass away without much spiritual advantage." Mr. Mather, jotting down hastily for the printer, the intelligence that comes post from Hadley, moralizes thus: "It is as if the Lord should say He hath a controversy with every plantation, and therefore all had need to repent and reform their ways." "This sore contending of God with us for our sins," writes John Pynchon to his absent son, "unthankfulness for former mercies and unfaithfulness under our precious enjoyments, hath evidently demonstrated that He is very angry with this country, and hath given the heathen a large commission to destroy." And Minister Hubbard, from his Ipswich study, where rumors come flying in of the untimely cutting off of the flower of Essex by Indian hatchet, groans out, "God grant that by the fire of all these judgments, we may be purged from our dross and become a more refined people, as vessels fitted for our Master's use."

The inhabitants of Deerfield, warned by repeated attacks, had been driven from their homes and were huddled together in two or three houses, poorly protected by palisades, and defended by a handful of soldiers. To the men, *who* with gun and sickle in hand, went out to harvest the fruits of their summer's labor, the smoke from some distant chimney was a terror, lest they should return to find the remnant of their little settlement in ashes. While as straggling bands of Indians on their murderous errand passed near the forts, the women watched and waited within, in an agony of fear, lest some beloved one might not return at nightfall. The noonday was thick with horrors, and a thousand phantoms of dread, haunted the darkness and silence of midnight. The wind shrieked and groaned through the forest, as if with pre-monition of impending disaster. To their frightened fancy, the patter of the autumnal rain, was the tramp of the approaching foe, and the rustle of the leaves, as they sped before the September gale, the final rush of their savage assailants. Compelled at last to seek security and shelter for their families in the better protected settlements, the men of Deerfield reluctantly prepared to desert the homesteads they had won with much toil from the wilderness.

The last bag of wheat was at length filled, the golden corn lay heaped on the great ox-carts, the feather beds and other treasures of thrifty housewifery carefully disposed atop, and the march for Hadley began. The feeling with which they saw the day breaking over the mountain, as they wended their way through the meadows on that ever memorable morning, the 18th of September, 1675, was, no doubt, one of mingled relief that the long suspense was ended, and of resolute confidence that they should return in the spring, to occupy the fields to which they now bade a regretful farewell. No foreshadowing of their awful fate, seems to have rested on their hearts. Joyfully their households awaited them at Hadley, joy turned all too soon to bitter sorrow, when the few that escaped told there, how the little stream, known before as Muddy Brook, had been baptized anew and consecrated forever, with the blood of eighteen of the sturdy yeomanry of Pocumtuck, and many a valiant soldier besides. Goodwife Hinsdale wept for her husband and three stalwart sons slain in the fight, and remembered with unavailing penitence, how the year before she had flouted his authority. Upon the ear of William Smead, mourning for his boy of fifteen, Mr. Mather's Latin *"Dulce et decorum est, pro patria mori,"* fell unheeded; and vainly did brave Sergeant Plympton strive to hush the wailing of his old wife Jane, for Jonathan, the staff of their declining years, now lost forever.

After the massacre at Muddy Brook, the garrison was withdrawn from Deerfield, and the enemy soon laid in ashes all that remained of that hopeful plantation. Some brave spirits, however, still clung to the hope of resettlement. These, exasperated by the news, in the early summer of 1676, that the Indians, not only had their rendezvous at the Great Falls, where they were laying in large stores of fish for their next campaign, but were actually planting corn on the rich intervales of Deerfield, gladly volunteered, under the heroic Turner, to dislodge them. By his defeat of the Indians at the Swamscott Falls, Philip's war, so called, was virtually ended. A few months later, the pallid hands of that once haughty chieftain were shown as a spectacle in the streets of Boston. His ghastly head set up on a pole in Plymouth, afforded the occasion for a public thanksgiving, and the body of Weetamoo,[2] his constant ally, more implacable in her resent-ment than even he had been, lay stranded by the ebbing tide, the once beauteous form now sodden and repulsive, the long hair, which the proud dame was wont to dress so carefully, all knotted with sea-tangle, the features once so gaily adorned, all begrimed with the ooze and slime of Taunton River.

The dispersion of their foes made the surviving settlers of Deerfield anxious to return there. The prospect of passing another winter with their families in the overcrowded dwellings of Hadley and Hatfield, was not agreeable to them, and they feared lest a union of the settlements might be effected, which would deprive them forever of their Pocumtuck heritage. Though the presence of prowling bands of Indians in the valley, made any attempt at resettlement hazardous, Quentin Stockwell would not be dissuaded from his purpose. Of Stockwell's previous history, but little is known except that he was from Dedham. There his name appears on various tax lists, from 1663 to 1672, when he removed with his wife to Hatfield, and thence the next year to Deerfield, where the Rev. Mr. Mather found a quiet home with them. That he was a man of energy and courage, appears from his being the only Deerfield man, who, in the autumn of 1676, dared begin to rebuild his ruined home. Driven from his work by the Indians, who burned his half-finished house, he fled again, most probably to Hatfield, where, with other Deerfield people, he spent the winter. He was, however, far from content. The birth of his child made him doubly anxious to shelter himself under his own roof-tree, and the next summer he succeeded in persuading old John Plympton, Benoni Stebbins, and one or two others, to return with him to Deerfield, where the former had already built himself a house, eighteen feet long.

It was the morning of the 19th of September, 1677. A year had passed since the close of the war, and the people of this valley, relieved of their apprehensions, were beginning to resume their usual occupations, when the shrill war-whoop rang through the frosty air, and a party of Indians, descending with fire and slaughter upon Hatfield, ran thence with seventeen captives, mostly women and children, towards Deerfield.

It was near sunset of one of those tranquil, New England autumn days, we know so well. Naught of melancholy was in the song piped by a belated August cricket, and the striped snake crawled from his hole to bask in the sunshine, as if he half believed summer had come again. The witch-hazel threw into the lap of October a wealth of blossoms, which June could never extort from her. A crown of gold, gemmed with opal and amethyst, rested on the brow of the western hills; the swamps were ablaze with the flame-colored sumachs. The mountain, already in shadow, seemed like some massive temple, where in stoles of scarlet and purple and gold, stood maple and oak and chestnut, like cardinal, bishop and priest, to offer a sacrament of peace. No sound in the woodlands, save now and then as a leaf rustled down softly and was silent. The squirrels as they frolicked among the branches, ceased their chatter, startled by the echo of Quentin Stockwell's hammer, as it was borne up from the valley. A light heart was in his bosom, for he thought how snugly his little family would be housed before winter set in, and faster fell the strokes as the sun declined. Nearby, sat little Samuel Russell, watching with delight the great chips as they fell from under John Root's axe, when suddenly "with great shouting and shooting," the Indians came upon them. Dropping their tools, and seizing their guns, the men fled towards the swamp, where Root was instantly shot, and Stockwell after brave resistance, was at last overpowered and compelled to surrender or die.

"I was now by my own House," says Quentin, "which the Indians burnt the last year and I was about to build up again, and there I had some hopes to escape from them. There was a Horse just by which they bid me take. I did so, but made no attempt to escape thereby because the enemy was near, and the beast dull and slow, and I in hopes they would send me to take my own Horses, which they did, but they were so frighted that I could not come near to them, and so fell still into the Enemies hands, who now took me, and bound me, and led me away, and soon was I brought into the company of other Captives, that were that day brought away from Hatfield, which were about a mile off; and here methought was matter of joy and sorrow both, to see the Company; some Company in this condition being some refreshing, though little help anyways.

Then were we pinioned and led away in the night over the mountains, in dark and hideous wayes, about four miles further, before we took up our place for rest, which was in a dismal piece of Wood, on the east side of the mountain.

We were kept bound all that night. The Indians kept waking, and we had little mind to sleep in this night's travel.

The Indians dispersed, and as they went made strange noises as of Wolves and Owls and other Wilds Beasts, to the end that they might not lose one another, and if followed they might not be discovered by the English.

About the break of Day we Marched again and got over the great river at Pecumptuck River mouth, and there rested about two hours. There the Indians marked out upon Trees the number of their Captives and Slain as their manner is. Now was I again in great danger; A quarrel arose about me, whose Captive I was, for three took me. I thought I must be killed to end the controversie, so when they put it to me whose I was, I said three Indians took me; so they agreed to have all a share in me. I had now three Masters, and he was my chief master who laid hands on me first, and thus was I fallen into the hands of the very worst of all the Company; as Ashpelon the Indian captain told me; which captain was all along very kind to me, and a great comfort to the English. In this place they gave us some Victuals which they had brought from the English. This morning also they sent ten Men forth to Town to bring away what they could find, some Provision, some Corn out of the Meadow they brought to us upon Horses which they had there taken. From hence we went up about the Falls, where we crossed that River again, and whilst I was going, I fell right down lame of my old Wounds that I had in the War, and whilst I was thinking I should therefore be killed by the Indians, and what Death I should die, my pain was suddenly gone and I was much encouraged again."

As they recrossed the river at Peskeompskut Falls, the Hatfield captives remembered with satisfaction, how Benjamin Waite had piloted brave Turner to his great victory at this very spot; and a gleam of hope cheered their hearts at the thought, that he would not be less active in the pursuit of the foe, who now bore his helpless wife and children into cruel captivity. Stockwell continues, "We had about eleven horses in that Company, which the Indians used, to carry Burthens, and to carry Women. It was afternoon when we now crossed that river. We travelled up it till night, and then took up our Lodging in a dismal place, and were staked down and spread out on our backs; and so we lay all night, yea so we laid many nights. They told me their Law was, that we should lie so nine nights, and by that time, it was thought we should be out of our knowledge. The manner of staking down was thus: our Arms and Legs stretched out were staked fast down, and a Cord about our necks, so that we could stir no wayes. The first night of staking down, being much tired, I slept as comfortable as ever. The next day we went up the river, and crossed it and at night lay in Squakheag meadows, and while we lay in those meadows, the Indians went a-hunting, and the English army came out after us."

Dividing into many companies to elude pursuit, they again crossed the river. About thirty miles above Northfield they re-crossed it to the west, and being quite out of fear of the English, lay there encamped about three weeks. On this last march Stockwell's three masters went off to hunt, leaving him with only one Indian, who fell sick, so that as he says, "I was fain to carry his Gun and Hatchet, and had opportunity and had thought to have dispatched him, and run away, but did not, for that the English Captives had promised the contrary to one another, because if one should run away, that would provoke the Indians, and endanger the rest that could not run away."

Life was dear to him, escape was easy, the thought of his child sorely tempted him to try it, but he remembered that if one should run away it would endanger the rest, and resisted. No knightlier deed was ever done. Not the dying Sidney putting aside the proffered cup of water from his fe-vered lips, more deserves our reverence, than Quentin Stock-well refusing liberty, and life for aught he knew, lest his gain might prove another's loss. While encamped here, Stockwell says, "they had a great Dance, (as they call it), concluded to burn three of us and had got Bark to do it with, and as I understood afterwards, 1 was one that was to be burnt, Sergeant Plimpton another, and Benjamin Wait his wife the third: though I knew not which was to be burnt, yet I perceived some were designed thereunto, so much I understood of their language: that night I could not sleep for fear of next dayes work, the Indians being weary with that Dance, laid down to sleep, and slept soundly. The English were all loose, then I went out and brought in Wood, and mended the fire, and made a noise on purpose, but none awaked, I thought if any of the English would wake, we might kill them all sleeping, I removed out of the way all the Guns and Hatchets; but my heart failing me, I put all things where they were again. The next day when we were to be burnt, our Master and some others spake for us, and the Evil was prevented in this place."

The tale is simply told, but no rhetoric could add to its pathos. The frightful orgies, whose dolor, says an eye witness, "no pen though made of harpy's quill, could describe;" the council fire and hellish pantomime, by which Quentin understood that some were destined to the stake; the savage brutes at length satiated with rioting, heavy and stupid with sleep, their usual precautions forgotten; the lonely watcher, his soul racked with torturing anguish, meditating on the chances of escape; his desperate resolution to attempt it, and noisily replenishing the tire with the double purpose of testing the vigilance of his foes and the wakefulness of his friends; cautiously removing the weapons, where they may be ready for his purpose, and then, as hope dies within his breast, as carefully replacing them, with the despairing consciousness that failure would only hasten the captives' doom, with never once a thought of leaving them to their fate and seeking safety for himself in flight,—all this is pictured with awful vividness.

At this period, there was trouble between the Mohawks and the Christian Indians, on account of the neglect of the latter to pay their customary tribute to the warlike lords of the Mohawk valley.

Six Mohawks, fully armed, had been seized near Boston while hunting, and thrown into prison by the authorities there. A party of Mohawks with a scalp, and two Natick squaws as captives, having passed through Hatfield on the very day before the assault upon that town, the opinion prevailed that it was made by them. Distracted with grief, Benjamin Waite, one of the bereaved husbands, hastened immediately to Albany to demand redress, but returned with the assurance that the New York Indians were innocent of the affair. A fortnight had elapsed since the capture, and the distressed people of Hatfield could learn nothing of the fate of their friends, when Benoni Stebbins, having escaped from his captors, returned with definite information concerning them. His relation as given by himself to the Northampton post-master, October 6th, 1667, is a curious document. He states that his captors were "river Indians, Norwattucks, save only one Narragansett, twenty-six in all, eighteen fighting men, two squaws, the rest old men and boys; that they came from the French whither they had fled at the end of the war, and intended to return there again to sell the captives, having been encouradged that they should have eight pounds apiece for them."

They also gave Stebbins the comforting assurance that the French Indians intended "to come with them the next time, either in the spring or winter, if they had sucses this time." The party having encamped thirty miles above Northfield, as we have already seen by Stockwell's narration, a part of the company was sent to "Watchuset hills to fetch away some Indians that had lived there through the war." Stebbins accompanied them, and having been sent out with two squaws and a mare to pick huckleberries, he says he "got upon the mare and rid till he tired the mare, and then run on foot and so escaped to Hadley, being two days and a half without vituals."

Wachusett hills, as often spoken of by the historians of Philip's war, included a much wider geographic extent than in our day. The expedition alluded to is mentioned in Pynchon's letter which follows, as having been made to "Nashaway Ponds."

Simultaneously with the attack upon Hatfield, Wonaloncet, a Merrimac sagamore, always peaceable and friendly toward the English, a praying Indian, in whose wigwam Mr. Eliot often held meetings, was spirited away with some of his people, by Indians from Canada, and never permitted to return. It is quite possible that the detachment accompanied by Stebbins was sent to seek this very party. Intelligence of Stebbins's return was forwarded immediately to Major Pynchon at Springfield, who at once despatched the following letter to Albany, in the hope of inducing the Mohawks to undertake the recovery of the other captives.

"These for his honored ffriend Capt. Salisbury, Commander-in-Chiefe at ffort Albany—Hast, Post Hast, for his Majestie's special service.

Springfield, Oct. 5, 1677.

Capt. Salisbury—

Worthy Sir:—

Yesterday morning I rec'd yo'r kind linis by Benj. Waite, whereby I understand yo'r sympathy with us in o'r sad disaster by ye Indians: and yo'r readiness in making greate Inquiries, and greate foirwardness to do what Possible lyes in you for us, w'ch I have abundant cause to acknowledge, and do most thankfully accept. . . . . and as to your opinion of the Maquas being free, and assuring me of their innocency, I do fully concur with you, having satisfaction fr'm what you wrote, and from Benj. Wake's relation. But to put it out of all doubt, God in His Providence hath sent us one of o'r captivated men, Benoni Stebbins by name, w'ch is ye occasion of these lines to yo'rself. . . . . So desire ye to put ye Maquas upon Psueing their and our enemys, there being greate likelihood of their overtaking them. Benoni Stebbins came into Hadley last night in ye night, whose relation was sent to me, w'h being but an hour since I had it, I Psently resolved upon sending Post to you."

Then follows a minute account of the capture and flight toward Canada with Stebbins's escape.

"He says," continues Pynchon, "that one of the Indians from Nashaway Ponds, seems to be a counsellor w'h they have consulted much; and spoke of sending to the English, but at last resolved for Canada, yet talkt of making a forte a greate way up the river, and abiding there this winter, and also of carrying the captives and selling yrn to ye French, which he concludes they resolved on, but make but slow passage, concludes it may be twenty days ere they get to
ye lake . . . .

In his postscript Pynchon adds:

"Ben Wait is gone home, before the Intelligence came to me. He talkt of goeing to Canada before, and I suppose will rather be For-ward to it now than Backward."

So good an opportunity for opening a correspondence with the New York Indians, with a view to their pacification and to the recovery of the captives was not neglected by our Government. The six Mohawks released from prison, were sent home bearing formal letters of apology for their seizure, with a demand for the Natick squaws, and a remonstrance against future depredations on the Christian Indians, together with diplomatic assurances of the "special respect" of Massachusetts for the Macquas.

The tidings of Stebbins's escape caused fear and trembling among the remaining captives. Stockwell was informed of it by Ashpelon, the captain of his party, who seems to have treated the English with the utmost kindness, and whose shrewd mediation saved them more than once from dreadful death.

"He met me and told me Stebbins was run away, and the Indians spake of burning us; some of only burning and biting off our Fingers by-and-by. He said there would be a Court, and all would speak their minds, but he would speak last, and would say, that the Indian that let Stebbins run away, was only in fault, and so no hurt should be done us, fear not: and so it proved accordingly."

A fortnight after the seizure of Stockwell and his friends, some of the same party fired the mill above Hadley, and being overpowered were let go, on condition of returning soon to treat for the release of their captives.

Stockwell says that Ashpelon was much for it, but the Sachems from Wachusetts when they came, were much against it, yet were willing to meet the English, only to fall upon and take them. Ashpelon charged us not to speak a word of this, as mischief would come of it.

While they lingered at this encampment, provisions became so scarce that one bear's foot had to serve five captives for a whole day's rations, and they began to kill their horses for food. At length resuming their journey, they reached a small river about two hundred miles above Deerfield, by Stockwell's reckoning, where they separated into two companies. The division to which he was attached passed over "a mighty mountain," which they were eight days in crossing, though they "travelled very hard." They suffered greatly on this march.

"Here 1 was frozen, and here again we were like to starve. All the Indians went a Hunting but could get nothing; divers dayes they Powwow'd but got nothing, then they desired the English to Pray, and confessed they could do nothing; they would have us Pray, and see what the Englishman's God could do. I Prayed, so did Sergeant Plimpton, in another place. The Indians reverently attended, Morning and Night; next day they got Bears: then they would needs have us desire a Blessing, and return Thanks at Meals: after a while they grew weary of it, and the Sachim did forbid us. When I was frozen they were very cruel towards me, because I could not do as at other times. When we came to the Lake we were again sadly put to it for Provisions; we were fain to eat Touch-wood fryed in Bears' Greace.

At last we found a company of Raccons, then we made a Feast; and the manner was, that we must eat all. I perceived there would be too much for one time, so one Indian that sat next to me, bid me slip away some to him under his Coat, and he would hide it for me till another time; this Indian as soon as he had got my Meat, stood up and made a Speech to the rest, and discovered me, so that the Indians were very angry, and gave me another piece, and gave me Raccoon's Greace to drink, which made me sick and Vomit. I told them I had enough; so that ever after that they would give me none but still tell me I had Raccoon enough; so I suffered much, and being frozen was full of Pain, and could sleep but a little, yet must do my work. When they went upon the lake, they lit of a moose and killed it, and staid there till they had eaten it all up.

After entering upon the lake there arose a great storm but at last they got to an island and there they went to Powowing. The Powwow said that Benjamin Waite and another Man was coming and that storm was raised to cast them away. This afterwards appeared to be true, though then I believed it not."

Continued storms kept them cruising among the islands for about three weeks, during which time the Indians themselves were almost starved. Stock well was days without food. The lake being now frozen, they went upon it with little sleds upon which they drew their loads. Faint with hunger and pain, after repeated falls upon the ice, 'T was so spent," continues the narrator,

"I had not strength to rise again, but I crept to a tree that lay along, and got upon it, and there I lay; it was now night, and very sharp weather: I counted no other but I must die there; whilest I was thinking of Death, an Indian Hallowed, and I answered him; he came to me, and called me bad names, and told me if I could not go he must knock me on the head: I told him he must then so do; he saw how I had wallowed in that Snow, but could not rise; then he took his Coat, and wrapt me in it, and went back, and sent two Indians with a Sled, one said he must knock me on the Head, the other said No, they would carry me away and burn me."

On seeing his frozen feet, however, they relented, carried him to a fire and gave him broth, which revived him so much that at daylight he and Samuel Russell, the eight years old child taken from Deerfield, went upon a river on the ice. A strange and sad companionship. Russell slipping into the water, was called back by the Indians, who dried his stockings, and sending the two ahead again with an Indian guide, they ran four or five miles before the rest came up to them. The poor little boy complaining of faintness, told Stockwell, who was much exhausted, that he wondered how he could live, for he himself had ten meals to Stockwell's one. Stock-well was then laid on a sled and they ran away with him on the ice. He says "The rest and Samuel Russell came softly after. Samuel Russell I never saw more, nor knew what became of him."

A halt of three or four days was made at Chambly, where Stockwell was kindly treated by the French, who gave him hasty-pudding and milk, with brandy, and bathed his frozen limbs with cold water. He was treated with great civility by a young man, who let him lie in his bed, and would have bought him, had not the Indians demanded a hundred pounds for him. To prevent his being abused, this young man accompanied Stockwell to Sorel.

From Sorel the captives were taken to the Indian lodge two or three miles distant, where the French visited Stock-well, and it being Christmas, they brought him cakes and other provisions. The Indians having tried in vain to cure him, he asked for a chirurgeon, at which one of them struck him on the face with his fist. A Frenchman nearby remonstrated and went away, but soon after, the Captain of the place with twelve soldiers, came and asked for the Indian who had struck the Englishman. Seizing him, he told him he should go to the Bilboes and then be hanged.

The Indian was much terrified at this, as also was Stock well, but the Frenchman bade him not to fear, the Indian durst not hurt him.

"When that Indian was gone," he says, "I had two masters still. I asked them to carry me to that Captain, that I might speak for the Indian. They answered I was a fool; did I think the French-man were like to the English, to say one thing and do another?— they were men of their words, but I prevailed with them to help me thither, and I spake to the Captain by an Interpreter, and told him I desired him to set the Indian free, and told him what he had done for me, he told me he was a Rogue, and should be hanged, then I spake more privately, alleging this Reason, because all the English Captives were not come in, if he were hanged it might fare the worse with them : then the Captain said, that was to be considered: then he set him at liberty, upon this condition, that he should never strike me more, and every day bring me to his House to eat victuals."

The magnanimity of his captive so delighted the Indian that he embraced him, called him his brother, treated him to brandy, and carried him off to his wigwam, where all the other Indians shook hands with him and thanked him. The next day according to promise, Stockwell was carried to the house of the Captain, who gave him victuals and wine.

"Being left there a while," says he, "I showed the Captain and his wife my fingers, who were affrighted thereat and bid me lap it up again and sent for the chirurgeon who when he came said he could cure me and took it in hand and dressed it. The Indians came for me;........I could not go;........That night I was full of pain; the French were afraid I would die; five men did watch with me, and strove to keep me chearly, for I was ready to faint: oft-times they gave me brandy; the next day the chirurgeon came again, as he did all the while till May. I continued in the Captain's house till Benjamin Waite came, and my Indian master being in want of money, pawned me to the Captain for fourteen beavers, or the worth of them, which if he did not pay, he must lose his pawn, or sell me for one and twenty beavers. He could get no beavers, so I was sold, and in God's good time set at liberty and returned to my friends in New England."

Thus ends the sorrowful narrative of one of that little company, ruthlessly torn from home and friends on that bright September day, two centuries ago—a strong man in the prime of life;—but who shall tell the woful sufferings of the old man of four-score, the tender babes, and helpless women, who with him were first to tread that cruel way into Indian captivity, travelled later by so many weary feet? Benjamin Waite, shuddering at its horrors for his delicate wife and three little girls, determined to follow and share their fate, if he could not recover them. Stephen Jennings, another Hatfield man, whose wife and children were among the captives, joined him.

The attempt of the Government to enlist the Mohawks in its service, for the pursuit of their common enemy having failed, the General Court, in answer to a petition from Hatfield, issued an order for the recovery of the captives, and resolved that all incidental expenses should be defrayed by the colony.

On the 24th of October, 1677, Waite and Jennings set forward on their mission of love. They bore a commission and letters from the Governor and other influential persons, explaining the object of their journey, and bespeaking the aid of the New York and Canadian authorities in promoting it. By way of Westfield, they reached Albany on the seventh day and immediately presented their credentials to Capt. Salisbury, Commandant at the post. Convinced by the discourteous manner of this arbitrary officer, that he had no desire to forward their enterprise, they did not comply with his orders to call upon him again before leaving town, but went at once to Schenectady to procure an Indian guide for their journey. Enquiring who the strangers were, the Dutch were told that they belonged in Boston; whereupon declaring that the Englishmen said that Schenectady belonged to Boston, and acting doubtless under secret orders from Salisbury, they remanded them to Albany. There they were detained as prisoners till an opportunity offered to send them down to New York for examination by the Governor and Council. These proceedings forcibly remind one of the fable of the wolf and the lamb. New York had never forgiven Massachusetts for her occupation of Connecticut River, and was ready to seize upon the slightest pretence for a quarrel. The existing ill-will appears in the minutes of the council concerning the examination of Waite and Jennings where Waite is reported as denying the accusation brought against him that he had said that Schenectady belonged to Boston, pretending some mistake, they not understanding one another's language. It was finally resolved to allow them to proceed on their voyage, and with an order from Capt. Brockholes, then acting as Governor, that no further obstacles should be interposed, they were sent back to Albany.

Waiting in the hope of finding ice on the lakes, and also delayed by the difficulty of obtaining a guide, the 10th of December arrived before these sorely tried men could perfect the arrangements for their perilous march through the wilderness. The French guide whom they had hired, failing them at the last minute, a Mohawk Indian offered to conduct them to Lake George. Much to their disappointment on arriving there, it was free from ice. Finding an old canoe, the Indian refitted it, and after drawing for them on birch bark a rough draft of the lakes over which they were to pass, he bade them adieu. Three days took them to the outlet of Lake George, and carrying their canoe two miles across the portage, they reached the shore of Lake Champlain on the 16th of December. Here they took to the ice, but after a day's journey it proved too weak to bear them, and sadly retracing their steps, they carried the canoe forward to open water, and again embarked. Imagine the desolation of these sorrow-stricken wayfarers, as they floated for days without food in their frail skiff, buffeted and tossed by the wintry winds and icy waters of that unknown sea.

Sustained through all their hardships by that mighty affection which gives us strength to bear all and dare all for our beloved ones, and protected in all dangers by that Providence which notes the sparrow's fall, they made land at last on New-Year's day. Hastening forward, and greatly refreshed on the way by some biscuits and a bottle of brandy left by some hunter in a deserted wigwam, they passed Chambly, then a frontier settlement of ten houses. Before reaching Sorel, they came upon an Indian encampment, where Jennings was overjoyed to find his wife. With sobs and broken speech she told him all she had endured, and how it had fared with the rest; how Samuel Russell and little Mary Foote had been killed on the way; how Goodman Plympton had survived the perils of the journey only to be murdered at the end; and how, after all had been continually threatened with burning, this old man was selected as the victim, and led to the stake by his friend and neighbor, Obadiah Dickinson, had walked serenely to his dreadful death. Groans burst from the lips of the two men as they listened to the harrowing details, but restraining their indignation, they hurried off to bargain for the redemption of their beloved ones. At Sorel they saw five more of the company, two of whom had been pawned by the Indians for rum. "Waite's wife with all the rest of the captives was found in the Indian lodges in the woods beyond. Stopping only to comfort her with the joyful tidings of her speedy release, Waite and Jennings pushed on to Quebec, where they were kindly received by the Governor. Glad of an opportunity to make return for a favor lately done him by the English Government, Frontenac aided them in collecting the captives and procuring their ransom, which was effected by the payment of £200.

On the 19th of April, 1678, the redeemed captives with their deliverers, escorted by four gentlemen of Frontenac's household and a guard of French soldiers, began the home-ward march. Travelling leisurely and hunting by the way as occasion required, they arrived at Albany on the 22d of May, whence a messenger was at once sent post haste with the following letters from Stockwell and Waite to their friends at Hatfield:

Albany, May 22, 1678.

"Loving Wife:—Having now opportunity to remember my kind love to thee and our child and the rest of our friends, though we met with great afflictions and trouble since I see thee last, yet here is now opportunity of joy and thanksgiving to God, that we are now pretty well and in a hopeful way to see the faces of one another, before we take our final farewell of this present world. Likewise God hath raised up friends amongst our enemies, and there is but three of us dead of all those that were taken away. So I conclude, being in haste and rest your most affectionate husband till death
makes a separation. Quintin Stockwell."

" To my loving friends and kindred at Hatfield:—These few lines are to let you understand that we are arrived at Albany with the captives, and we now stand in need of assistance, for my charges is very great and heavy and therefore any that have any love to our condition, let it move them to come and help us in this strait. Three of the captives are murdered: old Goodman Plympton, Samuel Foote's . daughter and Samuel Russell: All the rest are alive and well and now at Albany. 1 pray you hasten the matter, for it requireth great haste. Stay not for the Sabbath, nor for the shoeing of horses. We shall endeavor to meet you at Canterhook; it may be at Housatonock. We must come very softly because of our wives and children. I pray you hasten then. Stay not night nor day, for the matter re-quireth haste. Bring provisions with you for us.

Your loving kinsman,

Benjamin Waite.

At Albany written from mine own hand as I have been affected to yours all that were fatherless, be affected to me now, and hasten and stay not, and ease me of my charges.

You shall not need to be afraid of any enemies."

Copies of these letters were sent to the Governor and Council at Boston, who had previously appointed a day of fasting, and who immediately issued an order recommending "that on that day the ministers and congregation manifest their charity for the captives by a contribution and that for the quickening of the work Benjamin Waite's letter be publicly read that day in all the churches."

After tarrying five days in Albany, the party went on foot twenty-two miles to Kinderhook, where men and horses awaited them. At Westfield many old friends and neighbors from Hatfield met them, and their progress thence was like a triumphal procession, every neighborhood turning out to greet them. Two proud and happy men were Benjamin Waite and Stephen Jennings, as they headed the cavalcade into Hatfield street that May morning, each bearing in his arms his new, little daughter, and tears streamed from every eye as crowding round to welcome home the wanderers, the people passed from one to another the two little babies, born in bondage and christened in commemoration of the sorrows of their mothers, Canada Waite and Captivity Jennings. It may interest some to know that both children grew to womanhood, and that the former became the grandmother of the late Oliver Smith, gratefully remembered by many in the Connecticut valley.

Stockwell's experience of Indian hospitality seems to have disgusted him with frontier life, and the year after his return he removed to Suffield, Conn. That others still cherished the hope of finally possessing their lands in peace is proved by the following:

"To the honoured Generall Court of the Masachusetts Bay now setting in Boston ye 8th 3, '78:

Rigt Worshipfull : . . . .

We do veryly hope your thoughts are soe upon us & our condition that it would be superfluous to tell you that our estates are wasted that we find it hard work to Live in this Iron age to Come to the years end with Comfort; our houses have been Rifled & burned —our flocks & heards consumed—the ablest of our Inhabitants killed—our plantation has become a wilderness—a dwelling place for owls,—& we that are left are separated into several townes— Also our reverand & esteemed Minister, Mr. Samuel Mather hath been invited from us & greate danger ther is of o^r loosing him; all which speaks us a people in a very misirable condition, & unless you will be pleased to take us (out of your father-like pitty) & Cherish us in yor bosomes we are like Suddinly to breathe out o^r last Breath. Right Honoured The Committie appointed to manage o^r affairs for us the Rev. Mr Mather who hath not yet quitte forsaken us, & we the Remaining Inhabitants loyfully doe desire that we might return & plant that place againe. Yet we would earnestly begg. . . . . . that we may Repossess the Said plantation with great Advantage Both for the advancing the cause & Kingdome of Jesus & for o^r own saftie & comfort. . . . ."

The petition then enlarges upon the drawback they have heretofore encountered, in the fact that the best land is held by the proprietors, who are likely never to settle in Deerfield, and declare that Mr. Mather and they are of opinion "the plantation will be spoiled if these men may not be begged or will not be bought out of their rights." They conclude as follows:

"All judicious men who have any acquaintance with it, Count It as Rich a tract of land as any upon the river; they Iudge it sufficient to entertain & maintain as great number of Inhabitants as most of the upland townes, alsoe were it well peopled it would be as a bulwark to the other townes; also it would be a great disheartening to the enemie & veryly (not to make to bold with your worship's patience) It would mightily Incourage and Raise the hearts of us the Inhabitants yoʳ poor & Impoverished servants."

The prayer of the petitioners was not answered. The matter was referred by the Court to the proprietors, and no further attempt to rebuild Deerfield was made until 1682.

EUNICE WILLIAMS.

Towards the middle of the seventeenth century, on the bank of the ice-bound St. Charles, rose a hut, with the high sounding name of Notre-Dame des Anges. Two feet above its low eaves rose the drifted snow. Within, great logs blazed in the "wide-throated chimney," before which, on a wooden stool, at a rough, board table, sat Paul Le Jeune, Superior of the first Jesuit Mission at Quebec in New France. The trees in the neighboring forest cracked with the frost like the report of a pistol. Le Jeune's ink and his fingers froze; but late into the night, bribing his Indian teacher with tobacco, he toiled away at his declensions, translating his *Pater Noster* and *Credo* into "blundering Algonquin." Then, wrapped in his blanket, which was soon "fringed with the icicles of his congealed breath," he snatched an hour's rest, and waking with the dawn, with a hatchet broke the ice in his cask for his morning ablutions, and began his labors afresh.

"From Old France to New," says Mr. Parkman, "came succors and reinforcements," and a year before Harvard College was founded, there was at Quebec, the beginning of a school and a college for Huron boys and French youth. "Our Lady" smiled upon Paul Le Jeune's missions; and as in the days of Poutrincourt, the wealth and patronage of the ladies of the French Court sent the first Jesuit to New France, so the success of these later missions at Quebec, and of the newly consecrated Ville Marie de Montréal, was in great measure due to the zeal and romantic devotion of Madame de La Peltrie, Marie de L'Incarnation, Mdlle. Jeanne Mance, and Marguerite Bourgeois; and no one can read the story of Paul Le Jeune and his associates as related by themselves, without mingled admiration and respect for the founders of Roman-ism in Canada.

Meanwhile, with a kindred zeal, that noble apostle, John Eliot, sat in his little study at Roxbury, patiently translating the English Bible into the Algonquin tongue for the benefit of the Indians near Boston, often meeting them at Nonantum hill, after the duties of his own pulpit were discharged for the week, and there expounding to them it's simple truths. Nor was this the end of his labors for their improvement. Believing that civilization, or civility, as he calls it, should go hand in hand with religion, he instructed the sachems in agriculture and the use of tools, bought spinning-wheels for the squaws, and not neglecting the primer for the Catechism, founded schools for their pappooses, rewarding their diligence with the gift of a cake or an apple. At last, when he had established his praying Indians, as they were called, in a village of their own at Natick, the town of Dedham was indemnified for the loss of land appropriated to their use, by a grant of eight thousand acres elsewhere; and what is now Deerfield was the spot selected.

We of to-day, looking upon the fruits of two hundred years of culture, do not wonder at their choice, and we can scarcely realize how resolute and pious must have been the hearts, and how strong the hands, of the men and women, who in 1671, began the settlement of Deerfield. A rude life they led for the first few years, with no school, no meeting-house, and no settled minister; though Samuel Mather, son of Timothy of Dorchester, ministered to them in 1673, boarding at the time with Quentin Stockwell. Driven from their heritage by the savage hordes of Philip, it was not till 1682 that an effort at resettlement was made.

In the senior class at Harvard at that time, was John Williams, a studious youth, son of Deacon Samuel Williams of Roxbury. Graduated from a class of three, of whom two were Williamses, John Williams, then but twenty-two years of age, after studying divinity, was ordained minister of Deerfield, in 1688. There would seem to be little in the position of pastor to a frontier settlement to attract a young man born and educated at the metropolis; and without doubting that Mr. Williams was mainly actuated by that missionary spirit, which characterized the preachers of that period, it is possible that a previous acquaintance with the Northampton lady, whom he married the year after his ordination, made him more willing to accept the call to Deerfield. This was Eunice Mather, a cousin of the first minister of Deerfield, daughter of Rev. Eleazer Mather, and descended on her mother's side from John Warham, a noted Puritan Divine of Exeter, England.

Eunice Williams, second daughter, and sixth child of Rev. John Williams, was born September 17th, 1696. She was the middle child of eleven, all born to her parents within sixteen years. Though nothing can be definitely stated of her childhood previous to 1704, we may suppose that her five little brothers and sisters, whose births are recorded as rapidly succeeding her own, monopolized the attention of the mother with whom Esther, the eldest daughter, was more naturally associated in the care of the younger ones; while the father, busy in providing for his rapidly increasing family, and much occupied with his parish duties, devoted the little leisure that remained, to planning for the education of the older boys. So I fancy Eunice a pale, delicate, dark-eyed child, left pretty much to her own devices for the first six years of her life.

Let us glance at the Deerfield of that period. We see it all,—the palisade enclosing the Garrison House, the parsonage and many humble dwellings; the forts or stockaded houses outside; the old meeting-house, a square edifice, from the middle of whose foursided roof, sprang the belfry,—emp-ty, truth compels me to state, for the bell, whose echoes sounded so pleasantly in our ears for many years, has recently been silenced forever by the indefatigable antiquary: the people, with names and, doubtless, faces so familiar to us,—valiant, hard-working, God-fearing men; heroic, much-enduring, pious women. Only the location of the school-house, where Eunice probably went to school, is missing. But though the fathers and mothers of that time were for the most part uneducated, they had a school-house, and in Eunice's day as in ours, a Barnard was the noted school dame of the village; public-spirited, like her of our time, bequeathing large legacies to the schools. Eunice was a good reader, and knew her Catechism by heart. Mr. John Catlin was then school committee and I have no doubt, that when he visited the school, Eunice felt very much as we have on similar occasions; and that being the minister's daughter, she was plied with longer words and harder questions than the rest; and that she privately told Martha and Abigail French that she didn't like their grandfather at all. She liked to go to Deacon French's, who lived on what is now the site of the second church parsonage. The Deacon was the blacksmith of the village, and his shop stood a few rods west of his house. Eunice would stand hours watching him, as he beat into shape the plough-shares, that had been bent by the stumps in the newly cleared lands. As the sparks flew up from the flaming forge, she thought of the verse in the Bible, "Man is born unto trouble as the sparks fly upward," and wondered what it meant. Too soon, alas, she learned.

The Indians for a time held in check by the defeat and death of Philip, were beginning again to desolate the scattered villages. When in 1689, they settled old scores with Major Waldron at Dover, they killed Richard Otis, and took his wife and baby with other captives to Canada. Scalping parties hovered perpetually about Deerfield, and the newborn settlement was soon baptized in blood.

When in 1702, Dudley left England to assume the govern-ment of Massachusetts, it was evident that the English queen could not overlook the insult offered her by Louis XIV. As ever since the peace of 1698, the Canadian government had lost no opportunity of exciting the eastern Indians to hostility, under the pretext of protecting them from the encroachments of the English, it was inevitable that war between the two nations in the Old World, must be followed by a renewal of atrocities in New England. As a precautionary measure, Dudley appointed a conference with the sachems, in June, 1703, at Casco, and repairing thither with his suite, was met on the 30th, by Hopehood of Norridgwock, Wanungunt of Penobscot, and Wattanummon of Pennacook, with their chief sagamores. In stereotyped phrase, the new governor said, that commissioned by his victorious queen, he had come as to friends and brothers, to reconcile all differences since the last treaty. The Indian orator in turn assured him, that peace was what they desired above all things, and in language as poetical as it was false, declared that "as high as the sun was above the earth, so far distant should their designs be of making the least breach between them." Both parties then heaped up fresh stones upon the pillar called the Two Brothers, that had been set up at the last treaty, and

the ceremonies ended. A few weeks later, Bomazeen boasted that though several missionaries from the French had tried to seduce them from their allegiance, they "were as firm as the mountains, and so would continue as long as the sun and moon endured."

Truly has Penhallow said, "Their voice was like the voice of Jacob, but their hands like the hands of Esau," for in six weeks after, they with their Canadian allies, set the whole country in flames. New York was protected by her treaty with the Six Nations, and the whole brunt of the war fell upon Massachusetts and New Hampshire. Deerfield being the most remote settlement, and easy of access from Canada, was especially exposed. It had, however, a watchful sentinel at its outpost, in the person of Col. John Schuyler at Albany, who often sent intelligence of the movements of the enemy, and thus warded off the danger. A mission of converted Mohawks, (Iroquois,) whom the Jesuits had persuaded to leave their native towns, and settle on the St. Lawrence under the wing of the church, had at this time a fort at Saint-Louis, now Caughnawaga, nine miles above Montreal. They naturally allied themselves with the French, while those of their tribe who remained in the place of their nativity, came under the sway of the English. The praying Indians of the Mohawks, whose principal village was at Caughnawaga, forty miles distant from Albany, were in the habit of visiting their relatives at the Saint-Louis mission, and news of the threatened attacks upon Deerfield, was frequently brought by them to Albany on their return, and communicated by Schuyler to the authorities in New England.

In the autumn following the conference at Casco, Zebediah Williams, and John Nims, his half-brother, were taken from the north meadows in Deerfield and carried to Canada. So impressed was the Rev. Mr. Williams with a presentiment of the danger hovering over the town, that both in the pulpit and out, he urged the utmost vigilance upon his people. The old fable of the boy and the wolf was acted over again, and the savage foe, stealing from the forest at midnight upon the fold, found the guardians sleeping, and fell with rapine and murder upon the little flock. The story is an old one and needs no repetition here. But who can tell the horror stamped forever upon the heart and brain of Eunice, by the sights and sounds of that awful night? Suddenly waked from the untroubled sleep of childhood, to see the hideous faces of demons bending over her; dragged by bloody hands from her warm bed, hurried through the room where she sees her father, bound hand and foot, helpless to protect her, and afraid to pity lest he may hasten her doom; over the door stone, where her little brother lies dead, and by his side, gashed and bleeding, the faithful black woman, whom next to their mother, they loved; out into the cold winter night, reddening now like the dawn, in the glare of the burning village, and so to the church, the child is borne. Pine torches flaring in the hands of the dusky warriors, lighted up the scene within. The enemy's wounded, groaning in agony on the floor; old men praying and calling on God for deliverance; women speechless and despairing, among them her mother pale and wan; her playmates shrieking with terror; infants wailing with cold and hunger;—huddled there in woful companionship, while the mocking fiends completed the work of destruction. At dawn, the shivering captives began their weary march. The impression made upon the tender mind of the child, by the dreadful scenes of this night and the twenty-five succeeding days, may explain the fact of her reluctance to return to the home of which she had re-tained only this frightful remembrance.

In the distribution of the captives, Eunice fell to the lot of a Mohawk of Saint-Louis. Whether

her beauty pleased his Indian fancy, or her forlorn condition melted his savage breast to pity, it is certain that she was treated with more consideration by her master, than her companions were by theirs. When her little feet were weary, he lifted her to his brawny shoulder, or bore her tenderly in his arms. Wrapping her warmly in his blanket, he drew her on a sledge over the icy rivers, spread her bed softly with thick hemlock boughs when they camped at night, and selected the choicest morsels from his hunting for her food, often stinting himself that she might have the more. Seeing her playmates butchered in cold blood by their cruel masters on that fearful journey, the little innocent clung to her protector with the trustfulness of childhood, and the two strange companions learned to love each other well. On their arrival in Canada, she was carried at once to his home, and thus separated entirely from her family. At the earnest prayer of her father, who was at Montreal, the governor sent a priest with him to endeavor for her ransom. But the Jesuit at the Saint-Louis mission would not permit Mr. Williams to enter the fort, assuring him that it would be labor lost, for the Macquas would part with their hearts sooner than with his child. Accompanied by the governor, Mr. Williams finally obtained an interview with Eunice, who with sobs and tears begged and pleaded that he would take her away from that dreadful place. Soothing her as well as he could, though her sorrow must have rent his heart, her father heard her say her Catechism and told her she must pray to God every day. The seven years old child assured him that she had not once omitted to do so, "but," said she, "a wicked man in a long black gown comes every day, and makes me say some Latin prayers which I cannot understand, but I hope it may do me no harm." She told him how the savages profaned the Sabbath, and promised him that she would always keep it holy. For a few minutes again before his release, Mr. Williams was permitted to converse with his daughter. The Governor's wife, seeing his deep-seated melancholy on her account, had Eunice brought to Montreal, where she told him of the methods used to drive heretic children to the bosom of the mother church.

It is a mournful picture. The Jesuit with his slouched hat looped up at the sides, in a long black cassock, a rosary at his waist, and a scourge in his hand. The timid English girl, scion of a grand old Puritan stock, cowering in abject terror on her knees before him. Rebaptized Margaret, with the sign of the cross on her brow and bosom, Eunice is alternately threatened with punishment and allured with promises. She is told tales of her father's conversion, frightened with pictures of fiends tormenting the souls of little children, and beaten for refusing to make the sign of the cross. All offers of ransom were refused for her, and when she entreated to be allowed to go home, she was told that if she went she would be damned and burned in hell forever, a threat terrible to the ears of a child bred in the Puritanic fear of the everlasting fire. Fond as her Indian master was of her, he was powerless to protect her from these cruelties. While he did not deny the justice of the claims made for the restoration of the prisoner, he always asserted that he could not release her without an order from the governor, whose subject he was. On the other hand, the governor pleaded his fear of the king's displeasure, lamented his want of authority to command the Indians, who, he said, were his allies and not his subjects. The priests, appealed to as a last resource, scornfully repelled the implied suspicion, and declared that humanity forbade them to interfere to separate the child against her will, from the master whom she loved as her father.

After the blow fell upon the devoted town of Deerfield, Schuyler did not relax his efforts to protect New England. He openly protested against the maintenance of neutrality in New York, whereby the marauders passed unmolested, to attack the people of Massachusetts; and remonstrating in their name with the Governor of Canada, he said, he had thought it his "duty to God and man to prevent as far as possible, the infliction of such cruelties as had too often been committed on the unfortunate colonists." In all negotiations for the redemption of English captives he was especially act-ive. He sent out friendly Indians as scouts into the enemy's country, and reported faithfully to our governor all that he could learn of the designs of their captors in regard to them. He was much interested in the restoration of Eunice, and all that we know of her condition after her father's release is gleaned from hints in his correspondence. In a letter to Col. Partridge, commanding at Hatfield, dated Feb, 18, 1706-7, he says, "As to Mr. Williams Daughter, our spies. . . . . . are returned, who as they were hunting, saw Mr. Williams daughter wth the Indian who ownes her. She is in good health, but seemes unwilling to returne, and the Indian not very willing to part with her, she being, as he says, a pritty girl but perhapps he may Exchange her if he can gett a very pritty Indian in her Rome, which he must first see, you may assure Mr. Williams I will do all that lays in my power to serve him, as I have formally wrott to him, and indeed to all others that are prisoners." In conclusion, after notifying Col. Partridge of certain movements of the enemy, he says: "I wish you and us may be all on our guard, and God preserve us all from such bloody enemies." In another letter to Partridge on the nth of August, 1707, he notices the return of two trusty Indians whom he had sent as "spys" to Caughnawaga in Canada, and who reported a party of the enemy at Otter Creek on their way to New England, and also "that they see Deaken Sheldon of Deerfield at Montreal, who walked the streets, but was told he was deteind and had not liberty to goe home." Schuyler adds, "Do be on your guard to pre-vent your people from falling into the hands of these bloody savages; but I cannot enlarge, for I will have the messenger ride this night, and it is now ten o'clock."

Mr. Sheldon went at least three times to Canada, in behalf of Eunice and others, and on the above occasion was not allowed to return, there being another expedition on foot against the English. Deacon Sheldon's kind offices seem to have produced some relenting in the heart of Eunice's master, for I have before me a letter written from her cousin in Northampton, to her brother in Roxbury, dated Aug. 4, 1707, which says, "A post came from Albany last Saturday night, that brought letters from Canada, also a letter from Albany, that saith, 'Ye Indian, Eunice's master, saith he will bring her in within two months.' "

One can picture the quiet little village on that Saturday night. All work laid aside, the Puritan Sabbath already begun; the pious psalms of the different households borne out upon the summer air, and perhaps the solemn voice of the pastor, as with the remnant of his once happy family, he prays for the return of the captive still languishing in chains afar; the sound of horse's hoofs, as the messenger rides post from Albany, sent by Peter Schuyler to announce that Eunice's master will bring her within two months; the stir in the village, as the glad tidings spreads from house to house. Hope beating high in the bosoms of some, with the thought that now, perhaps, they may rejoin their beloved ones, long since torn from them by a fate more cruel than death; sorrow in some at the renewed remembrance of those that can never return.

Saddest of all is the remembrance of the ten years old girl at Caughnawaga, in the wigwam of her master. It is always her master and never a hint that any, even of the rudest of her sex, surround her. She may have heard that he has promised at last to take her home, and perhaps begs him with tears not to wait, but to go at once. He tells her, perhaps, that her father has ceased to care for her, that he has left her alone, and taken her brothers and sister home with him; that her mother is dead and her father has a new wife, who will beat her if she goes home; that she is to stay with him, till some young brave claims her as his squaw. It may be that she still weeps obstinately, and that he drags her to the priest, to be terrified into obedience.

The two months pass, and no tidings yet of Eunice at Albany. Seven years elapse; seven weary years of alternate hope and despair since her capture,——when, one summer morning, a strange visitor ascends the broad steps of the old Province House in Boston. She glides through the spacious doorway and into the grand reception room, where she gazes about her with a half frightened, half curious air. The governor is there with several gentlemen. "Who is she? What does she want?" he asks. "An Abenaki squaw," the usher replies, "who demands her children, captured by the English some time since, and now in Boston." A thought strikes the governor. He will exchange the children of this woman for Eunice. An interpreter is sent for. "The white man's axe is laid at the foot of the forest tree," says the Abenaki, "its branches are lopped away and it will soon die." The pappooses are brought, and while the mother fondles her young in savage fashion, the interpreter answers for the governor. "Among the hills," he says, "a shepherd fed his peaceful flock, when a wolf sprang upon them, and some were killed, and others driven far away. Day and night the shepherd grieves for the youngling of his flock, gone astray.

In the north the white lamb bleats, but cannot find her way back. Let the Abenaki bring her back to the shepherd, the white chief says, and her pappooses shall be restored to her; the branches shall be safe and the forest tree shall live again." "One touch of nature makes the whole world kin." "The Abenaki knows where the white lamb is hid. She will go, and before so many moons are gone, the shepherd shall have his own again." Another fierce embrace of her children, and the squaw strides forth into the wilderness. How she sped on her quest, is shown by the following extract from a letter in our archives, written by Father Meriel in Canada, to Mr. Johnson Harmon at Shamblee:

Sir:

Since you are gone, a squaw of the nation of the Abnakis is come in from Boston. She has a pass from your Governour. She goes about getting a little girl daughter of Mr. John
Williams. The Lord Marquis of Vaudreuil helps her as he can. The business is very hard because the girl belongs to Indians of another sort, and the master of the English girl is now at Albany. You may tell your Governour that the squaw can't be at Boston at the time appointed, and that she desires him not to be impatient for her return, and meanwhile to take good care of her two papows. The same Lord chief Governor of Canada, has insured me in case she may not prevail with the Mohoggs for Eunice

Williams, he shall send home four English persons in his power for an Exchange in the Room of the two Indian children. You see well, Sir, your Governour must not disregard such a generous proffer as according to his noble birth and obliging genious Ours makes. Else he would betray little affection to his own people." . . . . . .

Again Deerfield is agitated with rumors of the speedy recovery of Eunice Williams. Hope again visits the heart of her unhappy father, to be again dispelled by disappointment.

In a letter to the French governor, dated Nov. 10, 1712, Dudley, impatient of the delay, says: "I have in my Keeping one Indian sachem of Quebeck, one other sachem of your Indians near in blood and kindred to the woman that has Mr. Williams's daughter, which I will exchange for her,—or otherwise I will never set them free."

Meantime, having notified Schuyler of his interview with the Abenaqui squaw, and warned him to keep a sharp lookout for her return, he receives at last the following letter from Peter Schuyler:

 ' '*May it please your Excellency,*

Yo^r Excellency's Letters of ye 6th and 10th Currant for Expresse have Received together with five letters for Monsr Vaudreuil gov^r of Canida which have deliver^d to ye french officer Dayeville[1] who goes from hence y^e [19] Instant & have taken his Receipt for three Letters as you Designed which is here Inclosed as to what your Excellency mentions Relating to Mr. Williams his doghter, the squaw nor she is not come her yet nor have I heard anything of her Coming altho I shall be very glad to see them and do assure your Excellency If they come together or be it y^p squaw alone I shall use all possible meanes to get the child exchanged Either as your Excellency proposes or what other way the squaw will be most willing to Comply with. In the meantime shall Inform my Selfe by all opportunities whether the said Squaw & Child be coming here or if they be anywhere nearby. Your Excellency may depend that whatever I can do for ye obtaining of ye s^d Child shall at no time be wanting. So shall take leave to subscribe my Selfe

        Your Excellency
           Most humble & Obedient
                Servant
                    P. Schuyler.

Albany, Dec. 19, (?) 1712."

Accompanying this letter in our Archives, is the following: "Received of Coll. P. Schuyler, three French letters sent him from Governor Dudley, directed to Monsr Vaudreiul, govern'r in Canada which Letters I promise carefully to Convey & Deliver to ye said Govern^r in Canada as soon as I shall arrive there witness my hand this 19th December 1712

[Signed]   Dageuille. "

Father Meriel had written that the French governor would give four English captives in exchange for the two Abenaqui pappooses. It had now become evident that he would not give one; that one being Eunice Williams.

Months later than the date of Schuyler's letter, and the return of Dageuille to Canada, the squaw appeared alone at Albany. The same old story is repeated. The child Eunice refuses to leave her master. He is loath to compel her. Such influence is brought to bear upon Dudley, that he dares not reject the offer of the Canadian government. Four New England households are made happy by the return of their beloved ones; the squaw and her babies are sent home; but Eunice Williams, the child of so many prayers, the object of the solicitude of so many sorrowing hearts, the coveted prize of two governments, is still a helpless captive.

In the spring of 1713, John Schuyler, impatient of the long suspense, and fully confident of his own ability to mediate effectually between the two powers, undertook the weary journey to Canada. His letter[1] to Governor Dudley explains itself :

> *"May it please your Excellency:—*
>
> I thought it my duty immediately w'thout any further Omission, to signify to Your Excellency my return from Mont Reall to Albany, upon yᵉ 15th of this instant June with Monsʳ Bolock and three more, and nine prisoners, a list of their names is herein inclosed. I sett them forward for New England with Samel Ashly and Daniell Bagg upon the 100 th instant. I have not herein incerted the charges; by reason I cann't make up the Accᵗˢ till yᵉ officers return to Canada; I have likewise enclosᵈ for Yoʳ Excellency my Memoriall that touches the concern of yᵉ Revᵈ Mr Williams yᵉ Minister at Dearfeild for his Daughter. My indefatigueable Pains therein came to no purpose. If yʳ Excellency hath the Returns of peace I hope to receive them; and then shall dispatch them away as directed. I found a great fatigue in my Journey to and from Canada and waded through many Difficulties in yᵉ way wᵗʰ the Prisonirs To Dilate thereon would be prolix. I now beg leave to assure your Excellency of my Effection and Zeal to every yoʳ Commands and that in all Sincerity I am May it Please Yoʳ Excels
> Yoʳ most obedient humble Servᵗ
> John Schuyler.
> Albany June yᵉ 18ᵗʰ 1713"

The memorial accompanying this letter is a remarkable State Paper. The writer's sanguine hope, after his conference with the fair-spoken De Vaudreuil; his indignation at the iniquitous marriage, calmed by the explanation of the priest; his gentle and chivalrous reception of the girl bride; his patient and repeated pleading with her to return to her afflicted father; his unrestrained anger at her continued obstinacy; and the silent grief which overwhelms him at the thought of his fruitless mission, as he leaves her to her Indian lord;—all are told with a simple pathos, to which the words of another cannot do justice. It is therefore given entire.

"A true and perfect Memoriall of my proceedings Jn behalf of Margarett Williams now Captive amongst ye Jndians at the ffort of Caghenewaga Jn Canada, Jnsisting upon her Reliese and to persuade her to go home to her father and Native Countrey, it being upon the instant and earnest desire of her ffather now Minister at Dearfeild in New England. J arrived from Albany at Mont Reall on ye 15ᵗʰ of Aprill last, 1713, Where J understood y^t Monsr de Vaudruille, Govern^r and chief of Canada, was expected then every day from Quebeck. Upon which J thought proper not to mention anything touching the aforesaid Captive, untill his Excellency should be here himself: and accordingly when he arrived here J propos'd the matter to him, who gave me all the Encouragem^l J could immagine for her to go home, he also permitted me to go to her at the ffort, where she was, to prepare if J could persuade her to go home. Moreover, his Excellency said, that wth all his heart, he would give a hundred Crowns out of his own pockett, if that she might be persuaded to go to her Native Countrey: J observing all this, then was in hopes J should prevaile with her to go home. Accordingly J went to the ffort at Caghenewaga, being accompanied by one of the King's Officers and a ffrench Interpreter, likewise another of the Jndian Language Being upon the 26 Day of May. Entring at the Jndian ffort J thought ritt first to apply myself to the priests; As J did, Being two in Company, And was informed before that this infant (As J may say) was married to a young Jndian, J therefore proposed to know the Reason why this poor Captive should be Married to an Jndian, being a Christian Born (tho neerly taken from the Mother's Breast and such like Instances &c) Whereupon the priest Sett forth to me Such good Reasons wth Witnesses that myself, or any other person (as J believe) could fairly make Objection against their Marriage; (First, s^d he they came to me to Marry them) very often wch J always refus'd with good words and persuasions to the Contrary, But both continuing in their former resolution to Such a Degree that J was constrained to be absent from ye ffort three Severall times, because not Satisfyed mySelf in their Marriage; Untill at last after Some days past they both came to me, and s^d that they were Joined together. And if he would not marry them they matter'd not, for they were resolved never to leave one the other.   But live together heathen like; Upon wch J thought proper to Join them in Matrimony and Such like Reasons as aforesaid the priest did plainly Sett forth and after some further discourse, J desired the priest, to let me see her at his house, ffor J knew not where to find her upon which he sent for her, who prsently came with the Jndian she was Married to both together   She looking very poor in body, bashfull in the face but proved harder than Steel in her breast, at her first Entrance into the Room J desired her to sitt down, wch she did, J first Spoak to her in English, Upon wch she did not Answ^r me; And J believe She did not understand me, she being very Young when she was taken, And liveing always amongst the Jndians afterwards, J Jmployed my Indian Languister to talk to her; informing him first by the ffrench Interpreter, who understood the English Language, What he should tell her and what Questions he should Ask her   Accordingly he did J understood amost all what he said to her; And found that he Spoak according to my Order, but could not gett one word from her.   Upon which J desired the priest To Speak to her, And if J could not prevaile wth her to go home to Stay there, that She might only go to see her ffather, And directly return hither again,   The priest made a long Speech to her and endeavored to persuade her to go, but after almost half an hours discourse-could not get one word from her; And afterwards when he found She did not Speak, he again Endeavoured to persuade her to go and see her ffather   And J seeing She continued unpersuadable to speak; J promised upon my Word and honour, if she would go only to see her ffather, J would convey her to New England and give her Assureance of liberty to return if she pleased—the priest asked her Severall times for answer upon this, my earnest request And fair offers wch was after long Solicitations *zaghie oghte* which words being translated into the English Tongue, their Signifycation is *may be not;* but the meaning thereof. amongst the Jndians is a plaine denyall, and these words were all we could gett from her; in almost two hours time that we talked with her. Upon this my eyes being allmost filled with tears, J said to her mySelf. had J made such proposals and prayings to the worst of Jndians J did not doubt but have had a reasonable Answere and consent to what J had s^d. Upon wch her husband seeing that J was so much concerned about her replyed had her ffather not Married againe She would have gone and Seen him long Ere this time, But gave no further reason and the time growing late and J being very Sorrowfull that J could not prevail upon nor get one word more from her, J took her by the hand and left her in the priest's house.   John Schuyler."

De Vaudreuil sent a letter to Dudley by Schuyler, on his return, in which he says, "Colonel John Schuyler, to whom I have caused to be delivered nine of your captives,. . . . . will tell you in what manner Mr. Williams's daughter received him, and how he could never oblige her to promise him anything but that she would go to see her father, as soon as peace should be proclaimed. I am surprised at the little justice you do me in what you say to me about the marriage of that girl with a savage of the Sault. I am much more chagrined at this than you are, on account of her father for whom I have absolute respect; but not being able to foresee this, it was impossible for me to prevent it."

Schuyler's ill success did not prevent further efforts for the redemption of Eunice. On the 27th of June, 1713, shortly after the receipt of the above memorial, Governor Dudley writing to congratulate the Governor of Canada upon the return of peace acknowledges the receipt of his letter of the 12th inst. and acquaints him of the arrival of "John Schuyler and the nine English prisoners that accompanied him being far short of the number I justly expected should have been returned me; who would doubtless have been very forward to have come home, had they been allowed soe to doe when I have long since dismissed and transported at their own Desire and Choice, at my charge, all the French prisoners that were in my hands, and am in the hourly expectation of receiving an order directed to yourself from the Court of France, requiring the same on your part (a copy of which I have now in my hands), I have no satisfactory explanation to my complaint of the treatment of the Reverend Mr. Williams's daughter, referring to her marriage with a Salvage, and the unaccountable detention of her. She is to be considered as a minor within ye age of consent to make choice for herselfe being carryd away early in her infancy before she had discretion to judge of things for her own good. I hope you will interfere with all good offices to free her from the Impositions made on her tender years, that she may be rescued from those miseries she is thoroughly obnoxious to, and restored to her father." Dudley adds, that immediately upon the receipt of the order from the French King, for the release of the captives he "shall put that affair into such a disposition that I may be provided to transport and fetch home my people: and I desire you will cause them to be drawn near together, that the messengers I shall employ on that service may easily and speedily come at speech with them."

The order above alluded to having been received, Commissioners were sent by Gov. Dudley to Canada, to negotiate the redemption of Eunice and the other New England prisoners. At the head of the Commission was Capt. John Stoddard, son of the Rev. Solomon Stoddard, second minister of Northampton and second husband of Eunice's grandmother Mather. Capt. Stoddard's journal, printed from the original manuscript, is before me, and though it contains little pertaining especially to Eunice, it gives us a clue to so much of the romantic story of some other captives, that the substance of it is here given.

On the 5th of November, 1713, Capt. Stoddard, accompanied by Eunice's father, set out from Boston, reaching Northampton on the 9th. Here they were joined by Capt. Thomas Baker, Martin Kellogg and two others. Baker and Kellogg had both been carried captive with Eunice to Canada, whence the former had almost succeeded in escaping, but was recaptured and sentenced to the stake. The fire was already lighted, when with a bold dash he broke from his captors, and sought refuge in the house of one LeCair, a Frenchman, who bought him of the Indians for five pounds. The governor hearing of his attempt, put him in irons and kept him four months closely confined. When again at large, he, with Kellogg, Joseph Petty and John Nims, all Deerfield men, made his escape in 1705. Their sufferings on the way home were dreadful. Exhausted with fatigue and hunger, they fell upon their knees and prayed fervently for deliverance, when a great white bird appeared to them, such as they had never seen before. The despairing men eagerly seized and tore it in pieces, ate its quivering flesh and drank the warm blood, revived by which they finally reached Deerfield in safety.

By way of Westfield and Kinderhook, Stoddard and his party on horseback, reached Albany in four days from Northampton. Detained in Albany by a thaw which rendered the river impassable, they at last resumed their journey on the 22d of January, by way of Saratoga and Crown Point. Some-times on snow-shoes, sometimes in canoes, and sometimes running on the frozen rivers, they reached Chambly, whence they were conveyed in " carryalls " to Quebec, arriving there on the 16th of January.

The next day, they presented their credentials to the governor and demanded the prisoners. De Vaudreuil gives them his word of honor as a gentleman and an officer, that all prisoners shall have full liberty to return, and with great condescension promises his blessing to all who will go. He tells the commissioners to go freely among the prisoners, and to send for them to their lodgings. Much pleased with their reception, and full of the hope of soon regaining their long-lost relatives, they take their leave. Hearing soon, however, that the priests and some of the laity are practising to pre-vent the return of the prisoners, they complain by letter to the governor, to which he replies that he "can as easily alter the course of the waters as prevent the priests' endeavors," adding that upon reflection he cannot grant liberty to return to those of the English who are naturalized, but only to such as are under age. They answer with clear and cogent argu-ments, against the naturalization pretext, and expose its inconsistency with De Vaudreuil's oft-repeated declaration that he did not care how few English stayed in Canada, the fewer the better for him and the country.

For better communication with Eunice and the other Deerfield captives, the commissioners return to Montreal, where in March they hold another conference with the governor. With the air and speech of men who know that truth and justice are on their side, they reproach him with his breach of faith in throwing obstacles in the way of the departure of the prisoners, when he had at first pretended to favor it; and sick with hope deferred, they demand to know the worst they have to expect. "Heaven forbid ! " said Dora's papa to David Copperfield, "that I should do any man injustice; but I know my partner. Mr. Jorkins is not a man to respond to a proposition of this nature; "—and lamented the severities which he was compelled to practise, by the invisible and inexorable Jorkins. In like manner the governor protests that nothing is nearer his heart than the liberation of the prisoners, which only the fear of the king his master, prevents his effecting at once; and at length he hints, that if the so-called naturalized persons can be smuggled to a point below Quebec, Captain Stoddard may take them on shipboard as he drops down the river, and the government will not interfere.

One reads the sorrow and anxiety in the heart of Mr. Williams, as he demands that "men and women shall not be entangled by the marriages they may have contracted, nor parents by children born to them in captivity." The governor concedes that French women may return with their English husbands, that English women shall not be forced to stay by their French husbands, but about the children of such marriages, he is not so sure.

John Carter, a Deerfield youth of Eunice's age, having expressed his willingness to go by land, if only he may go home, the governor says, "If John will say this before me, he may go." Carter being sent for is at first awed by the governor's presence and denies that he has any desire to return, but afterwards repeating what he had before said to Mr. Williams, De Vaudreuil is very angry, uses the lad roughly, and tells him he is to wait for the ship. This scene is frequently re-enacted, till John at last is overpowered, re-tracts his wish, and remains forever in Canada.

Mr. Williams is forbidden to have any religious talk with the captives, and they are not allowed to visit him on the Sabbath. The "Lord Intendant," hearing that Mr. Williams had been abroad after eight o'clock in the evening to discourse upon religion with some of the English, threatens

if the offence is repeated, to confine him a prisoner in his lodgings; "for," says he, "the priests tell me you undo in a moment all they have done in seven years to establish the people in our religion,"—an unpremeditated compliment to Mr. Williams's power as a preacher.

When Mr. Williams begs that his child may be restored to him, she being a minor, and the circumstances of her education preventing her from knowing what is best for her, the governor says if her Indian relatives consent, he will compel her to return with her father. The government interpreter is sent to talk with her and her Indian relatives. The latter profess that she may do as she pleases. Knowing what this amounted to in John Carter's case, Mr. Williams, after an interview with his daughter at Caughnawaga, where he found the prisoners "worse than the natives," has a conference with the priests of the mission at the house of the governor, who makes a show of interceding in behalf of the afflicted father. The Jesuits reply coldly, that those of Caughnawaga are not held as prisoners, but have been adopted as children, and cannot be compelled to return against their wishes, but will be left to entire freedom. Too well Mr. Williams knows the freedom which the mother church of the Jesuits leaves to its adopted children. The commissioners solicit her deliverance as a favor which will be appreciated by the sovereigns of the two nations, and suitably acknowledged by the governors of both provinces. At last, Mr. Williams, overcome by his feelings, represents to the Jesuits that it cannot benefit them to retain such children, while they "cannot but be sensible that their parents are much exercised about them," and with tears streaming down his face, pleads that they will do in the matter as they would be done by. Vain appeal to the heart that knows not the force of paternal love.

In such discussion weeks were spent. The disappointment of Captain Stoddard, who with his personal interest in the restoration of Eunice to her family, had also hoped to render a signal service to his government; the conflict in the soul of Mr. Williams, as he tried to reconcile his natural affection as a parent, and his spiritual anxiety as a Protestant minister for the salvation of the child's soul, with a due submission to what seemed to be the over-ruling decrees of Providence for her; and the impatience and indignation of Martin Kellogg and Captain Baker, who would doubtless have preferred to make a short cut through the difficulty by running off the prisoners and taking the chances of recapture,—all this is easier imagined than described.

The expression of their feelings being limited by their ignorance of the French language, and the inconvenience of speaking by an interpreter, they poured forth their souls in letters, in which the straightforward, plain dealing of the English Puritan, appears in striking contrast to the circumlocution and diplomacy of the French Jesuit.

On the arrival of the brigantine Leopard from Boston, a final demand was made for the captives.

The commissioners, finally compelled to abandon all hope of Eunice's return, insist that Madame Le Beau[1] shall be allowed to depart; and desire that Ebenezer Nims and his wife and child may be sent for, they being anxious to return but afraid to say so, "till they see themselves clear of all danger from the Indians." Nims, then seventeen years old, had been carried captive from Deerfield in 1704, and adopted by an Indian squaw. Sarah Hoit, a maiden of eighteen, was taken at the same time. When after some years, her cap-tors were about to resort to force to compel her to marry a Frenchman, she had offered to accept as her husband any one of her captive neighbors who would thus free her from her troublesome suitor. Ebenezer gladly offered himself.

They were married at once, and at this time were with their baby boy at Lorette, eagerly hoping for deliverance. The governor promises that a horse or cart shall be sent for Nims's wife who is ill, and that all the family, unaccompanied by priest or Indian, shall be brought to Quebec. Captain Stoddard sends his own physician to assist her on the journey. He returns with the information that the woman is able to walk to town, and that he has been grossly insulted by the Jesuit priest at Lorette. Nims is sent, accompanied by "divers Indians," but at last by the persistence of Stoddard, all are assembled and put on board. The next day a great concourse of Indians came from Lorette, and demanding to see Nims, were assured by him that he wished to go home. Then they insisted upon his giving up his child, which he refusing, was permitted to return with his family to his native town. Years after, the Deerfield records tell how "Ebenezer Nims, Junior, having been baptized by a Romish priest, in Canada, and being dissatisfied with his baptism, upon consenting to the articles of faith," was baptized anew by good Parson Ashley.

One more effort was made by the Bishop, and high officials to prevent Madame Le Beau from going, but in vain.

On the 24th of July, 1714, after nine months absence from home, the commissioners set sail, having effected the deliverance of but twenty-six prisoners; as Stoddard sadly remarks, "Not having received the promised list from the governor; without having our people assembled at Quebec, or half of them asked whether they would return or not, or one minor compelled; having never seen many of our prisoners while we were in the country."

This was the last official effort for the redemption of Eunice Williams. In 1740, their faithful friends, the Schuylers, brought about an interview between her and her relatives, and yielding at last to their importunities, she in later years thrice revisited the place of her nativity. That she insisted upon returning to her Canadian home, and finally died there at the advanced age of ninety, is to my mind, no more than her marriage, a proof of her preference for savage haunts and modes of life. It is well known that English girls, captured at the same time, were forced into marriages with the French and Indians, utterly repugnant to their feelings. At the time of Eunice's memorable visit to Deerfield, children had been born to her, and to the maternal instinct, the strongest passion of which the human soul is capable, even filial affection must yield.

If we admit the statement that her Indian husband assumed the name of Williams, this, and the name of her father bestowed upon her eldest child, prove the lingering fondness in her heart for her kinsfolk. Although robbed of the Christian name given her by her father in baptism, she would not renounce the name of her race.

Another proof that the heart of Eunice Williams never ceased to turn in love towards the home of her infancy, and that she spared no pains to perpetuate this affection in her descendants, is afforded by their visit nearly a hundred years later, to the spot from whence, on February 29, 1704, she had been painfully torn. Weighing carefully the evidence, it seems indisputable that it was Romanism warring against Protestantism, Jesuit against Puritan, that held Eunice Williams eighty-three years a captive.

ENSIGN JOHN SHELDON.

A noted place is the Plym's mouth in Old England. On its blue waters have floated ships of Tyre and merchantmen of Massilia, Keltic coracle and Roman galley, Saxon keel and Norman corsair. Gallant fleets with fair foreign brides for English princes, have sailed into Plymouth harbor. Hither, too, came false Philip of Spain, on his way to his luckless wedding; and hence the pride of England's navy went out to chastise his insolent Armada. Not for these will the Plymouth of England be forever famous; nor because it was there the Black Prince landed with his royal captives, after Poitiers; nor because Drake and Hawkins, and other noted navigators, proceeded thence on their voyages of discovery: but because it is the port from which those nobler heroes, our Pilgrim Fathers, sailed when they came to establish freedom and justice in the New World, planting here the world-renowned colony of Plymouth in New England, the little seed which has grown and blossomed into the grandest Republic on the globe.

Ten years later than the Mayflower, with no less precious burden, and following in her track, another ship sailed out of Plymouth harbor. Before the landing of the Pilgrims, the coasts of Massachusetts Bay were familiar to the west of England seamen, and in 1623, "the merchants of the western counties had grown rich on the profits of the New England fisheries."

Among the more moderate Puritans of the west country was Rev. John White, rector of Trinity church in Dorchester. Though his name is believed to have headed the list of the "Adventurers for New Plymouth," thus showing his sympathy with the pilgrimage, he seems, at the same time, to have been a man to whom, personally, the mere externals of religion were of no vital consequence. Quaint old Fuller describes him as "a constant preacher, so that in the course of his ministry he expounded the Scriptures all over and half over again.........A good Governor, by whose wisdom the town of Dorchester (notwithstanding a casual merciless fire) was much enriched,—knowledge causing piety, piety breeding industry, and industry procuring plenty into it.........

He absolutely commanded his own passions, and the purses of his parishioners, whom he could wind up to what height he pleased, on important occasions." His motives and agency in the settlement of Massachusetts are well known to every reader of our early history. In 1629, he wrote to Endicott "to make a place for sixty more families from Dorsetshire, to arrive the next spring," sundry persons from that and the adjoining counties being desirous to come over and .settle together as an independent community.

A great ship of four hundred tons, the "Mary and John", was chartered at Plymouth, and in March, 1630, "many goodly families and persons from Devonshire, Dorsetshire and

Somersetshire," began to assemble there. "Great pains," says the historian, "were evidently taken to construct this company of such materials as should compose a well-ordered settlement." Here were those two reverend servants of God, Mr. John Warham and Mr. John Maverick, as their spiritual guides. Here were Ludlow and Rossiter, whose position as magistrates of the company, entitled them to be political counsellors of the plantation. Here were Captain John Mason, and others of military experience, to whom they could trust in case of Indian attack. Here, too, were many whose names are familiar to us, through their descendants, men past middle age, like Thomas Ford and William Phelps, with adult families and ample fortunes, whose presence lent dignity and character to the emigration; others, like Israel Stoughton and Roger Clap, stout-hearted, strong-armed young men in the prime of life both married and single, on whom the brunt of the actual labor of the new settlement would rest.

With them to the embarkation came the faithful pastor, John White. He had been the soul of the enterprise, and many of them were his friends, neighbors and parishioners. How solemn must have been the scene, unequalled except by the memorable parting of Robinson and his flock, when, gathering them together in the new hospital for a day of fasting and prayer, he preached to them, as he and they well knew, the last sermon they would ever hear from his lips; his final words of encouragement, as they bade farewell forever to home and native land.

In the afternoon of the same day, the people organized themselves into a church under the ministers whom he had appointed, they formally expressing their acceptance of the office without further ordination; and on the 20th of March the "Mary and John" dropped down Plymouth harbor and took her solitary way across the ocean. "We were of passengers many in number, of good rank," says Roger Clap; "so we came by the good hand of the Lord through the deep, comfortably, having preached or expounded of the word of God every day for ten weeks together, by our ministers."

After a passage of seventy days, the ship arrived at Hull. The place provided for the colony by Endicott was on the Charles River. Whether Captain Squeb supposed he had reached there, or whether he dared not venture farther into the bay without a pilot, is uncertain; but much against their will, he put his passengers and their cattle ashore on Nantasket point. Ten of the party, putting some of the goods into a boat, set out in search of a place for a permanent settlement. Threading their way in and out among the islands, they finally landed at Charlestown, went up the river as far as Watertown, and camped for a day or two on a spot to this day known as Dorchester fields.

"We had not been there many days," says Roger Clap, who was of the party, "though by our diligence we had got up a kind of shelter to save our goods in, but we had order from the ship to come away.........unto a place called Mattapan, because there was a strip of land fit to keep our cattle on.........so we removed and came to Mattapan."

The story of the first settlement of Massachusetts is so simply told by the actors in this grand drama, that we can hardly realize the magnitude of the enterprise. Think of the luxury and ease relinquished, the sorrow of parting forever from home and country, the anxieties, discomforts and dangers of a ten weeks' passage, and the terrible wilderness to be subdued before the most common wants of life could be supplied.

Notwithstanding the scarcity and sickness of the first year, the colony at Mattapan, which in honor of the patriarch White, had received the name of Dorchester, grew and prospered. But the current of emigration, already set firmly to the westward, was not to be stayed at Mattapan. Rumors of rich bottom-lands on a great river to the west, bred discontent with the rocky soil on which they had first planted themselves. This, fostered by the political ambition of some who were disappointed of preferment in Massachusetts, led the Dorchester colonists to determine upon removal.

"Come with me now," says Cotton Mather, "to behold some worthy and learned and genteel persons going to be buried alive on the banks of Connecticut, having been first slain by the ecclesiastical persecutions of Europe." At midsummer of 1635, a few pioneers from Dorchester reached the Great River, and near the Plymouth trading house, set up two years before by William Holmes, began to make preparation for a settlement. On the 15th of October, "the main body of the emigration, about sixty men, women and children" set forth from Dorchester on the long and toilsome journey to the valley of the Connecticut. Like a bit of romance from the middle ages,—like the vanguard of some great army of Crusaders, seems the march of this valiant little band.

Day after day in the beautiful October weather, driving their cattle before them, they wound their way through the trackless wilderness, a compass their only guide. The brill-iant leaves of autumn fluttered softly to their feet as they tramped through the tranquil forest, singing their pious hymns; and the frolicsome squirrel, scared from his harvesting, ceased his chatter as they passed. With prayer and praise, for fourteen days they journeyed on, but when they reached their destination, the autumnal glory had departed, the leafless trees sighed and shivered in the wintry gale, and the cold gray river gave them sullen welcome. We will not dwell upon the horrors of that winter. The spring brought many of their friends, who had been left behind at first, and the little settlement, known to us in later times as Windsor, was called Dorchester, a name dear to the hearts of so many of those weary Pilgrims.

Among "the precious men and women," whom we may supposed to have come with the Dorchester Company in 1630, and to have borne their share of the trials and sufferings of the new settlements, were Isaac Sheldon, his wife, whose name is unknown, and their infant son. Of his ancestry we

have no definite knowledge. The name was at that time an honorable one in England, and is still found among the nobility and gentry of several English counties. In the list of "The worthies of Somersetshire since the time of Fuller," is the name of "that most munificent and generous prelate," Gilbert Sheldon, born in 1598, "descended from the ancient family of Sheldons of Staffordshire," and Archbishop of Canterbury in 1663.

Isaac Sheldon's name appears in Dorchester in 1634, as of Warham's congregation, but not of the church. He removed to Windsor with the emigration of 1635, and there we find him four years later, the owner of a house, barn, orchard and home lot. The following, from Windsor town records, evidently referring to his son, then a young, unmarried man, seems to prove that Isaac, the elder, was not living at this date:

"Sept. 13, 1652. It is assented that Isaac Sheldon and Samuel Rockwell shall keep house together in the house that is Isaac's, so they carry themselves soberly, and do not entertain idle persons, to the evil expense of time by night or day."

In explanation of the above, it may be said that the statutes of our fathers for the prevention of vice were many. The family was next in sacredness to the church. Every newly-wedded couple was expected to set up a home, and at once to enter upon household duties. In good old Colonial days, the young husband could not lounge away his evenings smoking at his club, while his bride dawdled away hers in the petty gossip of boarding-house parlors; and married persons of either sex, remaining long in the colony without their respective partners, were made to send for them, or were themselves ordered back to England as disreputable. No inhabitant was admitted unless approved by the town, and every householder was called to strict account for his visitors, and made answerable for their good conduct and solvency.

In Windsor, "no master of a family" might "give habitation or entertainment to any young man to sojourn in his family, but by the allowance of the town," and "no young man that had not a servant, or was not a public officer, might keep house by himself without permission from the town under a penalty of twenty shillings a week." Wherefore, in 1652, his father being dead, Isaac Sheldon, Junior, then about twenty-three years of age, obtained permission to live on the homestead, and to take as his companion, Samuel Rockwell, a son of one of the early settlers also deceased. The arrangement was of short duration, for Isaac having married Mary Woodford in 1653, sold out to Rockwell the same year, and with his wife and infant daughter, removed to Northampton, among the first settlers of that town.

Isaac and Mary Woodford Sheldon were blessed with thir-teen children. John Sheldon of Deerfield, their second son and third child, was born in Northampton, Dec. 5, 1658. Among the companions of his childhood, were John and Benoni Stebbins, sons of John Stebbins of Northampton, and grandsons of old Rowland Stebbins of Springfield. In 1679, while yet lacking a month of his majority, he married their sister, Hannah Stebbins, she being then but fifteen years and four months old. The boy husband and his child wife remained in Northampton until after the birth of their first two children; but the pioneer spirit was born in him, and we find him soon, with his young family, among the founders of a frontier settlement, as his father and grandfather had been before him.

In another story are detailed the unsuccessful attempts at the settlement of Deerfield up to 1682. Among the very first of those by whom the town was permanently established, were John Sheldon and his wife's brothers, John and Benoni Stebbins.

John Sheldon is first mentioned in the town records of Deerfield in 1686, when he was chosen on a committee "to lay out all the woodlands." By this same meeting the Dorchester schoolmaster, John Williams, was called to be their pastor. The same year Sheldon was chosen on the first board of Selectmen, and re-elected almost every year until 1704. The legislative and executive powers of this board were then very great.

When in 1689, the people rose in their strength against Andros, and a "council for the safety of the people" headed by old Simon Bradstreet, the last of the Puritans, summoned a convention of delegates from the several towns of Massachusetts to deliberate upon the future government, it was a bold but justifiable act. Successful or not, it was treason; and if unsuccessful, its movers would pay the penalty. No town meeting appears to have been called in Deerfield, but John Sheldon did not hesitate. He, as Chairman of the board of Selectmen, took, with them, the responsibility of sending Lieut. Thomas Wells as delegate to the convention, signing with them his credentials as "We the Town of Deerfield." After the massacre at Schenectady, the town of Deerfield

"Att a Leagall Town meeting Feb^r 26. 1689-90 Voted that y^r shall be a good sufficient fortification made upon the meeting hous hill:. . . . .

Thatt all persons whose families cannot conveniently and comfortably be received into ye houses y^t are already upon ye meeting hous hill and shall be wthn the fortifications: such persons shall have habitations provided for y^m wthn s^d fortifications att the Town charg but any p^{r}son or p^{r}sons ye shall provide habitations for y^{m}selves shall be exempt from ye charges afores^d :

That Sgt Jn° Sheldon Benoni Stebbins & Edward Allyn shall have full pow^r to appoint where every persons hous or cellar shall stand w^t bigness y^a shall be."

On the death of Lieut. Thomas Wells, in 1691, his brother Jonathan was appointed in his place, and Sheldon, who had been also recommended by John Pynchon for the lieutenancy, was made ensign. In 1693, we find him deacon of the church; the next year, on the committee to build a new meeting-house, and on various other committees; and in 1696, on the committee to seat the meeting house. In 1697, he, with Jonathan Wells, was appointed to look over old papers and "direct the Town Clerk to record such as should be recorded." To the discretion and labors of this committee, Deerfield owes the preservation of four pages of very valuable matter on its town records. On these records, we find no busier man than John Sheldon, none whose voice was more often sought in the prudential affairs of the town. He was chosen to measure the meadow lands, and to settle the bounds between neighbors. He served as tythingman and school committee, and was very often moderator of the town meetings. In short, John Sheldon was a prominent man in the early history of Deerfield, successfully administering those important town offices, which require the most prudent foresight, and the most candid and impartial judgment.

While under the watchful care of John Sheldon, and others as faithful, the puny settlement was struggling for an existence, the mine for its destruction was already in train. Glance for a moment at the situation: Romish New France in the north; Romish

New Spain at the south; between these, as between the upper and nether millstones, Protestant New England and New Netherlands occupying the debatable ground; for years a political struggle for territory between the three last named. The Lieutenant-General of Canada sends over the ice and snow, and nails his arms to the trees on the English limits; the English quietly push towards Acadia, and hold their ground at the Great Bay of the north. The treacherous savage, ready to trade his peltry or sell his prowess to the highest bidder, to-day tears down the King's

crest from the trees and carries it in derision into Orange, and to-morrow begs the Lieutenant-General to send him "black gowns" to teach him about the Frenchman's God. There are plots and counterplots. The black gown writes to Canada "that the Governor of New York, who is coming to speak to the Five Nations, has sent a shabby ship's flag, bearing the arms of England, to be set up among them, which is still in the Mohawks' public chest" and he knows not when it will see day.

Complications arising from the accession of the Prince of Orange, and later, the succession of Anne to the English throne, afford the excuse for more open hostilities. In the French Archives of the period, may be found the links of that chain by which the pastor and people of Deerfield were to be held in bondage. There, in detail, is the policy of the French, which is by embroiling the eastern Indians with the English, under the pretext that the latter have encroached upon their hunting grounds, to incite them to fall upon the frontier towns: then under the plea that being at war with the English they can no longer live on English soil, by promises of support and protection, to induce them to remove near to Quebec and Montreal, whither they will attract much trade, and where they will become a powerful ally of the French in the prosecution of the war,

There are protests from the Canadian Governor against the trespasses of the English; threats of the French King of what will happen to Boston if the English do not keep within their limits; the fears of Frontenac that the Acadians may incline to the English, "as they are too far from French succor in case of trouble" between the two nations. There are instructions from the French minister to the Governors of Acadia and Canada, so to manage affairs that the Abenakis shall find it more advantageous to live by war than by the chase; notes on the political services of Fathers Rasle and Bigot; letters of commendation and gifts of money to Father Thury for his share in the bloody work; reports of the conferences of the chiefs with the governor at Quebec, and the diplomatic falsehoods and fair promises of the latter; lists of presents and supplies for the Indians: Brazilian tobacco, ver-milion, kettles of all sizes, blue serge, a jacket with gold facings, a shirt, hat, pair of shoes and stockings for one of the chiefs, and a "shift for his daughter, of whom he was very fond;" orders for "tufts of white feathers," costing a few *centimes* in Paris, to designate the savages in night attacks; weapons, and provisions, flour, molasses, butter, and "plenty of brandy, without which they will not act efficiently."

Ever since the building of her stockade, Deerfield had been in a state of alarm. Repeated sallies had been made by the enemy, and several of the inhabitants had been killed, and others carried into captivity. The distress of the people will be seen from the following extract from a letter of their pastor to the governor praying for an abatement of taxes, and dated Oct. 21st, 1703:

"We have been driven from our houses & home lots into the fort, some a mile, some 2 miles, whereby we have suffered much loss,...........the whole town kept in; our children of 12 or 13 years and under, we have been afraid to improve in the field, for fear of the enemy;.........we have been crowded together into houses, to the preventing indoor affairs being carryed on to any advantage & must be constrained to expend at least 50£ to make any comfortable provision of housing if we stay together in cold weather: so that our losses are far more than would have paid our taxes..........

　　　　i would request your Excellency so far to commiserate as to do what may be encouraging to persons to venture their all in the frontiers, ...and that they may have something allowed them in making the fortification; we have mended it, it is in vain to mend, & must make it all new, & fetch timber for 206 rod, 3 or 4 miles if

we get oak."

Thanks to the Deerfield historian, whose study of the "Antient Records" seems to have come to him by direct descent, we can reconstruct the village as it was in the winter of 1703-4. In the north-west corner of the rebuilt fortifications, stood the house of Ensign John Sheldon, a two-story front, 42x21, and a one-story lean-to or kitchen. It needs no description. The appearance of the "Old Indian House," as it was called ever after that fatal day, is familiar to many. He had built it in 1696, to accommodate his growing family. It was probably the largest and the best in town, and the hospitalities to this day so generously dispensed on that spot, began with Landlord Sheldon.

Lulled by frequent false alarms into a fatal sense of security, John Sheldon and his neighbors slept soundly on the night of the 29th of February, 1704. The bitter cold penetrated even his well-built dwelling, the drifted snow lay piled outside against the palisades, the wind shrieked as it tore the dry branches from the trees and hurled them far over the frozen crust; but no consciousness of unusual danger disturbed their slumbers. Yet with the rushing of each fitful gust, running with it from the north and pausing as it ceased, the cruel foe was creeping stealthily nearer to the little hamlet. The stormy night was well-nigh spent, the guard lay heavy in his first sleep, when "the enemy came in like a flood." Pouring over the palisades, heaving and tossing like the angry billows of a stormy sea, roaring and rushing to and fro within the fortification, the horrid crowd surged about the houses of the defenseless people. Roused by their hideous yells, the sleepers woke bewildered to find themselves surrounded by dusky faces fiendish with fresh war paint. Resistance was vain; some were instantly murdered; others, powerless from fear, were fiercely torn from their warm beds, bound hand and foot, and hurried out half naked into the bitter night. Deafened by the tumult, blinded by the glare of torches, driven like sheep to the shambles, they were huddled together in the meeting house, where but yesterday their faithful shepherd had folded his flock in peace. Confusion and terror reigned. The place which they had been taught to regard as the house of God was now defiled and desecrated. There, where so lately their voices had mingled in prayer and praise, could now be heard only the groans of the wounded, the wailing of women, the shrieks of the children and the tremulous voices of the aged calling on God to "remember mercy in the midst of judgment."

Hard by, in the house of Benoni Stebbins, seven heroic men, bravely seconded by their wives, for three hours kept at bay the combined force of French and Indians. With their children clinging to them in fright, unceasingly the women moulded the bullets, resolutely the men stood at their posts. The leaden hail beat steadily down upon the assailants. Fiercer and higher on the keen air, rose the yells of the baffled foe.

Not far away, in his own house, pinioned and helpless, but calm and steadfast, the pastor of the little flock, surrounded by his terrified family, as he "was able committed their state to God, praying that they might have grace to glorify His name, whether in life or death."

For a time, the well-built and firmly bolted door of John Sheldon's house proved an effectual barrier against the savages. Sacred historic door! Door of the ark of the covenant wert thou to our fathers in the olden time. Built of no costly material, thy posts were not inlaid with shell; no gold adorns thy panels. Heart of oak art thou, fit type of the heroes who framed thee; sturdy and strong in their defence as they, in defence of their liberty,—ye yielded never! More to us than Grecian sculptures are thy carvings by Indian tomahawk, and thy wrought spikes, more precious than bosses of silver and gold!

Maddened at last by their baffled efforts, they hacked and hewed at it till the hole was cut, which is still to be seen in it. Through this they fired at random, killing Sheldon's wife, who was dressing herself in bed in the room at the right of the door. Finally swarming in at the windows and rudely awaking Mary Sheldon, a maiden of sixteen, from sweet dreams of her lover, they captured her and her young brothers, Ebenezer and Remembrance; and killed their little sister, Mercy, a child of three years. Their eldest brother, John, had married three months before, Hannah Chapin of Springfield. During the preparation of the bridal outfit, her mother, loath to have her encounter the perils of a frontier settlement, yet with that strange inconsistency with which we often make a jest of the saddest things in life, advised her to have a pelisse made of unusual thickness, as she might need it if she were carried off by the Indians. On the first alarm she and her husband, who were occupying the east chamber of his father's house, jumped together from the window. Spraining her ankle, and unable to save herself, she urged her husband to leave her and alarm the nearest village. At her entreaties he stripped up a blanket, and binding it about his bare feet, ran to Hatfield. His heroic bride was captured with the rest.

At daybreak, Hertel de Rouville rallied his troops for the retreat, and the shivering captives began their painful march. The sorrows of that awful journey cannot be described. Snow-blind and starving, with aching hearts, and frozen limbs, and bleeding feet, they staggered on for twenty-five days. Arriving at Chambly in detached parties, they were separated, some remaining with their Indian captors, others bought by the French of Montreal and Quebec.

Let us return to the desolated village whence they had been so cruelly snatched. Of the whereabouts of John Sheldon the elder, on that fearful night, we know nothing, but we cannot suppose him to have been idle or panic stricken. He may have been with the gallant band that fell upon the enemy's rear that morning, abandoning the pursuit only when retaliation threatened the captives. What must have been his feelings and those of his neighbors equally bereft, as they walked among the still smoking ashes of their once happy homes, searching among the dead and dying for traces of their kindred. His daughter, Hannah, whose husband, Joseph Catlin, was slain in the meadow fight, his little grandchild, and his married son, were all that were left of John Sheldon's family. In the spring days that followed, the scanty remnant of these three households sat round his cheerless hearthstone, and talked sadly of their dead, and of those far away in captivity worse than death. Vaguely at first he thought of their possible rescue, but as the gloomy summer wore on, his dream became a definite purpose, and he announced his determination to devote his remaining energies to the redemption of his children and townsfolk.

Meanwhile their captors were jubilant. Exaggerated reports of their success were made to the French Minister, by the Governor and the Intendant of Canada:

A letter of this period from De Vaudreuil to the Minister, says:

"The Sieur de Rouville. . . . . . desires, My Lord, that you would have the goodness to think of his promotion, having been, invariably in all the expeditions that presented themselves, and being still actually with the Abenakis. . . . . . The Sieur de Rouvilles party.

My Lord, has accomplished everything expected of it, for independent of the capture of a fort, it showed the Abenakis that they could truly rely on our promises; and this is what they told me at Montreal on the 13th of June when they came to thank me."

A letter to the Minister from the Governor and the Intendant of Canada, written at the same time, contains the following:

"We had the honor to report to you last year, My Lord, the reasons which had obliged us to embroil the English with the Abenakis, ... The English having killed some of these Indians, they sent us word of it, and. . . . . . demanded assistance.

This obliged us, My Lord, to send thither the Sieur de Rouville an officer of the line, with nearly two hundred men who attacked a fort in which according to the report of all the prisoners, there were more than one hundred men under arms; they took more than one hundred and fifty prisoners, including men and women, and retreated, having lost only three men and some twenty wounded."

A deputation of the Abenakis waited upon their "father," the governor, "to bear witness to the pleasure he had given them in avenging them against the English," and he in turn, congratulated his "children" upon their united victory over their "common enemy." Mr. Parkman says, "Except their inveterate habit of poaching on Acadian fisheries, the people of New England had not provoked these barbarous attacks."

The correspondence between the governors of the two provinces during several years previous to the sacking of Deerfield, in which one or the other is constantly demanding or receiving satisfaction for the seizure of vessels, shows that privateering was common to both parties even during a nominal peace. In one of these poaching expeditions, the English had seized a Frenchman, known in our annals as Captain Baptiste, who had proved himself a spy and a traitor in the service of both governments, and who was, moreover, a wholly unprincipled fellow, having besides his Acadian wife, several others in different parts of the world. As from his knowledge of the coast, he was very necessary to the Acadian government, one Le Févre was sent to Boston in the autumn of 1702, to demand his release. War having been in the meantime declared, Dudley detained Le Févre, and flatly refused to surrender Baptiste. In concluding his letter to the governor of Port Royal, he says, "As for the exchange of prisoners, when I shall be advised of the settlement of a cartel properly, I shall embrace it as being very useful. In the meantime I must desire that the subjects of her Majesty the Queen, my Sovereign Lady, may have the good fortune to keep themselves out of the Inconveniences of a captivity, though never so easy and short." How grievously this hope was disappointed, we have already seen.

When the Deerfield pastor and his fellow captives reached Canada, the "Governor told me," says Mr. Williams, "that I should be sent home as soon as Captain *Battis* was returned and not before, and that I was taken in order to his redemption."

In April, 1704, and again in August, Dudley despatched letters by way of Albany, to the Canadian governor, upbraiding his conduct of the war as unlawful and unchristian. "You have boasted," he says, "of massacring my poor women and children, and carrying away into a miserable captivity the reste, and they are made a matter of trade between the Savages and the subjects of your master, under your government. . . . . . I write you this to tell you that such treatment of Christians will be esteemed barbarous by all Europe, and I expect you to withdraw all these Christian captives from the hands of savages, and return them to me, as I have several times returned your people to Port Royal, and shall continue to do, until I have your reply to this."

In his August letter he offers an equal exchange of prisoners, and threatens reprisals if a more honorable treatment of the captives is not guaranteed. "I cannot admit the pre-text," he says, "that the Indians have the right to retain these prisoners, because I would never permit a savage to tell me that any Christian prisoner is at his disposal." From Dudley's point of view, it seemed absurd for the Governor-General of New France to declare that he could not compel the Indians to give up their English captives.

The difficulties of his position will be better understood, if we remember that he had made the savages his tools, by promising them a chance to avenge themselves upon the English. Receiving no satisfaction from the French governor, Dudley, the last of September, proposed to his council that "Ar-thur Jeffrey, being attended with two French prisoners of war, be sent by way of Saint John's River to Quebeck, with letters to the governor, referring to the English prisoners there and to concert a method of exchange."

The departure of Jeffrey was doubtless prevented by the arrival of Jonn Sheldon at Boston. He was attended by young John Wells of Deerfield, whose mother, Hepzibah Belding, was one of the captives. On Wednesday, Dec. 13th, 1704, the governor acquainted his council that he had received no answer to his letter sent the preceding summer to the governor of Quebec, relating to the English prisoners, and that "it was doubtful if those letters found safe conveyance," . . . . . . "as also that John Sheldon and John Wells of Deerfield, who both had relations in captivity there, were now attending him, and very urgent to have license to travail thither, their being- also two French prisoners used to that Rhode, who have their relations here, that are willing to accompany the said Englishmen with his Excellency's letters, and to see them safely returned at the peril of having their near relations here exposed."

His Excellency proposed the conveying them by water to Casco, thence to take the direct course through the country to Quebec "in order to find out how many prisoners are in that country and to make way for their release in the spring."

Fortunately for John Sheldon, within the week Capt. Livingston of New York appeared in Boston, and "At a Council held in Boston on Tuesday, Dec. 19, 1704, His Excellency acquainted the Council, that since their last setting and advice for sending messengers to Quebec. . . . . . to negotiate the affair about the Exchange of Prisoners, he had discoursed that matter with Capt. John Livingston now in town who had been several times there, was well acquainted in the severall parts and the way thither from the upper towns of this province which he accounted to be more safe than to Travaile through the Eastern Country's and that said Livingston would undertake that service accompanyed with Mr. Shelden and Wells without any Frenchmen to have a hundred pounds for his service and his expenses borne. Upon consideration of the greater safety and certainty of this way and the charge saved of a vessel and men that must necessarily be Employed the other way, besides the fitting out the Frenchmen, and the inconveniencies that might happen upon their going: as also the accomplishment of Capt. Livingston for such a service. It was Advised that he be Imployed accordingly and his Excellency communicated his letters to the Governor of Canada to be sent by them."

Duplicates of Dudley's letters sent and unanswered during the preceding summer, were prepared and with them the following:

"Boston, Dec. 20, 1704.

Sir:

The enclosed were sent some time since by way of Albany; but fearing that they have miscarried I send you herewith Messrs. Livingston and Sheldon envoys, with John Wells,. . . . . to carry you this and to inform you that I have in my hands about 150 prisoners. . . . . On the return of my envoys with a list of my captives whom you have in your hands, I would willingly have yours transported this spring as far as Penobscot. . . . . Should the winter be so severe as to oblige my envoys to remain until the rigor of winter is passed, you will if agreeable to you, send an Indian to the fort at Casco Bay with a letter informing me when and where I may send a shallop to meet yours from Quebec, in order that the exchange may be made. . . . . You will have the goodness to let my envoys return as soon as they can safely do so, with your decision on this subject, in order that I may have your prisoners ready to deliver up on receipt of your reply in regard to those of my people now in your hands: and to grant my envoys opportunity for the freest conference with you as to what is most advantageous in this business.

> I am with all respect, Sir, your very humble and obedient
> servant."

With these credentials, Sheldon and his companions took the Bay Path for Deerfield, tarrying at Hatfield on the way to procure their outfit of Colonel Partridge.

I will not attempt to describe the stir in the village when it was known that Mr. Sheldon was there, *en route* for Canada, as an agent of the government in behalf of the suffering town. Pausing only for a brief good-bye, burdened with messages of love to the dear ones in bondage, and followed by the blessings of all, the party pushed on over Hoosac Mountain to Albany. We have a glimpse of them there, before they plunge into the pathless forest, in a scrap of paper containing an account, on which in Sheldon's handwriting, is endorsed, "what i paid to captain levenston at hotsoen river."

We need not go back to King Arthur for exploits of chivalry; our colonial history is full of them. This man, long past the daring impulses of youth ; this youth, whose life was all before him ; show me two braver knights-errant setting out with loftier purpose on a more perilous pilgrimage.

Three hundred miles of painful and unaccustomed tramping on snow-shoes in mid-winter, over mountain and morass, through tangled thickets and "snow-clogged forest," where with fell purpose the cruel savage lurked; with gun in hand, and pack on back, now wading knee-deep over some rapid stream, now in the teeth of the fierce north wind, toiling over the slippery surface of the frozen lake, now shuffling tediously along in the sodden ice of some half-thawed river; digging away the drifts at night for his camp; wet, lame,' half-famished and chilled to the bone, hardly daring to kindle a fire; a bit of dried meat from his pack for a supper, spruce boughs for his bed; crouching there wrapped in his blanket, his head muffled in the hood of his capote, eye and ear alert, his mittened hand grasping the hilt of the knife at his belt; up at daybreak and on again, through storm and sleet, pelted by pitiless rains, or blinded by whirling snow: what iron will and nerves of steel, sound mind in sound body, to dare and do what this man did.

Of the date of John Sheldon's arrival in Canada, we are ignorant. We can only guess at the impressions of the sturdy Puritan yeoman as he first stood upon the rock of Quebec, surrounded by "the appendages of an old established civilization." Strange sights and sounds must have greeted him as he sat in his inn on the great square. The "noisy bush-ranger" and the "befeathered Indian" swaggered about the door. "Plumed officers," with squads of soldiers in slouched hats, and "arquebus on shoulder," marched quickly at tap of drum up to the fort. Processions bearing relics of the saints, filed in at the cathedral door,—the gaunt Jesuit in black cassock and rosary, the gray gown of the Récollet friar, the Seminary priest in sable robe, with his band of boys in blue, pale nuns in white cornets and clad in serge, with their pupils, among whom is more than one English face. News of his arrival spread up and down the river, "reviving the drooping spirits of the captives." Far different was its effect upon their captors. Stephen Williams, the minister's son, was in the hands of a St. Francis Indian, who demanded forty crowns for his ransom. Mr. Williams had prevailed upon the governor to offer thirty. The savage stood out, and, leaving the boy with his wife, went off to hunt. "When Mr. Sheldon was come to Canada," says Stephen in his account, "my mistress thought there would be an exchange of prisoners, and lest the French should then take me away for nothing, she removed up in ye woods about half a mile from ye river, y^t if they came they might not find me." Having offended her a few days after, by slighting some heavy work given him to do, "the squaw," says the eleven-years-old child, "was very angry. 'I will not beat you myself,' says she, 'for my husband ordered me to the contrary, but will tell ye Jesuit, ye next time he comes.'......Within a day or two ye jesuit comes, she was as good as her word, did complain; he takes me out and whips me wth a whip wth six cords, several knots in each cord."

As soon as possible, the envoys delivered their letters to the governor, by whose permission Mr. Williams came up from Chateau-Richer, where he had been sent to prevent his interference with the conversion of his people by the Jesuits. From him Sheldon heard that his children were living, and John Wells learned the sad tidings of his mother's murder. He told them the harrowing tale of the march to Canada, and the details of the captivity. Deacon Sheldon was greatly exercised by his account of the craft and cruelty employed by the French "to ensnare the young, and to turn them from the simplicity of the Gospel to Romish superstition."

Mr. Williams doubtless accompanied the envoys to their first audience with the governor. The good deacon, in his home-spun garments, must have felt himself in strange contrast with the other occupants of the council hall; the governor majestic and surrounded by the brilliant uniforms of his guard; the haughty intendant; popinjay pages loitering about, stern old warriors bedecked with medals, gay young sprigs of the nobility in elegant apparel, "Jesuits, like black spectres, gliding in and out." As Mr. Williams saw the dignity of his fellow-townsman, unabashed by all this parade, he perhaps thought of the proverb, "Seest thou a man diligent in his business, he shall stand before kings; he shall not stand before mean men."

The deputies received little satisfaction from their conferences with the governor. "God's time of deliverance," says Mr. Williams, "was not yet come." Monsieur de Vaudreuil was civil and diplomatic. He says that the Indians are his allies, not his subjects; he has, therefore, no real right to demand the captives from them. They might perhaps be ransomed, but, "knowing Monsieur Dudley's resolution not to 'set up an Algiers trade' by the purchase of prisoners," he dares not take the responsibility. As to an exchange of those in the hands of the French, he hardly sees what basis for that can be arranged, since he learns by the list of French prisoners sent him that the governor of Boston has permitted some Port Royalists, who should have been sent home with the exchange, to embark for the West Indies. Moreover, there is Baptiste.

The days passed in alternation of hope and discouragement. Fair promises were succeeded by evasion and delay. Mr. Williams was refused permission to go up to Montreal to talk with his children and neighbors, and sent back to Chateau-Richer.

Leaving Mr. Sheldon to push the search for his children aid the other captives, many of whom had been put out of sight, Mr. Livingston set out for Boston on the 18th of March to state the situation of affairs and carry De Vaudreuil's letter to the governor, but returned to Quebec on the 26th, the ice being unsafe. On the 29th, Mr. Sheldon received a letter from his son's wife in Montreal, which probably gave him the first definite intelligence of his children. It appears to have enclosed a letter from one of her fellow-captives, who, on indirect evidence, I assume to be James Adams, captured at Wells, in 1703, with Samuel Hills and others. Of the letter and its enclosure, only the following scrap, in a beautiful handwriting, remains:

"I pray you my kind loue to Landlord Shelden, and tell Him I am sorry for all his Los. I doe in these few lines showe youe that God has shone yo grat kindness and marcy, In carrying your Daighter Hanna, and Mary in partickeler through soe grat a jorney far behiend my expectations noing how Lame they was, the Rest of your children are with the Indians. Remembrance lives near cabect, Hannah does Liues with the frenc In the same house I doe."

Mr. Sheldon's reply to his daughter-in-law is dated:

"Quebec the 1 of Aperl, 1705.

der child

this is to let you noe that i received yours the 29th of March

which was a comfort to me. . . . . .I am wheel, blessed be God for it, and i may tell you i dont here of my child as it [yet],   the saye is that he is in the wodes a hunten, remember my loue to Mr. Addams and his wife and judah Writ and all the reste as if named and my harty desire is that god would in his own good time opene adore of deliuerans fore you al, and the meanwhile let us wait with patiens one God for it, hoe can bring lite out of darkness and let us cast al our care one god who doeth care for us and can helpe us Mr Williams is sent down the riuer agane eighteen or twenty miles, I did enjoy his company about three wekes, wh^ch was a comfort to me, he giues his loue to al the captives there. My desire is that Mr Addams and you wod doe al you can with your mistress that my children mite be redeemed from the Indanes. Our post returned bake again in 8 days by reson of the badnes of the ise, they goe again the seckont of this month, and i desire to come up to Montreal the beginen of May. John Wels and Ebenezer Warner giues ther loue to al the captiues ther, and so rites your louen father

John Sheldon."

Between the date of the above and the seventh, on which the post is to start again, Mr. Sheldon is busy writing letters. The following, dated April 2d, 1705, is the remnant of that sent by this post to his son John, at Deerfield:

"deer could this fue lines are to let you noe i am in good helth at this time blessed be God for it. i may tell you that we sent away a post the 18th day of March, they ware gone 8 days and returned a gane by reson that the ise was soe bad. this may let you noe I receiued a letter from your wife the 29th of March and she was whel i may let you noe i haint sene none of my children but here they are gone a hunten."

On the 7th of April, Samuel Hills of Wells, who gladly gave his parole for the opportunity of visiting his friends, accompanied by two Frenchmen named Dubois, set out for Boston with letters from the envoys and the governor of Canada. They went across the country and down the Kennebec to Casco bay, arriving at Piscataqua on the 4th of May; and on the 15th, the letters brought by them were communicated by the governor at Boston to his council. De Vaudreuil re-

criminates in detail the accusations of the duplicate letters sent by Sheldon, "not having received them by Albany." Reiterating obstacles, and stating his terms for the return of the captives, he adds: "Mr. Livingston is a very worthy man, with whom I could soon agree upon an exchange, were not his powers limited. If you were sole in command in New England, as I am here, I should not have hesitated to take your word, and it would really have given me great pleasure to return to you by him all your prisoners. But as you have a Council, whose opinions are often divided, and in which you have but one vote, you must not take it ill that I demand a guaranty for the return of the prisoners on your side, more especially because I, on my side, having absolute authority, am always able to keep my pledged word."

The persistent importunities of Mr. Sheldon and Mr. Williams, aided by the friendly offices of Captain de Beauville, an officer of high rank, brought about the ransom of the minister's daughter Esther, one of Sheldon's children, his son's wife and two others unknown. The governor also purchased Stephen Williams from his Indian master, and Livingston told him at Sorel he was to go home with him, "which," says the boy, "revived me very much to think of going home, but the governor quickly altered his mind said I must not go."

In the first days of May, the envoys, with their five redeemed captives, set out on their journey home. The Sieur de Courtemanche, a distinguished officer, with eight French soldiers, accompanied them as escort, carrying duplicates of the governor's letters already forwarded by Hills. Shortly after the departure, four young men, Thomas Baker, John Nims, Martin Kellogg and Joseph Petty, disappointed at not having liberty to go home with Mr. Sheldon, escaped from Montreal, and after terrible suffering reached Deerfield in June, in an almost dying state.

Livingston and the French escort were probably left at Albany; Hannah Chapin Sheldon, safely returned to her father's house in Springfield; and Ensign Sheldon with the Sieur de Courtemanche, hurried on to Boston, where they must have arrived before June 5th, as a committee was appointed on that date to audit their accounts, "and to do it with all speed."

Hannah wrote from Springfield to her husband, on the 16th, that "she should be very glad to see him," and shortly after, she and the others were re-united to their friends in Deerfield. By his artful selection of a few captives for release, De Vaudreuil had quieted Mr. Williams, and rid himself of John Sheldon for a time. It is not probable that he expected Dudley to accept the terms offered by his messenger. The sending of Courtemanche with these instructions was done with the wily intent to gain time to rivet his prisoners' chains more strongly, and, as he himself avows in his report of the matter to the king, "to make himself acquainted with the country."

These instructions were: to be inflexible in his demands for Baptiste, "without whom there could be no exchange;" to demand the return of all the French prisoners in New England to Port Royal, giving his parole, that immediately upon information of their arrival there, all the English held by the French, (there is no mention of those in savage hands,) should be released and furnished with provisions and transportation for their return; to demand guarantees for the return of those Acadians who had been allowed to go elsewhere; to demand justice for an alleged murder of six Frenchmen; and, finally, to demand the release of one Allain, who, it was pretended, had been sent by the governor of Port Royal to negotiate an exchange, but who was held as a spy, his passport not being forthcoming.

On the 14th of June, 1705, "His Excellency acquainted the council with the advances he had made in his proposals to Mr. Courtemanche, relating to the exchange. . . . . and that the whole affair stuck at Baptiste, which Mr. Courtemanche insisted on as a particular article in his instructions, and declined to do anything unless Baptiste was included." The governor asks advice of his council, and desires "that certain of them with the Representatives take the matter into consideration, without speaking of the same without doors." The following day, the representatives sent a message to the governor "That he should use his utmost endeavors to obtain the exchange without releasing of Baptiste. But if finally it cannot be obtained without, that Baptiste be exchanged Rather than our Captives be retained in the hands of the Enemy."

Notwithstanding the injunction of secrecy, it was noised abroad that the governor intended to give up Baptiste. Whereupon a strong remonstrance against his release, was sent by the leading "merchants and sailors" of Boston. "If there were nothing else but the urgency of the French demanding him, it is a sufficient reason why we should preserve him to ourselves," they say. After much fruitless discussion, Dudley in his turn drew up proposals for the exchange. Courtemanche falling sick, or perhaps indisposed to return on foot, Captain Vetch, with an eye to trade at Quebec, offered to go with his vessel and convey him home. Courtemanche, who seems to have made himself agreeable in Boston, urged the governor to let his son, William Dudley, a young man of eighteen, bear him company to Quebec and return on the same vessel. Glad of an opportunity to acquire information and hoping thereby to obtain the release of some, the governor consented. "Bread, Beer, Flesh and Pease for a twenty days'" voyage are ordered aboard Captain Vetch's vessel, with "a Hoggshead of good wine as a present to the Governor of Quebec." The two Dubois are sent home by land; Courtemanche orders Samuel Hills to accompany him by sea. Dudley's dispatches are dated Boston the 4-15 July, 1705, and probably the vessel sails the next day.

Concerning the exchange, Dudley makes all proper concessions. It may take place at Mount Desert, whither he will send all the French prisoners on any day when De Vaudreuil will send the English there. He will buy none from the Indians, but if they are not at once rescued from them, he will retaliate and "your people will be reduced to accommodate themselves to a savage life as well as mine." He resents the insinuation that his authority is limited; he will send Allain home, and with him, in exchange for the two girls Mr. Livingston brought back, two strong men of Port Royal, captives here. "As to Baptiste I think Monsieur de Courtemanche has learned so many things about his dastardly conduct that you will agree with me that he is a rascal who does not deserve that you should want him back, and perhaps you will think he is not worth my keeping, wherefore I have resolved to send him with the others to the place of rendezvous, if the articles are accepted, and there will be an end of that business."

Not doubting that his terms will be accepted, he desires that his son may see the captives and help them to a speedy return, for fear that winter may overtake them. In case Mr. Williams should not wish to come with the others, if the governor will let him return with Captain Vetch, Dudley will provide an equally distinguished escort for any French gentlemen who may be prisoners in Boston.

The arrival of an English vessel in the St. Lawrence made a great stir. De Vaudreuil at first ordered her anchored fifteen leagues down the river, but finally had her brought up to Quebec, her sails removed and a guard put on board.

The details of young Dudley's sojourn in Quebec and the correspondence between Canada and the court of France on that subject are of exciting interest, but having no immediate connection with the Deerfield prisoners, must be omitted here. De Vaudreuil treated the Boston gentlemen politely and allowed them entire liberty in Quebec, but the wary intendant makes a merit of watching them closely during their stay in Montreal.

Mr. Williams came up from Chateau-Richer to see them, and was supplied by Captain

Vetch with money, but continuing to argue in season and out of season against Popery, he was sent back again. His son Stephen, Jonathan Hoit and a few others were allowed to go home with Mr. Dudley, whose negotiations towards the exchange were entirely unsuccessful. After a tedious voyage they reached Boston, where they had been long expected, on the 21st of November, 1705.

William Dudley was the bearer of new proposals to his father from the Canadian government, which not only included a full exchange, but were virtually a treaty of peace between the French and English in America, with the stipulation however, that "if not signed by the governors of Boston, New York and all other special English governors before the end of February, the articles should be null and void." The articles were rejected by the assembly and council at Boston, as not "consistent with her majesty's honor," and with thanks to Dudley for his past endeavors, it was left to him, upon advice with Lord Cornbury, to answer De Vaudreuil. To avoid their subsistence during the winter, and to set an example of generosity, Dudley early in December, sent home fifty-seven Port Royal captives, retaining Baptiste and others of importance.

On the 17th of January, 1706, the governor read to his council his answer to De Vaudreuil's proposals, "to be despatched to Quebec by Mr. John Sheldon, attended with a servant or two, and accompanied by two French prisoners of war."

Mr. Sheldon now appears upon the stage as a full fledged ambassador. His attendants were John Wells and Joseph Bradley, a Haverhill man, whose wife was languishing in her second captivity. They left Deerfield on the 25th of January, taking the same route as before, another dreary winter journey. They arrived, at Quebec in the beginning of March. Mr. Williams went up again for a few days to see Mr. Sheldon, and doubtless told him with indignation, the vigorous efforts of the priests to gain proselytes after Mr. Dudley's departure. "When Mr. Sheldon came the second time," says Mr. Williams, "the adversaries did what they could to retard the time of our return, to gain time to seduce our young ones to Popery."

Although the dispatches carried by Mr. Sheldon were not satisfactory to De Vaudreuil, he could oppose nothing to Mr. Sheldon's arguments, that he was in honor bound to release some captives in return for those already sent home by Dudley, and he at last reluctantly consented to release forty-three.

Captain Thomas More in his boat, the Marie, was to take them as far as Port Royal, with orders to the governor of Acadia to retain them there until "all the French prisoners without distinction" should be returned to Port Royal. Meantime the Marie was to proceed to Boston with Mr. Sheldon and his attendants, the two Frenchmen also returning with De Vaudreuil's ultimatum.

The Marie must have sailed soon after June 2d, the date of the governor's letter. She evidently stopped at Port Royal, for we have John Sheldon's account there of his "pocket expenses: the Doctor for John Wells," and "for two blankets and other things for yᵉ captives."

Whether Monsieur de Brouillant assumed the responsibil-ity of forwarding the captives with Mr. Sheldon, or how it was, we know not, but there is evidence enough that they arrived with him in the Marie at Boston on the first day of August. Mr. Williams, writing after his own redemption and before Mr. Sheldon's third expedition, says, "The last who came, in numbers between forty and fifty, with Mr. Sheldon (a good man and a true servant of the church in Deerfield, who twice took his tedious and dangerous journey in the winter from New England unto Canada on these occasions), came aboard at Quebec, May 30th, and after nine weeks' difficult passage, arrived at Boston, August 1st, 1706." On the 2d, Dudley informed his council of the letters "received yesterday, from the Governor of Canada by a Flagg of Truce with forty odd English prisoners." Who were the forty odd we know not. Sheldon's daughter Mary was one; James Adams, another. Mr. Williams was still in Chateau-Richer, and the intendant threatened "if More brought word that Battis was in prison, he would put him in prison and lay him in irons."

De Vaudreuil's letter also threatened reprisals if the Marie did not carry back tidings of Baptiste's release. One clause of this letter shows John Sheldon as an honest government official: "I have done myself the pleasure to honor the letter of credit you have given to Mr. Sheldon upon me. He has used it very modestly, and has demanded of me only 750 Livres." Mr. Sheldon's account shows how the money was expended. His landlords at Quebec and Montreal got a good part of it. The destitute captives were clothed; other interesting items are: "For acarriall to goe to see the captives at the Mohawk fort." "For a canoe and men to go from Quebec to visit Mr. Williams." "More paid to yᵉ Barbour for me and my men and for my Blooting." "Laid out for my daughter Mary for necessary cloathing." "More for my darter."

Mr. Sheldon's account being allowed, Wells and Bradley petitioned to be reimbursed for sundry expenditures, "snow-shoes and pumps," "a dog 15 shillings," and "besides there was a gun hired for the voyage, which said gun was broken in the discharging." Thirty-five pounds were voted to Mr. Sheldon, and twenty pounds each to the others for their services, over and above their outfit. While Mr. Sheldon was settling his affairs in Boston, young John Sheldon wrote him as follows:—

"Honored Father Sheldon:—After duty presented, these are to let you noe that I reseived your letter, which we desire to bless you for it. pray give my love with my wife's to sister Mary and all the rest of the captives. . . . . .I pray you to buy for me a paire of curtings and a feather bead, and a greaine coverlid and a necklace of amber.". . . .
. . . . .

No doubt these commissions were faithfully executed, and the "Old Indian House" was soon gladdened by the return of its master, and another of the long-sundered household.

A week after the arrival of the Marie at Boston, the council advised Dudley to reject the proposals brought by her, and "yet send away the French prisoners without exception to Port Royal and Quebec and demand ours in return, and to send a vessel forthwith to Quebec in hopes of seeing them before winter."

Captain Bonner and his vessel were hired; Mr. Samuel Appleton of the council was appointed as bearer of dispatches; and towards the last of the month the brigantine Hope, auspicious name in such a service, convoyed the Marie with Baptiste, and all but one of the French prisoners out of Boston harbor. Narrowly escaping shipwreck, they reached Quebec about the first of October. Mr. Appleton appears to have made himself pretty comfortable while the negotiations were pending, if we may judge from his tavern bill, on which I find beef and mutton a plenty, with ducks, broiled chickens and according to the fashion of that day, many bottles of *eau de vie*. There being no longer any excuse for retaining Mr. Williams, he and fifty-six others, among whom were his two sons and probably Sheldon's, came home with Mr. Appleton.

Mr. Williams says they left Quebec the 25th of October, but I find by the inn-keeper's bill that Samuel joined his father and Warham there on the 28th; that one of the boys was charged for breaking a glass on the 29th, and the board of the three is charged up to the 31st, so that unless their landlord was unusually rapacious we must take this as the day of their departure. After a stormy passage, they reached Boston on Nov. 21st, and were immediately sent for by the general court, then in session, where their pitiful appearance excited such commiseration that it was at once "Resolved that the sum of twenty shillings be allowed and paid out of the Publick Treasury to each of the captives this day returned from Canada." On Appleton's account, presented after his return, is the following item which must have made him doubly welcome to good Mr. Williams: "5 English Bibles, which Capt. Appleton carryed with him by order of yᵉ governor and council and given to the captives, 2 £ 13 s. 6 d."

On his return to Deerfield after his second expedition, John Sheldon entered again upon the town business. Within ten days after Mr. Williams landed in Boston, he was "chosen a committee to go down to the Bay to treat with Mr. Williams about returning to settle in Deerfield." I know not whether to admire more, the energy and courage of the people, or the fidelity and self-sacrifice of the pastor, in their action in this matter.

Early in 1707, by a vote of the town to build a house for the minister "as big as Ensign Sheldon's with a lean to as big as may be thought convenient," he was chosen on the building committee. But his country again needed his services, and he was not permitted to remain long with his re-united family. On the 14th of January, Gov. Dudley informed his council that there were about ninety English still held by the French and Indians of Canada, whom the governor had promised to return the coming spring, and proposed to have "a Person Leger at Quebec, to put forward that affair, and endeavor that all be sent, and that Mr. John Sheldon who has been twice already, may be employed with a suitable retinue to undertake a journey thither, on that service, if the season will permit." As we have already seen, John Sheldon was not one to permit the season to stand in the way of his serving the state. Accordingly, he left Deerfield on the 17th of April, attended by Edward Allen, Na-thaniel Brooks, and Edmund Rice. We have a hint of how it fared with him on his northward inarch, in this item from his account book: "Paid six livres to an

Indian to guide us into the way when bewildered." Mr. Sheldon was in great danger during this last journey to Canada, and his sojourn there. The French were exasperated by rumors of another invasion from New England, and the woods were full of small parties of Indians, on the war-path to the border settlements.

He arrived the 11th of May. His reception there was not the most courteous, as we learn by this letter from the court of Versailles to the governor of Canada: "His Majesty approves of your having spoken as you did to the man named Scheldin, whom that Governor (Dudley) sent you by land, in search of the English prisoners at Quebec, and even if you had had him put in prison with all his suite, it would have been no great matter." From Montreal, Mr. Sheldon wrote on the 20th of June, that the French were collecting forces there, being alarmed by the report of an approaching English fleet. He was not permitted to return until this excitement had subsided. In mid-summer, escorted by six soldiers under Monsieur de Chambly, who had secret orders to acquaint himself with the condition of things at Orange, he with seven more captives, came down Lake Champlain in canoes, arriving at Albany on the 24th of August. To Mr. Sheldon's annoyance, his escort were held as prisoners during their stay in Albany, by Col. Schuyler, who knew from friendly Indians in Canada the hostile attitude of affairs there, and he was sent with them down to Lord Cornbury at New York. Thence by Saybrook, New London and Stonington, now on horseback and now on foot, the captives came slowly home, and on the 18th of September, John Sheldon was in Boston and delivered his despatches to the governor in council, and gave a narrative of his negotiations.

In October, Mr. Sheldon is again in Deerfield, where he is appointed to manage for the town as a petitioner to the General Court for help towards Mr. Williams's salary. His name appears once more on the General Court records in November, 1707, on two petitions for aid in consideration of his own losses, and for his services and those of his attendants in his last journey, "in which they endured much fatigue and hardship and passed through great danger, sustaining also considerable damage by their absence from their Businesse." In answer, he was given fifty pounds for his services, thir-teen of which was to be paid him by a mulatto whom he had brought out of bondage, and a grant of three hundred acres, not to exceed forty acres of meadow land, was made him.

Shortly after this he removed to Hartford, where, in 1708, he had married a second time. In 1726, "being weak in body, yet through God's goodness to me, of sound mind and memory," he made his will, and died in 1734, at the age of seventy-six.

We need not search the rolls of heraldry for the pedigree of old John Sheldon. We have found him a brave man, and a good citizen, a tender husband and a loving father, true and faithful in all his private relations and public positions, a pillar of the church and state. What more need we ask ?

The great Archbishop Sheldon used to say to the young lords who sought his advice: "Be honest and moral men. Do well and rejoice." John Sheldon was both. He did well, and his descendants may rejoice.

MY HUNT FOR THE CAPTIVES.

There have been more noteworthy journeys to Canada than that whose fruits are gathered here.

There is that one abounding in thrilling experiences, from which Benjamin Waite and Stephen Jennings returned triumphant to Hatfield.

Many others, endured perforce by our captive ancestors with a fortitude never to be forgotten; and equally memorable those undertaken for their redemption.

Rev. John Williams thus writes of the most notable of these: "Mr. Sheldon, a good man and a true servant of the church in Deerfield, twice took his tedious and dangerous journey in the winter, from New England into Canada on these occasions."[1] Though, with the Redeemed Captive, I have "blessed God that deliverance was brought for so many," the number left behind could not be forgotten. As often as I have read in our annals the pathetic story, "taken captive to Canada, whence they came not back," I have longed to know their fate. The longing has become a purpose, and I have taken upon myself a mission to open the door for the return of the long-lost captives. I doubt if Deacon Sheldon himself was thought so demented, when he announced his intention of going to Canada in mid-winter to demand the release of his kinsfolk and neighbors, as I was, when I made known my purpose, to go to Montreal in December.

So with that apparent vacillation which often cloaks our firmest resolutions, I bought my tickets with the privilege of returning them, in ease of a heavy snow storm on the day of departure. The day and the storm arrived together, but I had set my hand to the plough, and even if it should prove a snow plough, there was no turning back. Two hundred years have robbed the winter journey from New England to New France of all its tedium and danger, and one needs all the reflected glory of his heroic ancestry, to reconcile him to the ignoble ease with which it is performed.

After two days of fruitless search for the trail of our cap-tives, I had begun to despair, when chance led me to the rooms of the Natural History Society. There, by a rare good fortune, I found a remarkable collection of the Old Régime, —priceless treasures, hitherto guarded jealously in the home, the convent or the church, now, for the first time, and probably the last, by the energy of the Numismatic and Anti-quarian Society of Montreal, brought together for a week's exhibition. This alone would have repaid me for my journey. There were portraits of Wolfe and Montcalm, and sil-ver mugs once owned by the latter. There were Champlain's autograph, and the patent of nobility conferred upon François Hertel and his posterity. Here I stood, face to face, with the illustrious founders of New France—soldiers, nuns, mission priests, Intendants, Governor-Generals, heroic martyrs, gallant captains and faithful viceroys of Louis XIV. The frank, sensible, practical, womanly and warm-hearted Marguerite Bourgeois; Madame de la Peltrie, the ardent and sincere, albeit romantic and sensational enthusiast; Pore Jogues, the refined, scholarly and pious missionary, with his poor, mutilated hands, and his deeply-lined face; timid, humble, self-distrusting, meek and patient as a lamb under

Indian torture, bold as a lion in defence of his faith. Laval, the highborn prelate, stubborn fighter for the supremacy of the church; Talon, the intendant, sagacious, alert, whose delicate face gives no hint of his energetic character; Charle-voix, cotemporary and historian of them all. Here were Boucher and d'Ailleboust, representatives of the old *noblesse,* and de Montigny, greatest of Canadian warriors; the same to whom Esther Jones and Margaret Huggins and poor little Elisha Searle, may have appealed for mercy for their kinsfolk slain at Pascommuck. And here were the Hertel brothers, faces all too familiar to our Deerfield captives, handsome and noble faces, nevertheless. These were the features first revealed to our woe-begone ancestry, in the light of their burning homes, nearly two hundred years ago. This decoration may have been De Rouville's reward for his successful attack on Deerfield. Those very eyes must have beamed gratefully upon Mary Baldwin Catlin, as she tenderly raised the head and moistened the fevered lips of the wounded French youth. This thought was an inspiration. An hour later I found myself on a bench in the church vestry, with a crowd of old women, anxious for confession, awaiting my turn to speak with the Curé of Notre Dame. At four o'clock when the early sunset of that northern latitude overtook me, one might have seen me perched upon a high stool, at a grated window, straining my eyes over the ancient record, and translating letter by letter from the old French, the following, in the handwriting of Father Meriel:

"On Monday, the 21st day of December, in the year 1705, the rites of baptism were by me, the undersigned priest, administered in the chapel of the Sisters of the Congregation, with the permission of Monsieur François le Vachon de Belmont, Grand Vicar of my Lord, the Bishop of Quebec, to Samuel Williams, upon his abjuration of the Independent religion; who, born at Dearfielde in New England, the 24th of Jan. O. S. [3d of Feb.] of the year 1690, of the marriage of Mr. John Williams, minister of the said place, and his wife Eunice Mather, having been taken the 29th of Feb. O. S. [11th of March] of the year 1704, and brought to Canada, lives with Mr. Jacques Le Ber, Esquire, Sieur de Senneville. His godfather was Jacques Le Ber. His godmother Marguerite Bouat, wife of Antoine Pascaud, merchant, who have signed with me."

Then follow the signatures of Senneville, Marguerite Bouat Pascaud and the unformed and tremulous autograph of Samuel himself. Dear lad! On this very spot he was sent to school, to learn to read and write French. The schoolmaster sometimes "flattered him with promises, if he would cross himself, then threatened him if he would not;" and finding promises and threats ineffectual, he "struck him with a cruel whip, and made him get down on his knees for an hour." For weeks, this went on, till at last, after many tears, "through cowardice and fear of the whip," says his stern, old Puritan father, "he was first brought to cross himself." From this to abjuration and baptism, was a natural step. Two days after his baptism, he wrote to his father in Quebec a strange letter, filled with accounts of the conversion of his fellow-captives to the Roman Catholic religion, and not one word of himself. "When I had this letter," says the heart-broken father, "I presently knew it to be of Mr. Meriel's composing, but the messenger who brought it, brought word that my son had embraced their religion. The news was ready to overwhelm me with grief and sorrow—anguish took hold upon me. I asked God to direct me what to do, and how to write, and to find an opportunity of conveying a letter to him." That letter, and Samuel's answer, may be read in "The Redeemed Captive."

Far into the twilight I sat there, spellbound by the old manuscript. How many tales it unfolded. True stories of real folks, far transcending in interest, any wonder book of fiction. I pictured the fourteen years old boy in the house of his so-called master. It was, doubtless, one of the best in the town, for Jacques Le Ber, shopkeeper at Montreal, had by industry and thrift made himself a fortune, and ambitious for his children had "got himself made a gentleman for 6000 livres. . . . . .so far had *noblesse* already fallen from its old estate."

Though Jacques Le Ber was the possessor of riches and a title,—though it pleased him to be called *Ecuyer* or Esquire, and to sign himself Seigneur de Senneville, he had had sore disappointment. His wife had died. His eldest daughter, his favorite child, instead of helping him, in the care of the younger children, had shut herself up at twenty-two, in her chamber, where for ten years she sat embroidering altar cloths and vestments, refusing to see anyone but her confessor, and the girl who brought her food. An odor of sanctity must have pervaded the house of Jacques Le Ber, and Samuel probably heard from her own sisters the story of Jeanne Le Ber. Ten years before he became an inmate of the family, she had retired to a cell which had been built for her behind the altar, in the new chapel of the nuns of the Congregation; and the boy and his master must both have thought of the family saint, so near and yet so far, as they stood by the altar when Samuel was baptized. It was kind in Jacques Le Ber to burden his household with the boy, and Samuel felt it; for he tells his father, in excuse for his conversion, that they told him (perhaps Le Ber's own children), that he had never been bought from the Indians, but was only sojourning in Montreal, and that if he would not turn, he should be given back to the savages, but that if he would he should never be put into their hands any more.

I wondered as I sat there putting the two ends of the story together, whether it was all so dreadful to the boy as it seems to us. Whether, as he waded from Jacques Le Ber's house to school, through that Canadian winter, he was ever gay and merry like other boys, and snowballed and frolicked on his snow-shoes. Or whether the thought of his mother slain, his father far away, his brothers and sisters scattered he knew not where, haunted him day and night. The priests spent whole days urging him to renounce his father's religion. To rescue from heresy the child of the Puritan preacher, was an object worth their labor, and they spared no pains nor argument to that end. When at last the ship came to take him home, they tried to frighten him with tales of shipwreck, and threats of eternal damnation. They told him if he would stay, the king would grant him a pension, and that his master, an old man and the richest in Canada, would give him a great deal of money; but that in New England he would be poor and homeless. It is a relief to remember that neither promise of preferment, nor the fear of poverty on earth and of hell hereafter, could keep him from home and native land.

When I walked back to my hotel, the stars were shining. The Montreal of to-day had vanished, and men, women and children from the Deerfield of 1704, thronged the snowbound streets of the old French town. Ville-Marie de Mont-Réal— what legend of the age of chivalry equals the romance of thy true history! The most brilliant conception of the imagination pales before the simple recital of the exploits of thy crusaders.

To all readers of "The Redeemed Captive" the name of Father Meriel is as familiar as that of Parson Williams himself. For the next two days I followed his steps in the old records as he went in and out among the captives. On the triumphant return of De Rouville from Deerfield, the Seigneur de Montigny, whom I have already mentioned as the greatest warrior of New France, was sent to the Connecticut valley with a party of French and Indians. Montigny attacked Pascommuck, a little hamlet of Northampton, occupied by five families, and known also as Northampton Farms. The Hampshire record is as follows:

"May 12 [13] Pascomok Fort taken by ye French and Indians being about 72. They took, and Captivated ye whole Garrison being about 37 Persons. The English Pursueing of them caused them to nock all the captives on the head, Save 5 or 6. Three they carried to Canada with them ; the others escap'd and about 7 of those knocked on the Head Recovered, ye Rest died."

Those carried to Canada were Esther Inghesson, [Ingersol] wife of Benoni Jones: Margaret Huggins, her niece, aged eighteen, and Elisha Searle, a little boy of eight.

Imagine the emotions with which I read the Canadian account of the Pascommuck story. It is so strange to find the homely names of *"un petit Anglois"* or *"unepetite Angloise"* and their fathers and mothers, old-time friends and neighbors of our own ancestry, done into French in Father Meriel's beautiful hand-writing as bright and clear to-day as if fresh from his pen. Stranger still it is to see them coupled with names of warriors and courtiers, who not only figure brilliantly in the annals of New France, but who once shared at Fontainebleau, the pleasures of the corrupt and splendid court of Louis XIV., who may have seen the rise and fall of the La Vallière and the Montespan,—and have lounged in the ante-chambers of Madame de Maintenon.

The old record reads like a novel, it is all so vivid. Instinctively I hold out my arms and whisper, "Don't be afraid," to the little Elisha Searle as I see him there, in his blue checked apron and shabby homespun, just as he was snatched from his mother's side. He stands there ready to burst into tears, clinging tight to the hand of Jean Baptiste Céléron de Blainville, with whom he lives. How he shrinks from the priest and the baptismal water, and turns half trustfully towards Dame Marie Anne Le Moyne de Chassaigne, his god-mother. It is all over now, and this is our last sight of little Elisha, or Elisée, as the French have it. His god-father, the Sieur de Blainville, has taken away the name given him by good Parson Stoddard, and when we meet him again, if we ever do meet him, it will be as Michel Searls. A year later, Margaret Huggins is baptized. Father Meriel tells us that she was the daughter of John Huggins and Experience Jones, born at Stony Brook in 1686, and baptized at Springfield four months later; that she was taken by the Abenaquis at Pascommuck, near Northampton, and carried by the Indians to St. Francis. From them she was bought by that illustrious exile, the Marquis de Crisafy, governor of Three Rivers, with whom she lived until August, 1706, when she was brought to Montreal. Her sponsors were Monsieur Etienne Robert and Marguerite Bouat, who seem to have been as zealous in the conversion of heretics as Father Meriel. I doubt not that her name re-appears later, where lack of time forbade me to look for her.

My next find was the story of Esther Jones, as Father Mer-iel wrote it out for Samuel Williams to copy and send it to his father. Between the lines it is easy to read the prolonged agony of that first year of captivity, ending for this poor woman in weeks of sickness in the hospital. There, "distempered with a very high fever, if not distracted," as Mr. Williams says, on their death beds, scarcely conscious of their acts, and "at first disdaining," she and Abigail Turbot yielded to the threats of the priests and the importunities of the nuns who took care of them, and, confessing the sins of their whole lives, abjured Protestantism, received extreme unction, died and were "honorably buried side by side, in the church-yard next the church," "close to the body of the Justice Pese's wife," writes Samuel, "all the people being present." What a picture these few lines recall. The beauty of that spring night on Northampton meadows; the stillness broken by the horrid war-whoop; the terror of those five families; the flaming farm-houses; the flight with the prisoners; the brave pursuit and the merciless slaughter; the three desolate ones, marching on to unending captivity; the meeting with some of their Deerfield friends in the Indian camp at Coos; the arrival in Canada ; their separation; the year of illness ending with the hospital, where Esther Jones finds her cousin, Abigail Turbot, who had been taken at Cape Porpoise, Me.;[1] finally, that gloomy Sunday afternoon in December, when both sufferers lay spent with the struggle, life ebbing fast from their fever-racked frames; grey-robed nuns flitting softly back and forth between them; black-gowned priests reiterating in low tones alternate threat and promise, their efforts at last successful; Father Meriel pressing forward with extreme unction for the penitents; Samuel Williams and other English prisoners looking on, awestruck at the scene; Madam Grizalem, as they call Christine Otis's mother, whose captivity has had a happier ending there too, let us hope as a kind mediator between the sufferers and their persecutors; the burial, at which "all the people were present;" the captives standing sadly about the open graves and wondering whose turn would come next; then, earth to earth, *requiescant in pace;* and Father Meriel hurries to the church vestry to write down before it is quite dark the record, which two hundred years later, shall be thus read by a descendant of Deerfield. So the curtain falls on the tragedy of Pascommuck.

In the attack on Deerfield, Sarah Jeffreys, widow of Thomas Hurst, and her six children were captured. The youngest, Benjamin or Benoni, was slain in the meadows. Sarah, eighteen, Elizabeth, sixteen, Thomas, twelve, Hannah, eight, Ebenezer, five, were carried with the mother to Canada, where they were probably separated. Widow Sara, the mother, was re-baptized, and appears on the Canadian records as Marie Jeanne. Ebenezer was baptized by Father Meriel on Sunday, Dec. 6, 1705, and the name of Antoine Nicolas was given him by his god-father, Monsieur Antoine Adhc-mar, registrar of the jurisdiction of Ville-Marie. His brother Thomas was carried to the Mission of Notre Dame de Lorette and baptized by Father Meriel at Montreal, on the 17th of January, 1706. We have heretofore believed that the Widow Hurst, with her two eldest daughters, was redeemed and returned to New England, Ebenezer, Thomas, and Hannah remaining in Canada. I am led to doubt this statement in regard to Elizabeth by the following extract from the Montreal register:

"On Monday, the 3d of October, 1 7 1 2 , after the publication of the three banns. I, the undersigned, Seminary priest of Montreal, with the permission of Monsieur François de Vauchon, Grand Vicar of the Bishop of Quebec, and with the mutual consent of Thomas Bécraft, weaver, aged thirty-three, son of Thomas Bécraft, deceased, and of his wife, Elizabeth Gay, of the Bishopric of Norwich in England, of the first part, and of Marie Elizabeth Hurst, aged twenty-three, daughter of the late Thomas Hurst, and his wife, Marie Jeanne Jeffreys of Deerfield, in New England, of the second part, both now living in this parish of Ville Marie, have married them and have given them the nuptial benediction in presence of Mr. John Thomas, master shipbuilder to the king, in this country, and of Daniel Joseph Maddox, friend of the groom, of William Perkins, step-father of the bride, of Thomas Hurst, her brother, and of several others, friends of both parties, who have signed this certificate according to law, with the exception of Thomas Hurst, who says that he cannot sign."

Then follow Thomas's mark and the autographs of Marie Françoise French, William Perkins, John Thomas, Jacob Gilman, Daniel Joseph Maddox, Joseph Bartlet and Meriel Prêtre. As the age of the bride corresponds exactly to that of Elizabeth Hurst, I am led to believe that Hannah went back with Sara and their mother to New England, and that Elizabeth, with the name of Marie added at her baptism, was left with Ebenezer and Thomas in Canada, where she married as above. The Marie Françoise French, who appears as one of the witnesses at the wedding of her friend Elizabeth Hurst, was a daughter of Deacon Thomas French and his wife, Mary Catlin. Deacon French was the town clerk of Deerfield, and also the blacksmith.

The deacon and his children,—Mary, aged seventeen, Thomas, fourteen, Freedom, eleven, Martha, eight, and Abigail, six—were captured. His wife and their infant John were killed on the retreat. Deacon French and his two eldest children were redeemed. Freedom was placed in the family of Monsieur Jacques Le Ber, merchant of Montreal, and on Tuesday, the 6th of April, 1706, Madame Le Ber had her baptized anew by Father Meriel, under the name of Marie Françoise, the name of the Virgin added to that of her god-mother, being substituted for the Puritanic appellation of Freedom, by which she had been known in Deerfield. She signs her new name, evidently with difficulty, to this register, and never again does she appear as Freedom French. I find her often as a guest at the marriages of her English friends. Her sister Martha was given by her Indian captors to the Sisters of the Congregation at Montreal. On the 23d of January, 1707, she was baptized *sous condition,* receiving from her god-mother the name of Marguerite in addition to her own. On Tuesday, November 24, 1711, when about sixteen, she was married by Father Meriel to Jacques Roi, aged twenty-two, of the village of St. Lambert, in the presence of many of their relatives and friends. Jacques Roi cannot write his name, but the bride, Marthe Marguerite French, signs hers in a bold, free hand, which is followed by the dashing autograph of the soldier, Alphonse de Tonty; and Marie Françoise French, now quite an adept in forming the letters of her new name, also signs. Two years later, on the 6th of February, at the age of twenty-one, Marie Françoise French married Jean Daveluy, ten years older than herself, a relative of Jacques Le Roi, her sister's husband. Daveluy could not write, but here, appended to the marriage register, 1 find for the last time the autographs of the two sisters written in full, Marie Françoise and Marthe Marguerite French.

Elizabeth Catlin, sister of Deacon French's wife, both daughters of Mr. John and Mary Baldwin Catlin, married James Corse, who died before the destruction of Deerfield, leaving her with three children, two boys and a little girl just the age of her cousin, Martha French. On her arrival in Canada, Elizabeth Corse, then eight years old, was taken by Pierre Roy or Le Roi, an inhabitant of St. Lambert, and on July 14, 1705, Pierre Le Roi's wife, Catharine Ducharme, and Gilbert Maillet, master mason, stood as sponsors at her baptism. She is allowed to keep her own name intact, though Father Meriel writes it Elizabeth Casse. The Canadian French sometimes pronounce the vowel a *ah* and sometimes *aw.* The latter doubtless represents the child's pronunciation of her family name, the r being entirely suppressed. With Pierre Le Roi's children, Jean, Jacques Barbe, and the rest, Elizabeth Corse grew up to the age of sixteen, when, on the 6th of November, 1712, she married Jean Dumontel of the same village. It is interesting to note that she named her first child Mary, in memory of her aunt, Mary Catlin French, and her second, Elizabeth, for her mother. Several with French names follow, among them a Pierre, which seems to hint at a kindly regard for her benefactor; Pélagie, the last, was born in 1728. On the 6th of January, 1730, Elizabeth Corse married, at St. Lambert, her second husband, Pierre Monet. It was in this very year that her brother James went up from Deerfield to look for her in Canada. How one longs to know whether he found her a widow, at the head of her young family, or whether he arrived too late for the second wedding. It seems hardly possible that his search could have been fruitless, or that the little colony of cousins and friends, settled in and near Montreal, could have escaped him.

Thanks to the detail of Father Meriel in his records, a thread of fancy maybe interwoven with these bare statistics. We may imagine the grief and loneliness of these three cousins, when, after the horror of their seizure and the suffering of the journey were somewhat abated, they found themselves separated among a people so different and speaking a strange tongue. No doubt good Catharine Ducharme was at her wits' end to know what to do with the wailing little girl, who had fallen to her share in the distribution of prisoners; and that Martha French gave the pious nuns of the Congregation no end of trouble. The solemn routine of the cloister must have been very irksome to the wayward child, who had been free to rove with her mates, at their own sweet will, up and down the beautiful street of Deerfield. We may suppose that, after Elizabeth's baptism, Dame Le Roi asked the Sisters to let Martha French go home with her to St. Lambert for a while; and that this arrangement was found to be such a relief to all concerned that the visits became frequent, and that Freedom, *alias* Marie Françoise French was of the party. It is possible that Mary Brooks, who was the same age, was there too. She had been baptized as Marie Claire the Sunday after Elizabeth Corse, and was living with the Seigneur Joseph de Fleury in Montreal. Gradually their homesickness wore away, and they grew to womanhood. We can picture these grandchildren of Mr. John Catlin, light haired, dark eyed—race type that we have known so well in later generations. No wonder that Jacques Roi and Jean Dumontel thought they had never seen maidens so winsome as Martha French and Elizabeth Corse, or that even grave, sober Jean Daveluy, with his thirty-one years' experience, was finally captivated by the beauty, vivacity and saucy wit of Marie Françoise French, who was probably living with her married sister at that time.

The condition of the people of Deerfield in the fall and winter of 1703-4 is pathetically described by Mr. Williams in a letter to Governor Dudley, which I have quoted in another story. Though their elders were depressed by foreboding and fear, the young people of the village seem to have gone on as usual. Early in December young John Sheldon rode down to Chicopee and brought home Hannah Chapin, his bride, on a pillion behind him, clad, perhaps, in that famous pelisse, which the gossips had quilted of double thickness, laughingly telling her she would need it when the Indians should carry her off to Canada,—so perilous was the situation at Deerfield considered. I must confess that I have always looked with less favor on two other marriages contracted that winter, that of Elizabeth Price to Andrew Stevens, the Indian, and that of Abigail Stebbins to James Denio, of whom all that we have hitherto known is that he was one of three Frenchmen then living in Deerfield. That these two girls, born of good Puritan stock, should have done this thing, and especially at a time when the very name of French and Indian was most hateful to the people of New England, has always shocked my sense of the fitness of things. Andrew Stevens, "the Indian," was killed at the sacking of the town. His young wife, with James Denio and his bride, Abigail Stebbins, her father and mother and the rest of their children were captured.

 John Stebbins, his wife Dorothy and their two sons, John and Samuel, came back. Abigail and her husband, her sister Thankful, and her brothers, Ebenezer and Joseph, remained in Canada; so also did Elizabeth Price Stevens. The latter lived for a time with the Nuns of the Congregation, and having made formal abjuration of the "Calvinistic heresy," was baptized on the 25th of April, 1705, her godmother, Marie Elizabeth Le Moyne, daughter of Charles Le Moyne, Baron Longueuil, giving her the added name of Marie. Father Meriel says that she was "born at Northampton, and was the daughter of Robert Price, Episcopalian, and of his wife, Sara Web, Independent, and widow of Andrew Stevens of Northampton." She signs the register as Marie Elizabeth Stevens, but the autograph looks as if her hand were held and the letters traced by another. On the 3d of February, 1706, at the age of twenty-two, she married Jean Fourneau, a master shoemaker. Among those present were Samuel Williams, "friend of the bride," Hannah Parsons, Marie Esther Sayrs, Christine Otis and Catharine Denkyn, all English captives. She died ten days after the birth of her seventh child, Nov. 4, 1716. Though we may object to his methods, we cannot have followed thus far the ministrations of Father Meriel without admiring his persistent efforts to save the souls of those whom he regards as heretics. According to his light he befriended the captives, and there can be no question of his sincerity. I felt sure that his unflagging zeal would sooner or later put Abigail Stebbins's name on the baptismal register. When I tell you that but for her marriage with the Frenchman I should not have been I and this sketch might not have been written, you will understand the satisfaction with which I read the following:

"On Monday, the 28th of May, 1708, the rites of baptism have been administered by me the undersigned Priest, to an English woman, named in her own country Abigail Stebbens, who born at Dearfield in New England, the 4th of January 1684 (N. S.) of the marriage of John Stebbens an inhabitant of that place, and of Dorothy Alexander, both Indépendants, having been baptized by the minister of that place some years after and married the 14th of February 1704 to Jacques Desnoions now Sergeant of Mr. de Tonti's company, came with him to Canada, towards the end of the following March, and lives with him at Boucherville. Her name Abigail has been changed to that of Marguerite. She has had for her godfather the High and Mighty Seigneur Phillippede Rigaud, Marquis de Vaudreuil, Chevalier de l'Ordre Militaire de St. Louis and Governor-General of New France; and for godmother, Marguerite Bouat, wife of Antoine Pacaud, royal treasury clerk

who have signed with me

according to the ordinance." The autographs follow:

Vaudreuil

Mgte Bouat Pascaud

Marguerite Stebben

Abigail's signature shows that she was over-powered by the presence of the *haut et puissant* Governor-General.

"Both Indépendants." How it stirs the dissenting blood in one's veins to read this of old John Stebbins and his wife Dorothy. How much in a little Father Meriel gives us. Here we have for the first time the real name and occupation of Abigail's husband, Jacques Desnoions, now Sergeant in Mr. de Tonti's company. That *now* banishes my life-long fear that the three Frenchmen in Deerfield that winter were scouts sent in advance by Hertel de Rouville. It is noticeable that Abigail Stebbins is not spoken of as the others have been, as "captured Feb. 29. 1704 and brought to Canada," but as having "come with her husband to Canada, and living with him at Boucherville." Here then was the clue. Boucherville was the home of Abigail's married life. On its parish records I must look for the births of her children. With reluctance I shut the Montreal register and set about going to Boucherville.

Easily accessible in summer, it was not to be thought of in midwinter, said the officials. Thought, however, is not so easily dismissed. The thing done often seems of so little worth, compared with the thing foregone. After groping awhile among the defective copies of parish records in the court house, the Gordian knot was cut by a suggestion from the lady from Philadelphia that we should get across the river by train *and* trust luck for the rest. Booming through the great bridge, we halted for a moment at Saint-Lambert, the adopted home of Elizabeth Corse and her cousins, and thence to Longueuil. Here the courtesy of our conductor was our luck. He gave us in charge to a clever French driver, in whose capacious sleigh, with only our heads visible above the bear skins tucked up close under our chins, we glided on to Boucherville.

The road from Longueuil to Boucherville is a forcible reminder of that modified feudalism which formed the basis of Canadian colonization. Longueuil and Boucherville are among the oldest seigniories granted by the king with patents of nobility to the more prominent colonists of Canada. Charles Le Moyne, Baron of Longueuil, the son of an inn-keeper at Dieppe, was a man of rare worth. The family founded by him is still eminent in Canada. Boucherville was the seigniory of Pierre Boucher, whose descendants, the De Bouchervilles, a family of distinction, still live on the spot. "The fief of the seignior," says Mr. Parkman, "varied from half a league to six leagues fronting on the river, and from half a league to two leagues in depth. The condition imposed on him may be said to form the distinctive feature of Canadian feudalism, that of clearing his land within a limited time, on pain of forfeiting it." This was to prevent the lands of the colony from lying waste. "Canadian feudalism," still quoting Mr. Parkman, "was made to serve a double end,—to produce a faint and harmless reflection of French aristocracy, and simply and practically to supply agencies for distributing land among the settlers.". . . . ."As the seignior was often the penniless owner of a domain three or four leagues wide and proportionally deep, he could not clear it all himself, and was therefore under the necessity of placing the greater part of it in the hands of those who could. But he was forbidden to sell any part of it which he had not cleared." He must grant it in turn to his vassals, on condition of a small annual rent. The usual grant from a seignior to his vassal included woodland and tillage. It was about a mile and a half in depth, with a narrow river frontage. The *censitaire* or tenant, *habitant* as he is still called, naturally built on the front of his lot, close by the river, which served as his highway, and as his neighbors did the same, a single line of dwellings, not far apart, was ranged along the shore, forming what is to this day called a *côte*. A continuous *côte* connects Longueuil and Boucherville. The picturesque beauty of the landscape and the splendor of that winter day are indescribable. The road of spotless white followed for seven miles along its southern shore the curves of the magnificent river. At the right, quaint old dwellings, each with its long well-sweep, its Lombardy poplars and its rude paling; the houses a story and a half high, built of stones and bits of rock of a rich brown color, irregular in size and shape, and imbedded in coarse, gray mortar; high, steep roofs, painted black or dull red, with curved and far projecting eaves; huge chimneys at the gable ends, built up from the ground outside; casement windows of different shapes and sizes, set without regard to external symmetry, and protected by heavy red wooden shutters; long, low barns, whose warped and weathered sides are crusted with yellow lichens, their roofs thickly thatched, the thatch bristling erect like a close cut mane, along the ridge-pole. Enormous ricks of straw were clustered in the angles of the buildings; shaggy, stout-legged horses huddled together in the barn yards, resting their necks on each other; clumsy Breton cows moved slowly about; dingy, heavy-fleeced sheep poked their noses down among the dead grass of the fields, which the winds had laid bare in spots. An *habitant* raking straw from a snow-topped rick was the only sign of human life. His boots of untanned deer skin, his blouse of blue homespun, belted with a scarlet sash, the tasselled peak of his red woollen cap falling to his shoulder, gave a bit of bright color to the picture. Behind the farm buildings lay a vast expanse of snow-drifted meadow, sparkling as if encrusted with gems; here and there a graceful elm in its naked beau-ty; and in the middle distance, rising abruptly from the plain, a pale blue mountain, vague and tender in the rimy atmosphere. At the left there was the low slope of the river's bank. Now and then the blackened thyrse of a sumach, or the dry pod of a milkweed rustled on its stalk, turning its buff satin lining to the light. Clumps of the red osier and yellow twigs of dwarf willows already gave promise of spring. At intervals immense blocks of ice jammed together, formed a rampart that cut off the view. Near Boucher-ville the river bank broadened into a great stretch of marsh, the haunt of innumerable wild ducks; and far beyond this the long, low Isles of Boucherville broke the otherwise dreary expanse of the gulf-like river.

Road and river, mountain and meadow are the same to-day as on that blustering March day in

1704, when at the dispersion of the captives at Montreal, Jacques de Noyon and his young bride wended the same way to his old home at Boucherville. Perhaps her husband, pitying her distress, had begged that her father and mother and her young brothers and sister might accompany them. The houses may have differed somewhat from those of to-day. Doubtless some were built of logs and daubed with clay. Whatever the material, the form was the same; "Such as the peasants of Normandy built in the reign of the Henries."

From the northern provinces of France, from Brittany, Normandy and Picardy, Canada was peopled. They came in such numbers that the king at last instructed his minister to inform the intendant that he needed his peasants for soldiers and could not afford to depopulate France in order to people Canada. Year after year, however, shipload after shipload sailed from Rochelle or Dieppe. An anonymous writer of the period describes them as "docile, industrious and pious." Mr. Parkman adds: "They seem to have been in the main, a decent peasantry. Some of them could read and write, and some brought with them a little money."

Renowned as is the town of Noyon in Picardy for its linen factories and its magnificent church of the thirteenth century, famous as the place where Charlemagne was first crowned and Hugh Capet elected king, it is still more famous as the birthplace of Jean Chauvin, or John Calvin, the great reformer. It is not unlikely that another John, born in Noyon at a time when surnames were unusual, came to be known as John of Noyon, or Jean de Noyon. Be this as it may, we may assume that among the emigrants who, notwithstanding the king's protest, sailed yearly from Rochelle or Dieppe, came Jean de Noyon, with his wife, Jeanne Fran chard, and Marin Chauvin of the Calvins of Noyon, with his wife, Gilette Ban. The women were Normans, from the neighborhood of Rouen. I have no doubt that their husbands were Picards, old friends and comrades in the town of Noyon. They were among the earliest settlers of Canada. On the 8th of December, 1650, Marie, daughter of Marin and Gilette Chauvin, was baptized at Three Rivers.

She married at fourteen, Rolin Langlois of Three Rivers, a man ten years her senior. He died within three months after his marriage, and the youthful widow married the same year Jean de Noyon of Three Rivers, she being then fifteen and he, twenty-three years of age. This was at the time when such an incentive to early marriage was offered by the king in yearly pensions to those who should become the parents of large families. Pierre Boucher was then governor of Three Rivers and his daughter married there at the age of twelve.

William, the oldest son of Jean de Noyon, and Marie Chauvin, the widow Langlois, was born about 1666. Their second son, Jacques, our James, was baptized at Three Rivers, Feb. 12th, 1668. Jean de Noyon, 2d, son of Jean and of his wife, Jeanne Franchard, and father of William and James, was an edge tool maker and a master of his trade. A man who could make bill hooks and felling axes must have been very useful in a new country, and I dare say that Pierre Boucher, governor of Three Rivers, offered him some inducement to become a tenant of his seigniory. Whether this be so or not he removed with his family soon after the birth of his second son, to Boucherville. There three more sons and five daughters were born to him, ten children in all. They probably ran about bareheaded and barefooted, in scanty clothing, and "grew stout on bread and eels." As I find no evidence that any of them became priest, monk or nun, I suppose that Jean de Noyon received annually three hundred livres of the king's bounty money. This, with what he could earn from his trade and the product of his tillage, supported the family. The eels of the St. Lawrence, smoked and salted, supplied them with much of their food. As they grew older the boys hunted and fished, and in winter, perhaps, helped their father to fell and hew timber for the market, getting in exchange the bare necessities of life. The general testimony concerning the Canadian youth of that period is that they would not work, but were idle and unruly, and as soon as they could handle a gun they spurned restraint and spent their time in the woods.

Household drudgery occupied the mother. The girls worked in the fields in summer but spent their winters in idleness. Domestic spinning and weaving were unknown arts in Canada at that time and hemp and flax were not cultivated till much later.

Jean de Noyon, master edge tool maker, died in 1692. Whether his eldest son, William, who had married three *years* before, lived with his mother and succeeded to forge and farm, I know not. At this time the disorders arising from the fur trade were at their height. In vain did the home government try to regulate or control this traffic. Licenses were granted, annual fairs established, to no purpose. Hundreds of young men took to the woods, carrying goods and brandy to exchange with the savage for peltries at their own price, to sell again at large profits. All the youth and the vigor of the colony was absorbed in this irregular trade. Men could not be found to till the seignior's acres. Farms ran wild again. Agriculture languished. Population diminished. A year or two of this free life in the wilderness made men averse to labor and loath to marry. The king was in despair. Severe edicts were followed by generous amnesties. The lawless vagabonds cared no more for one than the other. Neither threats of branding, whipping, hard labor at the galleys, nor promise of the king's grace and bounty could induce this army of *coureurs de óois*[1] to return to the duties and obligations of civilized life. So general was this outlawry, that at one time the intendant writes to the minister that "There is not a family of any condition or quality soever that has not children, brothers, uncles and nephews among them," and he expresses the fear that if absolute pardon is not offered them "they may be drawn to pass over to the English, which would be a general loss to the country." Again he writes: "The *coureurs de bois* not only act openly, but they carry their peltries to the English and try to drive the Indian trade thither." There is plenty of evidence that the English took advantage of the situation, paid the bushrangers twice as much for their beaver skins as the Canadian merchants and sold them merchandise at much cheaper rates.

Jacques, the second son of Jean de Noyon, would have been twenty-four years old at his father's death. It is hardly probable that under any circumstances he would have stayed at home under his brother's rule. Of his career up to the time of his appearance in Deerfield I am ignorant. As he was probably no better nor worse than his fellows, why may we not assume that he was a part of this general exodus of the young men? Official letters from the New York government confirm the French accounts of the attitude of the *coureurs de bois—Boss lopers* as they are called. On Aug. 17, 1700, David Schuyler writes to the Earl of Bellamont that Jean Rosie, the interpreter, whom Peter Schuyler mentions as an inhabitant of Albany and a very honest man although a Frenchman, "told him that there were thirty of the Principall Bush loopers, Canadians born, had combined together to come to Albany for passes to go to Ottowawa, for the governor of Canada would give them no passes there." In November of the same year Samuel York, a Portland man who had just been released from a ten years' captivity in Canada, and with Jean Rosie, a loyal citizen of Albany, passed frequently back and forth as envoys between New York and Canada, testifies on examination that many of the *coureurs de bois* are in the Ottawawa country, "in a sort of rebellion," refusing to obey the orders of the Canadian governor and "very desirous to come to trade here with the English, only fear the Five Nations will not suffer them to pass through their country." York and Rosie also told Governor Bellamont that these hunters had assured them they would come and offer their services to him and quit Canada forever. Evidently the governor did not discourage these advances, for on the 26th of October, 1700, two French bushrangers appeared in New York with the following petition:

"My Lord, We, Jean De Noyon and Louis Gosselyn, come to place ourselves under your Excellency's protection, in the hope that you will allow us to live and trade with King William's subjects in the town of Albany and grant us the same rights and privileges as others enjoy, in which case we submit ourselves with promise of fidelity to the laws of the government. We are commissioned by our comrades to assure you, if our request be granted, that twenty-two, all fine young men, will come to Albany next February. And after that we promise to bring, in the month of September of the year 1701, thirty brave fellows to the said town of Albany, all laden with peltry: and finally, we oblige ourselves further in good faith to bring, in the aforesaid month of September, on our return from hunting, ten or twelve of the principal Sachims of the Ottowawa Nations. Dated in New York, this 26. October, 1700.

DENOYON.L. GOSSELIN.

The governor acts cautiously, fearing the Greeks, even bearing gifts. This opportunity to trade with the Ottowawas and to seduce the Northern Indians from their allegiance to the French, is a strong temptation. In November he writes tentatively to the Lords of Trade, setting forth the advantages of beaver hunting in the Ottowawa country.

Who was the Jean de Noyon who was in New York in the autumn of 1700, as envoy from the rebellious *coureurs de bois?* Jean, the father of Jacques, was dead long before. Jean Baptiste, Jacques' brother, was but a lad of fourteen. It would be too daring a guess, for a matter of fact historian, that it was Jacques himself. It is not impossible that the translator of the petition may unconsciously have rendered Jacques as Jack, the nickname of John, and thus changed the name. This question is left to be solved by future research, either directly from Canada, or more likely by way of Albany.

Jacques de Noyon, a bushranger, discontented with his government and seeking a new home, came to Deerfield. That he was thirty-six years old and unmarried favors my theory that he had led a roving life. Flattered by the preference of the stranger, a man so much older than herself, the sober-minded Puritan girl was attracted by the gay *insouciance* of such a character. His vivacity and intelligence, his ardent temperament, his reckless courage, his songs and tales of wild adventure captivated her, and under his promise that her people should be his people, her God his God, she married him.

"The best laid plans of mice and men gang aft agley," and suddenly, in a most unexpected manner, Jacques de Noyon was restored to his native land. Perhaps his presence on that fateful night saved his wife's whole family from the tomahawk.

On his return to Boucherville, Jacques de Noyon probably found his mother and her three youngest children, a son and two daughters, living on the old spot. We can imagine the stir in the family at the return of the outlaw with his English bride and her relatives. In the following December the first child of Jacques de Noyon and Abigail Stebbins was born. On the 28th of December, 1704, in the parish church of Sainte-Famille at Boucherville, Father de la Saudray baptized "René de Noyons, born the 26th of the same month, son of Jacques de Noyon and Gabrielle Stebben, his wife living in this parish," Jean Boucher, Sieur de Niverville and Marie de Boucherville standing as sponsors to the child. In Gabrielle I recognize the attempt of De Noyon's mother and sisters to render into French, Abigail, the harsh English name of his wife. Other children followed in rapid succession. On the 12th of March, 1706, Father Meriel, who seems never to have lost track of a single Deerfield captive, baptized Marie Gabrielle, born the day before, Louise de Noyon, the baby's aunt, being her godmother.

Jean Baptiste was born August 11, 1707, and baptized the next day, his paternal uncle, for whom he was named, acting as godfather. This child died "in the communion of the holy Catholic church" exactly one year from the day of his birth.

Up to this time we have no clue to the occupation of Jacques de Noyon after his return to Canada. His life in the bush had unfitted him for farming; the forest was his element; a young family was pressing upon him for support; a soldier's life was most to his taste, and he became a sergeant in Air. de Tonti's company. This was Alphonse de Tonti, younger brother of the distinguished Henri de Tonti, friend and companion of La Salle. Father Meriel had never ceased importuning De Noyon to have his wife baptized into the holy Catholic church. She felt that the baptism which she had received from good Parson Williams was sufficient, and as her husband's long separation from church and priest had made him indifferent, he did not urge her. Now that he was turning his back on his former life and ranging himself on the side of law and order, and as at any moment he might be killed in battle, he probably thought it wise to secure for her the protection of the church. Accordingly one Monday morning in May, 1708, they paddled over in their canoe to Montreal, where, as we have already seen, she was baptized Marguerite. This was an eventful summer. On the 29th of June, her young brother Ebenezer, who was living with her, was baptized, receiving from his god-father, Jacques Charles de Sabrevois, captain of a detachment of the marine, the name of Jacques Charles. The certificate is signed by the priest, by De Noyon in a handsome handwriting, by De Sabrevois, and by the wife of the Seignieur Boucher as god-mother.

The fourth child of Jacques and Abigail Stebbins de Noyon, was born on the 12th of October, 1708, and named Jean Baptiste in memory of his dead brother. His aunt, Thérèse Stebbins, whom we remember as Thankful Stebbins of Deerfield, and who was living with her sister Abigail, was his godmother. In the record of baptism the baby's mother is called by her new name, Marguerite. The father was absent on this occasion, being doubtless with his company at Fort Frontenac, then commanded by Captain de Tonti. It is probable that Abigail's father and mother and brother John had ere this been released from captivity. Before the birth of their next child, Francois, baptized July 7th, 1710, Jacques de Noyon had removed his family to the Côte St. Joseph, another part of the parish of Boucherville. This must have been an equal relief to his mother and his wife. I fancy that the housekeeping now began to show New England thrift and industry, and that the noise of the shuttle and the cheerful hum of the spinning wheel were soon heard in the new home. Dorothée, named for her grandmother Stebbins, was baptized Oct. 3, 1711. Then followed Marie Joseph, who died in infancy, Jacques René, Marie Charlotte, another Marie Joseph, Marie Magdalen, and finally Joseph, born June 21, 1724.

René, the eldest of these children, when about ten years old, had been sent with a party of French and Indian traders to visit his grandparents in Deerfield. His grandfather Stebbins induced him to stay, and when the hunters were ready to go back René could not be found. Not understanding the boy's pronunciation of his own name, or wishing him to bear a more godly appellation, his grandfather called him Aaron. So René de Noyon grew up in Deerfield as Aaron Denio. In 1723, John Stebbins died. In his will he left one-eighth of his lands to each of his children then in Canada, to wit: Samuel, Ebenezer, Joseph, Abigail and Thankful, provided they would come and live in New England. Each one's share, if he died in New England, was to descend to his heirs; otherwise, to revert to those who remained in New England.

"Those that will not live in New England," says the old man, "shall have five shillings apiece, and no more.....Yet be it forever understood that if my daughter Abigail come not and tarry as above said, then Aaron Denieur, her son, shall be my Heir in her Room and Stead, provided Said Aaron continue in this Countrey then. After my decease and my wife's decease, Said Aaron shall enter upon that which should have been his mother's part, and possess it until his mother comes, but if She come not and fulfill the above said Conditions, and Aaron stays in New England and doth fulfill them, then the said eighth part of my lands to descend to said Aaron's heirs forever.".....And if some of my children, now in Canada, shall come and fulfill the conditions.......though the rest come not then my lands shall be divided between my son John and Aaron, and those that do come. . . . John having three times as much as one of the rest....

It is to be supposed that Jacques and Abigail de Noyon had heard at intervals from their son, and that René had informed his mother of his grandfather's death. His uncle John must also have notified his brothers and sisters in Canada of the conditions of their father's will. After much talk, Abigail decided to accompany her brother Samuel to Deerfield. It was certainly no mercenary motive that led her to undertake such a journey under the circumstances. Five shillings was to be her dole if she returned to Canada, and to husband and children she must return. But her heart yearned for the boy from whom she had been separated for years. She longed—who does not ?—

to revisit the home of her childhood and to see her old mother once more before she died. How or when the journey was performed, how long the visit lasted, and what was her escort on her return to Canada, I know not. I only know that in Deerfield, on the 27th of February, 1726, her thirteenth and last child was born.

The little Marie Anne, "born," so the record reads, "at Guerfil, in New England, on the 27th of February, 1726," was baptized at Boucherville on the 5th of November of the same year, her eldest sister, Gabrielle de Noyon, then the wife of Nicholas Binet, being her godmother.

Samuel Stebbins remained in Deerfield.

At the marriage of one of Abigail de Noyon's daughters at Boucherville in 1731, Nicolas Binet and Joseph Stebbins, uncle of the bride, both from the parish of Chambly, appear as witnesses.

About 1734 Joseph Stebbins married Marguerite Sanssoucy. He died the 23d of April, 1753, aged fifty-two. Their descendants still live in Chambly. Marie Chauvin, the mother of Jacques de Noyon, died in 1723, the same year as his wife's father.

Abigail de Noyon, born Abigail Stebbins of Deerfield, died at the age of sixty, and was buried at Boucherville, on the 15th of November, 1740. Her husband, Jacques de Noyon, aged about seventy-eight, was buried on the 12th of May, 1745·

Here ended my hunt after the captives. It was as if I had laid the ghosts of unburied shades that had wandered, restless, haunting my whole life. It was a sad satisfaction to find that these offsets from the first planting of Deerfield, though rudely transplanted, had not been utterly blasted; that when the sting of their first grief was over, these young men and maidens in their turn had loved, married, reared children, founded homes, and at length rested in peace.

TWO CAPTIVES.A ROMANCE OF REAL LIFE, TWO HUNDRED YEARS AGO.

The name of Somers Islands, corrupted in our time to "Summer Islands," was given to the Bermudas, not, as many suppose, on account of their genial climate, but because of the shipwreck there in 1610 of Sir George Somers and his companions on a voyage to Virginia. Up to that time, doubtless because of their dangerous coast, the "still vexed Bermoothes," had been known to the English as the "He of Divels, and reputed a most prodigious and inchanted place. . . . . . .never inhabited by any Christian or Heathen people."

The report of the shipwrecked men who dwelt nine months upon the islands, enjoying the balmy air, and finding the soil "abundantly fruitful of all fit necessaries for the sustentation and preservation of man's life," removed all fears of the He of Divels from the minds of the venturous youth of England.

Sir George Somers sold his claim to the Bermudas, to a company of one hundred and twenty, who got a charter for their settlement and in 1612, sent out sixty settlers. During the civil war in England, and immediately after, many persons took refuge there. The poet Waller invested money in Bermuda land, and Mr. Edmund Gosse thinks that he wrote his poem of the "Battle of the Summer Islands" as an advertisement of his plantation to his rich and noble friends. In exchange for the products of the Islands England sent cloth, which, says the poet,

"Not for warmth, but ornament is worn. . . . .

Such is the mould, that the blest tenant feeds,
On precious fruits,—and pays his rent in weeds;
With candy'd plantain, and the juicy pine,
On choicest melons, and sweet grapes they dine,
    And with Potatoes feed their wanton swine.

Tobacco is the worst of weeds which they

To English landlords, as their tribute pay.

So sweet the air,—so moderate the clime,
None sickly lives, or dies before his time;
For the kind spring which but salutes us here,
    Inhabits there, and courts them all the year."

Dear to the student of New England genealogies is a book entitled "Original Lists of Persons of Quality, Emigrants, Religious Exiles, Political Rebels, Serving men sold for a term of years, Apprentices, Children stolen, Maidens pressed and others, who went from Great Britain to the American Plantations from 1600 to 1700." According to this book, on the 13th day of September, 1635, the good ship Dorset, John Flower, Master, weighed anchor at London "bound for yᵉ Bermodas." Aboard her was a motley company, ninety-five passengers all told. Full half were lads under eighteen. Eight had already reached that important age. The rest were mostly young men under thirty-five, half a dozen of whom were accompanied by their wives. Among the passengers were two ministers, Rev. Geo. Turk and Rev. Daniel Wite or White. Two linger longest at the stern, as the ship slowly leaves her moorings, Judith Bagley, a lone, lorn woman of fifty-eight, apparently with no kith nor kin to keep her company, and James Rising, a resolute stripling of eighteen,—the only one of his name discoverable among the founders of New England.

To which of the afore-mentioned lists shall we refer this ship's company ? "What sought they thus afar?" For lack of present knowledge, I shall assume that love of adventure led James Rising to seek his fortune in the New World, and that he came, apprenticed for a term of years to labor in the Bermudas. Of his life there, we have as yet no details. Sugar and molasses became important exports from the islands, and New England afforded a good market for the latter ar-ticle, being then largely engaged in the distillation of rum from molasses.

"Att a general town meeting held at Salem on the 20th day of the 4th month of the year 1657 James Rising is received an Inhabitant into this Towne." About three weeks later, on the 7th of July, 1657, he married at Boston, Elizabeth, daughter of Robert Hinsdell, the sturdy pioneer of Dedham, Medfield and Deerfield. I conclude that he probably chose Salem as his home in New England, as being a port of entry for ships, freighted with the products of the islands. He was admitted as a member of the First Church in Salem, on the 22nd day of the 11th month, 1661, by a letter from his Pastor Wife or White of the church in Bermuda. On the 20th day of the 2nd month, 1663, his daughter Hannah was baptized in the First Church of Salem. Whether his two sons James and John, were older or younger than their sister is unknown.

Windsor, Conn., was at that time a leading commercial town, and carried on an extensive trade with the *West* Indies and adjacent islands. There was no bridge at Hartford, and Windsor became a noted port of entry, not only for coasters and West India vessels, but for English ships. The river was at all times full of vessels loading and unloading there, and "Windsor green, often heaped with goods" awaiting storage or transportation, "was lively with jovial sea captains" and sunburned sailors. Making and shipping pipe-staves was an important industry of this vicinity, and James Rising may have wished to add this branch of trade to his business. However this may be, he was "voted an inhabi-tant of Windsor," on March nth, 1668, and the next year he was formally dismissed by letter from the church of Salem to that of Windsor. There his wife died on the 11 th of August, 1669. Four years later he married the Widow Mar-tha Bartlett, who died in less than a year after her marriage. It is said that he kept the ferry at Windsor. To the contribution made by that town to the sufferers from Philip's war in other colonies, James Rising gave five shillings, his son John one shilling and sixpence, and his daughter Hannah, one and three pence.

The same year a grant of fifty acres was allotted to him in Sumeld, and in 1682 as a proprietor he voted at the organization of that town. There in 1688 at the age of seventy-one he died.

Of his daughter Hannah nothing more appears. His son James died unmarried two years after the father's death, being taken care of in his last illness by his brother John, who inherited his estate.

John Rising lived at Sumeld. His first wife was Sarah, daughter of Timothy Hale of Windsor. By her he had nine children. Josiah, their seventh child, was born Feb. 2nd, 1694. His mother died when he was but four years old, and his father soon married again. The stepmother, burdened with the care of a house full of children, the eldest of whom was but fourteen, probably found little Josiah, a robust boy of five, a trial to her patience. At some unknown period, probably on the birth of a new baby in 1702, he was sent to Deerfield to stay with his father's cousin, Mehuman Hinsdell.

Leaving little Josiah Rising with his cousins in Deerfield, we must go back and take up another thread of our story.

It is the morning of the 24th of September, 1667: the day when the County Court begins its fall session at Springfield. A crowd is already gathering at the ordinary, so the inn of the olden time was called, a room being always set apart there for the holding of the court. Men with pointed beards and close cropped hair, in tall steeple-crowned hats, short jerkins of a sad color with wide white wristbands turned back over the sleeves; leather belts, broad falling collars stiffly starched, tied with a cord and tassel at the throat, hanging down on the breast and extending round on the back and shoulders; full trousers reaching the knee, where they are fastened with a bow: long, gray woollen stockings, and stout leather shoes, broad, low and well oiled, complete the costume. Some of the younger men are in great boots rolled over at the top, and slouching in wrinkles about the leg.

The women are in steeple hats, not unlike those of the men,—and Mother Hubbard cloaks. Some are bareheaded or wear a handkerchief over the head, with white kerchief pinned straight down from the throat to the waist, white cuffs and long, white aprons covering the front of their gray or black woollen gowns. The boys and girls, miniature copies of their elders, except that the boys wear woollen caps with visors, and the girls, close fitting hoods of the same material.

A constable armed with a long, black staff tipped with brass, having three youths in charge, forces his way through the crowd. They have been sent by the commissioners at Northampton, to be tried and sentenced at Springfield. The culprits are pale and evidently frightened. The face of the youngest, a mere child, is swollen with weeping. The others, who are perhaps sixteen and seventeen years old, affect an indifference to their situation which their pallor belies. It is easy to see that the eldest is the most hardened of the three.

"In sooth they are not ill looking lads," said a gossip, "I marvel of what evil they are accused." "The little one is the son of Goodman John Stebbins our former neighbor," said another, "He numbers scarce twelve summers, yet m-thinks he is old in sin, for they say he hath entered the house of his stepmother's father, with intent to steal." "One Godfrey Nims is the ringleader of these villanies," put in a third. "He hath conspired with the others to run away to Canady, under the guidance of a drunken Indian varlet, who hath been hanging about Northampton of late." "It is believed that Goodman Hutchinson will intercede with the Court in behalf of Benitt," added the last speaker, "he hath lately taken the lad's mother to wife." "Poor boys," said a young mother, who led her little son by the hand, "I hope our Worshipful magistrate will mercifully consider their youth, and the shame to their parents."

"Our magistrate is a God-fearing man," replied a stern Puritan father at her elbow. He will deal justly with the malefactors, but it behooves him not to be merciful over-much. Our young men are getting overbold in their carriage. Our maidens wear silk in a flaunting manner, and indulge in excess of apparill to the offence of sober people. They must be taught to fear God, to obey the law and honor their parents."

"Ay, verily, it were better if they were more often admon-ished and scourged," interrupted a hard-faced woman, "and for my part I should like to see a score of lashes well laid on to the backs of these knaves I misdoubt if they get off with less."

The entrance of the magistrates and jurors put a stop to the talk, and the trial proceeded. The story is told in the records far better than I could tell it:

"Sept. 24, 1667. Att the County Court holden att Springfield, Capt. John Pynchon one of the Honored Assistants of this Colony presiding, "James Bennett, Godfrey Nims and Benoni Stebbins, young lads of Northampton being by Northampton Commissioners bound over to this Court to answere for diverse crimes and misdeeds comitted by them, were brought to this court by ye constable of y^t towne, wch 3 lads are accufed by Robert Bartlett, for that they gott into his house two Sabbath days, when all the family were at the Publike Meeting, on ye first of which tymes, they, viz Nims and Stebbins did ransack about the house, and took away out of diverse places of the house viz, 24 shillings in silver and 7 sh. in Wampum, with intention to run away to the ffrench, all wch is by them confessed; wch wickedness of theirs hath allso been accompanyed with frequent lying to excuse and justify themselves espec-ially on Nims his part, who it sems hath been a ringleader in the villanyes; ffor all which their crimes and misdemeands this corte doth judge y^t the said 3 lads shall bee well whipt on their naked bodies, viz Nims and Bennett with 25 lashes apeece and Benoni Stebbyngs with 1 1 lashes; and the said Nims and Stebbins are to pay Robert Bartlett the Summe of 4£ being accounted treble damage, according to law for what goods he hath lost by their means. Allso those persons that have received any money of any of the said lads, are to restore it to the s^d Robert Bartlett. But their being made to the Corte an earneft pirition & request by Ralph Hutchinson, father in law to ye said Bennet, and diverse other considerable persons, that the said Bennett's corporall punishment might be released, by reason of his mother's weaknese, who it seemed may suffer much inconvenience thereby, that punishment was remitted upon his father in law his engaging to this corte, to pay ffive pounds to ye County, as a fyne for the said Benitts offence; which $£ is to be paid to ye county Treasurer for ye use of Sd county. Allso John Stebbins Junior, being much suspected to have some hand in their plotting to run away, This Corte doth order ye Commissioners of Northampton to call him before y^m, & to examine him about that, or any other thing wherein he is supposed to be guilty with ye said lads and to act therein according to their discretion attending law. Also they are to call the Indian called Onequelat, who had a hand with y^m in their plott, and to deale with him according as they fynd."

The three thoroughly scared boys were sent back the next day to Northampton. There let us hope that little Benoni was taken from the grasp of the law, and put into his father's hands for chastisement. Bennett's fine was paid by his stepfather. As for Godfrey Nims he paid the penal-ty of his misdeeds at the whipping post in front of the meeting house. Alas for poor Godfrey! he lived in the age when a spade was called a spade. Lying was lying in good old colony days. Nobody thought of applying to the wild boy the soft impeachment of being an imaginative youth. The luckless wight had no indulgent friends to plead for him that "boys must be boys" and that wild oats must be sown. Wild oats were an expensive luxury in those days, as poor Godfrey found to his cost. Doubtless he was a disorderly fellow, yet without wishing to palliate his offence, I may say that he was without the good influences of a home life. There is no evidence of his having father or mother, kith or kin at Northampton. An active and excitable lad, with no legitimate scope under Puritan rule for his surplus energy, he fell in with the Indian vagrant, by whose tales of bush-ranging, his soul was fired to daring and reckless deeds. It is of such stuff that pioneers and heroes are often made.

Another turn of the kaleidoscope gives us a better picture of these impulsive youths.

It is the 18th of May, 1676. The sun, sinking behind the western hills, throws a golden glow over meadow and river. The Holyoke range is already in shadow. A force of about one hundred and forty-four men is gathered at Hatfield, awaiting the order to march against Philip's horde, for it was now the "generall voice of the people" that "it was time to distress the enemy and drive them from their fishing at Peskeompskut. Nearly all are mounted; a few on foot. Among the volunteers from Northampton are Godfrey Nims and James Bennett, comrades to-day in a righteous cause. Nims as usual with a dare-devil look in his eyes, resolute, careless and ready for any fate; Bennett more serious and subdued. The Reverend Hope Atherton, chaplain of the expedition, pours out his soul in prayer for the little army, and the cavalcade moves northward. Who at that moment remembered the youthful escapade of Godfrey Nims and James Bennett ? Surely not Mary Broughton, who stood sobbing among the women that watched their departure. She had married Bennett in 1674, not long after she herself, had had a brush with the magistrates. At the March Court of 1673, held at Northampton by Worshipful John Pynchon, Captain Holyoke and Deacon Chapin, Maid Mary Broughton had been severely admonished, and fined ten shillings for wearing a silk hood or scarf contrary to law. A sympathetic revolt against Puritan discipline may have attracted Bennett and Mary Broughton to each other. Their happiness was short-lived. On Saturday Nims brought her the sad news that Bennett had been killed in the Falls fight. In the spring of 1677, the young widow married Benoni Stebbins, her husband's dearest friend, another of the trio of bad boys of Northampton. Soon after his marriage Benoni Stebbins joined Quentin Stockwell and several other bold men who returned to Deerfield two years after the massacre at Bloody Brook, to begin a new settlement. There Stebbins worked early and late at the house to which he fondly hoped to bring his bride before winter should set in. At the end of their day's work on the 19th of September, 1677, they were surprised by twenty-six Indians from Canada under Ashpelon. Hurried up from the clearing to the mountain, they found there seventeen people from Hatfield who had been seized the same day, and with them, began the weary march to Canada. They were the first to follow that woful road, travelled later by so many New England captives. Crossing and recrossing the Connecticut, they journeyed rapidly by day. At night they lay stretched on their backs upon the ground, a rope about their necks, arms and legs extended and tied to "stakes so that they could stir nowayes." Halting thirty miles above Northfield, Ashpelon sent Benoni Stebbins back towards Lancaster, to notify a part of his band to join him on the Connecticut. On the return, Stebbins escaped on the 2nd of October and reached Hadley in safety. His own account taken down in writing on the 6th by the postmaster of Northampton, says that "being sent out with two squaws and a mare to pick huckleberries, he "got upon the mare and rid till he tired the mare, then ran on foot, and so escaped, being two days and a half without victuals."

Notwithstanding the sorrows and perils that so beset the life of Mary Broughton, her high spirit seems not to have been crushed. The following from the Court Records of March 26, 1678, shows that she never yielded a woman's right to make herself look as pretty as she could, and that she was upheld in her resistance by her admiring husband.

"Mary wife of Benoni Stebbins being presented to this Court for wearing silk contrary to law, and for that she agravates it by persisting in it, when as she was once presented before:

This court considering the agravation, and how unfit such things are in this day of trouble, did adjudge her to pay a fine of 10 shillings: As also Benoni Stebbins, openly affronting the court in saying he would not pay the money due for fees to the clerk of the Court; this Court judged him to pay as a Fine to the County 10 sh. forthwith, and committed him to the constable for the payment of the aforesaid fines."

Benoni Stebbins returned to Deerfield at its permanent settlement in 1682, becoming a prominent citizen there, and filling the highest town offices creditably to himself and acceptably to his neighbors. Mary, his wife, died in 1689.

About the time of Benoni Stebbins's marriage, Godfrey Nims had wedded the Widow Mary Williams and become the guardian of her little boy. He owned land in Deerfield in 1674, and if he were not, as tradition declares, one of the first three inhabitants, he and Benoni Stebbins with their families, were certainly among the earliest permanent settlers. Godfrey Nims, cordwainer, appears to have been an industrious and law abiding citizen. He was the first constable of Deerfield, being chosen in 1689, and later held other town offices.

In 1692 on his marriage to his second wife, Mehitable Smead, widow of Jeremiah Hull, he bought the lot on which the second church, the town house and Memorial Hall now stand, and built a house which was burned Jan. 4th, 1693-4. His little stepson, Jeremiah Hull, perished in the flames. The same year he bought the adjoining lot, building again on the site which has ever since been held by his descendants. When Joseph Barnard was wounded at Indian Bridge, and his horse killed under him, Godfrey Nims bravely took the helpless man upon his own horse, which being soon shot down, he was forced to mount behind Philip Mattoon, and "so got safely home."

Immediately upon Queen Anne's accession, the people of Deerfield began to make ready to meet the tempest from the north which they felt to be impending. The fort was "righted up," the school master was asked to help the selectmen "in wording a petition to the governor for help in the distress occasioned by a prospect of war." In the summer of 1703, Peter Schuyler warned the people of Deerfield that an expedition against them was fitting out in Canada. Those who had settled at a distance from Meeting House Hill, began to seek shelter within the palisade. Twenty soldiers were sent as a garrison to the settlement. On the 8th of October John Nims and Zebediah Williams, son and stepson of Godfrey Nims, while looking after their cows in the meadow, were captured by Indians, and carried to Canada. Such was the alarm and distress of the people, that they urged their minister to address the government in their behalf. The letter is a credit to pastor and people. In asking for relief from taxation as the fortification must be rebuilt, Mr. Williams says: "I never found the people unwilling to do, when they had the ability, yea they have often done above their ability." He speaks of the "sorrowful parents and distressed widow of the poor captives taken" from them, as requesting the governor "to endeavor that there may be an exchange of prisoners to their release." Parson Stoddard of Northampton also wrote to Governor Dudley in behalf of Deerfield. He tells him that the people are much depressed and discouraged by the captivity of two of their young men, and asks that dogs may be trained to hunt the Indians, "who act like wolves and are to be dealt withall as wolves." To this letter dated Northampton, Oct. 22, 1703, the following postscript is added: "Since I wrote, the father of the two captives[1] belonging to Deerfield has importunately desired me to write to your Ex'cy that you w^d endeavor the Redemption of his children."

Notwithstanding the general uneasiness, private affairs went on as usual. Birth, marriage, death, like time and tide, stay for naught. Winter wore to spring. The soldiers were still billeted in the homes of the people. The minds of all were tense with anxiety. The air was thick with omens. Sounds were heard in the night as of the tramping of men around the fort. March came in like a lion. The village lay buried in the snow, the people in sleep. In that hour before dawn when night is darkest and slumber deepest, the long-dreaded storm burst; unexpected at the last, like all long-expected events. On what a wreck the morning broke! Benoni Stebbins, after fighting for hours like a tiger at bay, lay dead in his house. In the southeast angle of the fort, Godfrey Nims's house was still burning, three of his little girls somewhere dead among the embers. His daughter, Rebecca Mattoon, and her baby, slain by the tomahawk. Ebenezer, his seventeen years old son, his stepdaughter, Elizabeth Hull, aged sixteen; his wife with Abigail, their youngest child, about four years old, already on the march to Canada.

His opposite neighbor, Mehuman Hinsdale, bereft of wife and child by the same blow,—also a captive, with the boy Josiah Rising, his little Suffield cousin, whom he had taken into his home and heart. Did Godfrey Nims and Benoni Stebbins in those hours of horror, remember how in their boyhood, they had "plotted together to run away to the ffrench" with Onequelatt the Indian ?

How Thankful Nims and her family were saved by a snowdrift: how Godfrey's wife was killed on the inarch: how Zebediah Williams died at Quebec, firm in the Protestant faith: how John Nims escaped from captivity, and was finally married in Deerfield to his step-sister, Elizabeth Hull: how Ebenezer Nims contrived to outwit the good priests, who were faithfully trying to secure his sweetheart's conversion by marrying her to a Frenchman: how Mehuman Hinsdale came back to Deerfield, and was again "captivated by ye Indian Salvages," are matters of history. But what of Abigail Nims and Josiah Rising?

Up to this moment, from the hour when cruelly roused from the innocent sleep of childhood, they were dragged towards the north, over the snowbound meadows and icy river, this question has been asked in vain. Thanks to the careful records made at the time by Canadian priest and nun, and thanks again to the kind help given me by Canadian priest and nun of to-day we can now follow the fortunes of the two captives, so rudely torn from home and kin.

In the history of New France there is no more interesting and romantic chapter, than that of the life and labors of Marguerite Bourgeois. To bring about the conversion of the savages by giving to their children a Christian education, was her dearest wish. Not only literally but figuratively did she plant the cross on the mountain of Montreal. In 1676, the priests of Saint-Sulpice built a chapel on the mountain and founded there a mission for such Iroquois and others, as wished to settle on the island of Montreal. In 1680, soon after the school for Indian boys was begun at the mission of the mountain, Marguerite Bourgeois sent two nuns of the Congregation there to teach the girls.

In 1685 forty Indian girls were in training at this school. It takes but a moment to tell the story, but the pain, peril and privation, the self-abnegation, the devotion by which this result was achieved, cannot be estimated. This Indian village, palisaded to protect the Christianized Iroquois from the attacks of their savage brethren, who were incensed against the converts, was an out-post of defence for Montreal itself. Destroyed by fire in 1694, through the carelessness of a drunken Indian, the fort was rebuilt of stone, with rude towers at each angle, two of which were set apart for the nuns and their school.

In 1701, disturbed by the opportunity afforded the Indians by their nearness to the town of obtaining strong liquors, yet unwilling to deprive Montreal of their help in case of attack from their enemies, the priests removed the mission to the other side of the mountain, to a picturesque spot called Sault au Recollet, on the bank of the Riviere des Prairies. There they built a church, modelled after the Chapel de Notre Dame de Lorette in Italy, and a house for themselves and their school. The Sisters of the Congregation also erected there a building for themselves and for a school for girls. The village and mission building were enclosed by a palisade with three bastions.

It was to the Sault au Recollet fort that our two captives, doubtless with others from Deerfield were carried at once on their arrival in Canada. The squaw Ganastarsi, probably the wife or mother of her captor, gladly took little Abigail into her bark wigwam, and Josiah Rising was led to that of his Macqua master. There they lived in true Indian fashion, rolling in the dirt with the pappooses and puppies with which the village was swarming, and quickly catching the Iroquois language. To Josiah, the savages gave the name of Shoen-tak8anni of which the French equivalent is *Il lui a ôté son village*. Abigail was known as T8atog8ach, which rendered into French is *"Elle retire de l'eau."*

The little four years old English girl, with her uncouth name, her pale face and her yellow hair, did not long escape the notice of the holy sisters of the mission. The following is a translation of her French record of baptism:

"On the 15th day of June of the year 1704, the rites of baptism have been administered by me, the undersigned, to a little English girl, named in her own country Abigail, and now Mary Elizabeth; born in Dearfielde, in New England the 31st of May, of the year 1700, of the marriage of Geoffrey Nimbs cordwainer, and of Meetable Smeed also deceased. The child, taken at the said place the eleventh of March last, and living in the wigwam of a squaw of the Mountain, named Ganastarsi. The god-mother was Demoiselle Elizabeth Le Moine, daughter of Monsieur Charles Le Moine esquire, Baron de Longueuil, chevalier of the order of Saint-Louis, and captain of a company,—with François Bonnet who says that he cannot sign.

Signed Marie Elizabeth Longueuil. Meriel, prêtre."

What the nuns of the Congregation did for little Abigail, was done for Josiah Rising by the good priests of Saint-Sulpice at the Sault au Recollet mission. He was baptized on the 23rd of December, 1706, being then about eleven years old. The name Ignace was given him, and it was as Ignace Raizenne on Canadian records, that I recognized Josiah Rising.

Picture the life of these children at the Indian fort. The dark, cold, smoky wigwam; the scanty clothing in which they had been snatched from home all rags and dirt, replaced at last by a blanket which was their dress by day, their bed at night; coarse and unpalatable food; corn pounded, soaked and boiled in unsavory pottage; roasted pumpkin a rare luxury. Better times came for the poor waifs when they could go to school. There they were decently clad, for Marguerite Bourgeois knew that the first step towards Christianizing any people, is to make them dress decently and to inspire them with a love of work. "If you can introduce petticoats and drawers into your mission," wrote Monsieur Tronson, "you will make yourself famous; nothing would be more useful, or fraught with better results."

At school, they learned to sing and chant, to read and write and to speak French. The catechism and creed were taught in French, as well as in English and Indian. The girls learned to sew and knit, to spin and make lace. The boys were instructed in carpentry, shoemaking, mason work and other trades.

But Sunday, so gloomy to the children of Puritan households, was the day of days to the girls and boys of the mission. Then Abigail went in procession with the other girls to mass and saw the gorgeous altar cloths and vestments, and the candles burning brightly, and the pictures of the saints, and little Jesus and his mother looking kindly down upon her. She sat close to Sister des Anges, and crossed herself and said her prayers, and felt very good and very happy; only she wished that Shoentak Sanni would just look at her; but he sat among the choir boys and sang away and never lifted his eyes from his book.

I like to think of the busy school days and cheerful Sundays of the little New England captives, thus cared for by gentle nun and kindly priest. We must not forget, however, that the "Oso" fort, as the New England captives called the fort at Sault au Recollet, had its sadder pictures.

Sometimes an Indian would come back from the town, enraged by the white man's fire-water, and bringing the news that some "Bastonnais" had arrived in Montreal. Every messenger from our government, no matter how far from Boston his home might be, was a "Bastonnais," in Canada.

Then Abigail's master would threaten to carry her into the woods, and Ganastarsi would be very cross, and call her Kanaskwa, the slave, and possibly, give the child a slap in the face,—for she had grown fond of T8atog8ach and did not mean to give her up to the Bastonnais if she could help it. Sister des Anges and the other nuns would seem distressed and anxious, and kept the little girl day and night at the convent, out of sight of any possible English visitors. Abigail was too young to mind much about any of this, but Josiah knew, and I dare say, asked the school master if he might not go home with the messengers. At this the priest would frown and speak sharply to the lad, reproaching him with ingratitude to the Indian who had saved his life. No doubt he would tell the boy what he himself sincerely believed, that if he went back to Protestant New England, his soul would be damned eternally. When Josiah's master heard about this, he beat the boy and sent him off to the woods with a hunting party.

Deacon Sheldon came back from his embassy in 1705 with but five captives, not having even seen his boys, who, he was told, had "gone a honten." Shortly after this, bitterly disappointed at not being allowed to go home with Deacon Sheldon, John Nims, Martin Kellogg, Joseph Petty and Thomas Baker ran away. It went harder with Josiah and the rest after this. Ensign Sheldon must have have kept the Sault au Recollet mission in a stir in the first years of the captivity. He was certainly there twice in the spring of 1706. Among his accounts is an item of 12 livres paid "for a carriall to goe to see the captives at the Mohawk fort," and "4 livres more for a second visit." He probably saw Josiah and Abigail at this time, but they were not among those whom he brought home. Grim and direful scenes our two captives saw, when the war parties returned with scalps and prisoners. Then two long rows of savages armed with clubs and hatchets, were formed at the gate of the fort. Between these the weary and footsore captives ran for nearly three-quarters of a mile, the savages mocking and striking at them as they ran. Then came the dreadful pow-wow, when the poor sufferers were made to sing and dance round a great fire, while their tormentors yelled and shrieked. The children saw many of their Deerfield neighbors brought into the fort in this way. Martin Kellogg in the fall of 1708, Josiah's cousin, Mehuman Hinsdell the next spring, and Joseph Clesson and John Arms in June, 1709, all ran the gauntlet at the Oso fort.

After John Sheldon's third journey to Canada in 1707, there had been no general exchange of prisoners. In the summer of 1712, the Canadian governor proposed that the English captives in Canada should be "brought into or near Deerfield, and that the French prisoners should be sent home from thence." Governor Dudley ordered Colonel Partridge to collect the French captives at Deerfield.

There must have been some excitement in the usually quiet town of Deerfield when it was known that the French captives were mustering there, especially when the dogged refusal of some to return to Canada was noised abroad. That Colonel Partridge met with some unexpected obstacles in dispatching the French captives is shown by the following extract from his letter to Governor Dudley:

Hatfield, July 1, 1712.

"I begg yor Excellency's excuse & tender Resentment. Off our repeated demur & delay of moveing towards Canada by the Frentch-men & o^r Messengers, which is wholie by the indisposition of the Frentchmen, Especially two of them, who will not be p^{r}suaded to go, neither by p^{r}suasions nor force, except they be carried, viz, Cosset & Laffever. the Capt. hath used all means with them, especially Cosset, in so much that I believe if they go into the woods together, they will murder one another before they get to Canada. Cosset positively refusing to go, Chuseing rather to Remayne a prison" all his days, as he saith, rather than go with him. The Captaine vehemently mad with him, as he saith, will kill him & its thought by their violent treatm^t one towards another, that murder had been done if o^r men had not p^{r}vented itt. They cannot speak together but some fall to blows. . . . . . .Laffever has been oposite of goeing all a Long & now it comes too positively opposes it, except he be forct. Yesterday I went up to Deref^d & two of the Frentchmen orderd him & the Frentchman to attend me in order to their goeing immediately away.". . . . .

When it was known that an escort was to be sent from Deerfield with the French captives, there was no lack of volunteers. Colonel Partridge continues:

"As to Messengers, severall offer themselves to go. . . . . . We had pitcht upon Ltt. Williams, with the consent of his ffather, who hath the Frentch tongue, Jonath Wells, Jno Nims & Eliezer Warner, but haveing in yor last letter a forbidd to any of Baker's Company, we pitcht on Lt. Wells, Sergt. Taylor, John Nims & Thomas Frentch, who also hath the Frentch tongue, but think the former most apt. . . . .

I have had no small fategue in this matter, but ye disappointment hath been on ye Frenchman's p^t as aforesaid."

On the above letter was the following endorsement: "Co'll Partridg: Honn^d Sir, I have all along been much against returning home: to Canada: but am now come to a Resolution that 1 will not go, except the Governor with yourself, doe compel me to return; which I hope you will not do; I have an Affection for the people and Countery; and therefore do not intend to lieue it untill there be a Peace; and then only for to give my Parents a vissitt and Returne againe from your humble serv't to command; this is La ffeveres words."

The party under command of Lieut. Samuel Williams, a youth of twenty-three, started from Deerfield on the 10th of July, returning in September with nine English captives.

Godfrey Nims had died some years before. Ebenezer was still in captivity and John Nims evidently went as the head of the family, hoping to effect the release of his brother and sister. I judge that in urging Abigail's return, John made the most of the provision for her in his father's will, as the story goes in Canada, that the relatives of the young Elizabeth, who were Protestants, and were amply provided with this world's goods, knowing that she had been carried to the Sault au Recollet, went there. . . . .and offered a considerable sum for her ransom ; and the savages would willingly have given her up, if she herself had shown any desire to go with her relatives. To her brother's entreaties that she would return with him she replied that she would rather be a poor captive among Catholics, than to become the rich heiress of a Protestant family,—and John came back without his sister and brother. About this time came Abigail's first communion. She walked up the aisle dressed in white, with a veil on her head, and all the people looked at her, and a bad Indian girl muttered, "Kanaskwa," [the slave].

Shoentak8anni, in his white surplice, swinging the censer, ringing the bell and holding up the priest's robe, seemed almost as grand as a priest himself, and it was all very solemn and very beautiful to the child. That was the summer when Hannah Hurst of Deerfield was married. Marie Kaiennoni, she was called at the Mission. She was seventeen, and Michel Anenharison, a widower of thirty-two. T8atog8ach heard them called in church. She wondered at Marie. Shoentak8anni was ever so much nicer than Michel. I think Father Quéré had his doubts about this match. He urged Marie to leave the Indians altogether, but she declared she wished to live and die among them. Sister des Anges heard her say this often. Father Quéré asked Monsieur Belmont what he ought to do about marrying them, and Monsieur Belmont said she must be treated as if she were really an Indian girl. Then Father Quéré told Thomas Hurst and Father Meriel, and as they did not forbid the banns, he married them.

A year passed. The treaty of Utrecht had been signed. Peace was proclaimed in London, and a grand *Te Deum* sung to Handel's music in St. Paul's Cathedral. In this interval of peace, renewed efforts were made by our government for the recovery of the English captives in Canada. Nothing daunted by the ill success of John Schuyler's mission, Captain John Stoddard and Parson Williams with Martin Kellogg and Thomas Baker as pilots and interpreters, and com-missioned by the government to negotiate for the release of the remaining captives, arrived in Canada the middle of February, 1714.

It is a long and tedious business. De Vaudreuil is vacillating and contradictory in his promises. He shirks the responsibility alternately upon the captives who have been formally naturalized; upon his king whom he fears to offend; upon the savages who claim the ownership of many and who he says are his allies, and not his subjects to command. Finally he says that he "can just as easily alter the course of the rivers, as prevent the priests' endeavors to keep the children."

The long sojourn of this embassy, its influence and dignity undoubtedly made a profound impression at the Sault au Recollet mission. What more natural than that Abigail Nims's captor, knowing that the English envoys were insisting on the return of minors and children,and fearing to lose his reward if general terms of release were agreed upon, should have fled with his prize to the Boston government, to secure the money for her ransom before Stoddard's return. This he could have done without the knowledge or consent of Mission priest or nun. Moreover, had they known his purpose, they would have been powerless to prevent its fulfilment.

Whether this theory be correct or not it was before the return of the envoys that Colonel Partridge on the 28th of July, 1714, wrote to the Council at Boston, giving an account of an "outrage in the country of Hampshire," a Macqua Indian, having brought to Westfield and offered for sale, a girl "supposed to be an English captive carried from Deerfield, it appearing so by her own relation and divers circumstances concurring." The Council at once advised that Capt. John Sheldon, then living at Hartford, should be the bearer of a letter to the Indian commissioners at Albany, demanding a strict examination of this matter. The result of Capt. Sheldon's mission is told in the Council Record.

"In Council Aug. 22, 1714. Upon reading a letter from the Commissioners of the Indian affairs at Albany by Capt. John Sheldon, messenger thither, to make inquiries concerning a young Maid or Girle, brought thither into Westfield by a Macqua and offered for sale, very probably supposed to be English and daughter of one [Godfrey] Nims, late of Deerfield, and carried away captive, the Commissioners insisting upon it that she is an Indian:

Ordered, that Samuel Partridge Esq. treat with the Macqua, her pretended Master, and agree with him on the reasonablest terms he can for her release and then dispose her to some good family near the sea side, without charge, for the present to prevent her fears; unless Capt. Sheldon will be prevailed with to take her home with him.

Paid John Sheldon for journey to Boston, from Northampton and back to Albany and back with his son, 17£, 16s, 7d for time and expenses.

In Council, Sept. 20, 1714. Ordered, that the sum of £25. be paid to Elewacamb, the

Albany Indian now attending with letters and papers from thence, who claims the English girl in the hands of the English and her Relations at Deerfield, and that a Warrant be made to the Treasurer accordingly. Also that a coat and shirt be given s^d Indian."

"Here," says Mr. Sheldon in his History of Deerfield, "the curtain dropped. After this not the slightest trace of Abigail Nims was found."

Had the story ended here, it would have been romantic enough ; but truth is stranger than fiction.

An interval of eight months elapses, and the curtain rises again:

ACT I.Scene i.

> *A marriage in the church of Notre Dame de Lorette, at the Sault au Recollet fort, on the Island of Montreal.*

DRAMATIS PERSONAE.
Abigail Nims, *aged fifteen.*
Josiah Rising, *aged about twenty-four.*
Soeur des Anges, *and other nuns of the Congregation.*
PèRE QuéRé, *a Mission priest.*
Iroquois Indians.

The ceremony is soon ended. Father Quéré records it on the parish register where it stands fair and clear to-day. Here is the translation:

"This 29th July 1715. I have married Ignace Shoentak8anni and Elizabeth T8atog8ach, both English, who wish to remain with the Christian Indians, not only renouncing their nation, but even wishing to live *en sauvages,* Ignace aged about twenty-three or twenty- four years,—Elizabeth about fifteen. Both were taken at Dierfile about thirteen years ago. [Signed] M. Quéré, prêtre S. S."

How Abigail Nims got back again to the Sault au Recollet from Deerfield, is the missing link in the story of her long life. But what more probable than that she should have run away. There is of course a shadow of doubt as to the identity of the captive bought of Elewacamb, with Abigail Nims. The girl had said she was a Deerfield captive: John Sheldon and Colonel Partridge believed her to be Abigail Nims, and had satisfied the governor and council that she was. They had bought her of Elewacamb, paid for her in lawful money and given him a bonus besides. It was not strange that the commissioners at Albany "insisted that she was an Indian." From her babyhood, for eleven years she had lived among the savages, and had become one. An orphan, a stranger, not knowing or caring for her Deerfield relatives, bred a Roman Catholic and irked by the straight-laced customs of the Puritan town and church, hating the restraints of civilized life, homesick and unhappy, pining for the nuns and for her free life in the wigwam of Ganastarsi, fearless and fleet of foot, she may have betaken herself to the woods, and somehow got back to the Macqua fort.

Fancy the joy at the Mission, when the stray lamb returned to the true fold. It was then, as I believe, that the priests, to settle the question forever, with much difficulty obtained the release of T8atog8ach and Shoentak8anni from their Indian masters. "They deserved this favor," says the historian, "for the odor of virtue which they shed abroad over the mission of which they were the edification and the model." Their speedy marriage and the emphasis laid in the record upon their wish to conform to the Indian mode of life, was to protect them from future importunities for their return to New England.

John Rising of Suffield died Dec. 1 1 , 1719. In his will he bequeaths to his "well-beloved son Josiah, now in Captivity, the sum of five pounds in money to be paid out of my estate within three years after my decease, provided he return from captivity." Josiah Rising and Abigail Nims, his wife, never returned. When in 1721 the mission was transferred to the Lake of the Two Mountains, the priests, charmed with the edifying conduct of Ignace and Elizabeth, with their industry and intelligence in domestic affairs, for their advantage and as an example to the mission at large, resolved to establish them in a permanent home of their own, and accordingly gave them a large domain about half a league from the fort.

There, they served as a pattern to the savages and to all the people round about, of patriarchal life and virtue, by their care in training their children in the fear of God, and in the faithful performance of their religious duties.

Abigail Nims, wife of Josiah Rising, died Feb, 19, 1748. In her last illness, she refused to leave off the hair shirt which she had always worn as penance. She left eight children, six daughters and two sons. Her eldest, Marie Madeleine, was a nun of the Congregation by the name of Sister Saint-Herman. Having learned in childhood the Iroquois language, she was sent as missionary to the Lake of the Two Mountains and there taught Indian girls for twenty-five years. When about ninety, she died in the convent at Montreal.

Four of the daughters of Ignace and Elizabeth Raizenne, married and reared families, many of whose members filled high positions in the Roman Catholic church. I learn from one of the ladies of the Congregation, who was the pupil of one of Abigail Nims's grand-daughters, that she has often heard from this teacher the story of her grandmother's life, and that she always laid particular stress on the fact that she refused to return to Deerfield when sent for.

The eldest son of Ignace and Elizabeth was a priest and *cure* of excellent character and ability. Jean Baptiste Jerome, their younger son, unable to carry out his wish to take orders, married and settled on the domain originally granted to his father. His house was a refuge for the poor, the orphan and the unfortunate. He regulated his household as if it were a religious community. The father and mother rose early and prayed together. Then both went to their respective labor, he to his fields,—she to her ten children. The hours for study, for conversation, for silence and for recreation were fixed by the clock. All the family, parents, children and servants, ate at the same table and while eating, the lives of the Saints were read. After tea the father explained some doctrinal point to children and servants. Then followed prayers and all went silently to bed.

Marie Raizenne, born in 1736, was the most distinguished of Abigail Nims's children. She entered the Community of the Congregation at the age of sixteen, and in 1778, under the name of Mother Saint-Ignace, attained the honor of being its thirteenth Lady Superior. She was deeply religious, full of energy and courage, of extraordinary talents and fine education. She is said to have possessed in a remarkable degree, the real spirit and zeal of Marguerite Bourgeois, and to have sought untiringly to revive this spirit in the com-munity of which she was the head. She died at the age of seventy-six.

Thus again did the blood of the martyrs of Deerfield become the seed of the church of Canada.

A DAY AT OKA.

General Hoyt in his "Antiquarian Researches," writes of the Deerfield captives, "Twenty-eight remained in Canada and mixing with the French and Indians and adopting their manners and customs, forgot their native country and were lost to their friends." The names of the twenty-eight who never came back follow. This list must now be corrected by adding to it the names of the Widow Hurst and her daughter Elizabeth, making thirty in all, and I doubt if the list is yet complete. We may congratulate ourselves to-day, on having found, within the last three years, eighteen of these exiles from home. Would that I could tell you these tales of the captives as they might be told; pathetic, full of incident, and glowing with romance as they are; but I can only transcribe the bare facts of their lives as I find them clearly recorded on the parish records of many a picturesque Canadian village, where they lived, died, and lie buried in nameless graves.

In the settlement of Deerfield, home lots were laid out and granted at Plum Tree Plain, now Wapping, as early as 1685. The little colony at Wapping consisted mostly of young men with their young families, nearly connected by blood or marriage. Thither came Thomas Hurst, freeman of Hadley, with his wife Sarah.

The people of Plum Tree Plain probably removed for safety to the town street, where Thomas Hurst died in 1702, leaving a family of six children. Among the captives of the 29th of February, 1704, were Widow Sarah Hurst, then about thirty-eight years old, and her children. The youngest was killed on the march. On their arrival in Canada the family was separated, some remaining in Montreal, Thomas and Hannah being sent, with several other Deerfield children, to the mission at the Sault au Recollet or Lorette, on the Riviere des Prairies, on the other side of the island of Montreal. The only one of Thomas Hurst's family who ever came back to New England was Sara, the eldest child.

With nothing to guide me, groping laboriously through pages of old French manuscript in the archives of Quebec, in the portfolios of ancient notaries of Montreal, dead and turned to dust a century and a half ago, in the parish records of both cities, finding here a little and there a little, and putting the disjointed fragments together, I had nearly succeeded in rehabilitating the Hurst family of six Deerfield captives, when 1 saw that for further knowledge of Thomas and Hannah, I must seek the records of the Oso fort. These were to be found at Oka, the Indian name for the village of the Lake of the Two Mountains on the Ottawa river, whither in 1720 the Sault au Recollet mission had been removed. By early morning train to La Chine where one drops perforce from the 19th to the early 17th century. Here, before 1615, the most important trading post of New France was set up by Champlain; and here, to-day, in good preservation, stand the great cobble-stone chimney and oven of Champlain's post, with the broad fireplace, by which Robert de La Salle later sheltered himself until he had built his palisaded village, a mile to the west, on the land granted him by the gentlemen of the Seminary of Saint Sulpice. Opposite me, across Lake Saint Louis, as I stood in the ruined doorway of La Salle's homestead, where he must so often have stood looking longingly westward, were the crumbling ruins of the Mohawk fort, where Eunice Williams and other Deerfield children sobbed out the first months of their captivity, and the low roofs of Caughnawaga, the cross gleaming from its picturesque steeple. Was it the wail of the Deerfield bell, a captive still, that floated faintly above the sullen murmur of the rapids? Who knows? Swan-like our boat glides on to Saint Anne, Bout de l'Isle, Tom Moore's Saint Anne, the house where he wrote his Canadian boat-song, in full view from our steamer. As we round the end of the island, at our right loom up the vine-covered towers of the ruined château de Senneville, the seigniorial mansion of Jacques Le Ber, "a Canadian feudal castle of the 17th century." While in captivity Samuel Williams, the son of the Deerfield minister, lived with Jacques Le Ber, a rich merchant of Montreal, whose chateau was then in process of building. Back from the river, on a hill, stands the old stone mill of the seignory, not unlike that at Newport, R. I., but more imposing, from its solitary and commanding position. A little to the northwest of the château, "Ottawa's tide" expands into the Lake of the Two Mountains, beyond which the twin mountains form the background of this beautiful picture. Nestling at their base and following the curve of the lake shore, is the Côte, or village of Oka, as the Mission of the Lac des Deux Montagnes is now called. On a finely wooded point, formed by the double curving

of the shore, the site of the ancient Iroquois fort, are the mission buildings, the church and the presbytery or priest's house. The convent stands where it stood in 1720, but the comfortless birch bark cabin, then occupied by Soeur des Anges, and her companion, the two devoted nuns of the Congregation, who gathered here their school of Indian girls, has given place to a modern gray stone building. Here another Sister des Anges, with two assistants, still teaches the little Indian girls their catechism. To her I was introduced by a letter from a nun of the mother house of the Congregation, of Montreal, whose friendship is very precious to me. Being herself the descendant of a New England captive, she takes the warmest interest in my work, and does everything in her power to help me. We were cordially received by the Lady Superior, who would not hear of our going to the inn, but gave us a room in the convent. The Sault au Recollet mission was the Canadian home of the two captives, Abigail Nims and Josiah Rising. There they went to school, there they were married; and that their virtues and their piety might be an example to the neighborhood, they were granted by the priests a large domain at the Lake of the Two Mountains, about a half a league from the fort.

"There are farms in Canada," says Mr. Parkman, "which have passed from father to son for two hundred years." The estate given to Ignace Raizenne, by the gentlemen of the Seminary in 1720, having passed from father to son for one hundred and seventy years, is now owned and occupied by Jean Baptiste Raizenne, great-great-grandson of Josiah Rising and Abigail Nims. I therefore left word with the shop-keeper of Oka, that if Mr. Raizenne should come into the village that day, he was to be told that a lady who could tell him about his New England ancestry was at the convent and would like to see him. In half an hour he appeared, and I am sure that I shall never again be treated with such distinction or welcomed with such frank hospitality as I was by that simple Canadian *habitant,* of which class he is a fine type.

A face of strong character, mobile in expression, with piercing black eyes; quick of apprehension, alert in manner, rapid in speech and gesture, with a lithe, agile and nervous frame. Naive, unconscious and enthusiatic, he showed the greatest delight in meeting one who came from the home of his remote ancestry, of whom he is very proud.

We gladly yielded to his desire that we should go with him to visit his *"propriété."* First, however, to the records. After dinner I presented myself at the Presbytery.

With the Apostle to the Indians at Oka, I had had an interesting correspondence, yet I had not been able to decipher his name, and had I known that he is a savant, considered the best living authority on the Iroquois language, I should hardly have presumed to make such demands as I have, upon his time and patience. This venerable father is as modest, kindly and simple as he is learned, and I owe him much. The greatest are always the simplest. Great poems, great pictures, great music, and great men.

The most careful reader of the mission records in Canada, finds, at the outset, an impenetrable veil shrouding their precious secrets, in the fact that the captives on arriving at the mission with their savage captors, were adopted into Indian families, receiving Indian surnames. Added to this, at their baptism by the mission priests, in nine cases out of ten, the names of their French sponsors, or of the saints of the Catholic church, are substituted for the Christian names given to them at their baptism in New England. It is only by the most persistent pursuit of isolated facts, hints, dates and names, through register after register, collating, and comparing them, that one finally evolves the stories of the captives.

These records are like the photographer's negative. They require patient and skillful manipulation and developing. At first all is a blank, a haze. By straining a little in one part, restraining a little in another, the picture begins to come, and when it does come, its contrasts of light and shade surprise and thrill one. The photographic distinctness of every detail of these lives, which, hidden from sight for nearly two centuries, are now suddenly revealed almost takes one's breath away. For example, when I first struck the trail of Abigail Nims, she was baptized as Elizabeth in Montreal and was said to be "living in the cabin of a squaw of the mountain." Of the Mission of the mountain, and its successive transference to the Sault au Recollet and to the Lake of the Two Mountains I then knew nothing. As I chased her from record to record, the little Elizabeth flitted before me like an elf, appearing as Elizabeth Stebin, Elizabeth Kanaskwa, Elizabeth Sahiak, Elizabeth T8atop8ach. When I finally ran her down as Elizabeth Nairn, married to a fellow-captive, Ignace Raizenne, I had no difficulty in recognizing the two little playmates who were living opposite each other in Deerfield on the morning of Feb. 29, 1704. My first clue to the Deerfield Hursts at Oka, on the Sault au Recollet records, was the birth of a son to Michel Anenharison and Marie Kawennaenni. This Marie I found to be Hannah Hurst. Doubtless her descendants still live at Oka.

At four o'clock, Jean Baptiste Raizenne drove to the convent gate. We clambered over the great wheels, into the *habitant's* cart, a revised edition of our dump cart, and taking his little daughter

Guilhelmine between us, we set out for the old homestead of Abigail Nims and Josiah Riseing. Though it was October, the sun was warm, and the sky and river a summer blue. Leaving the village, our road lay over high sand dunes, the relic of some old sea beach of the ancient continent. To stay these shifting sands, which are alike an ornament and a protection to the village, the Curé an intelligent and agreeable man, has planted on their slopes this year forty thousand young pine trees.

As we ploughed through these great drifts up and down, there was no sound but that of the sand sifting through our wheels and the sad murmur of the pines. At the foot of a tall black cross, planted in the yellow expanse of the plateau, an oasis in the desert, as it were, knelt a group of pilgrims on their way to the mountain chapel of Calvary.

As we struck into the primeval forest Jean Baptiste began to chatter with the volubility of a Frenchman. " *Voici la propriété du pauvre Ignace!"* "This is the estate of poor Ignace," he cried. "This road the captive made with his own hands." When we came in sight of the house, his excitement was intense. *"Marche, donc vite!"* "Go on quick!" he shouted to his horse, and to me, *"Voilà la vieille maison, la maison d'Ignace! oh, que je l'aime!"* "There is the old house, Ignace's house! oh, how I love it!" And it was *"voilà"* this, and *"voilà"* that, and finally, " *Voilà le bébé!"* as the little toddling thing met us at the kitchen door, and here we were under the very roof-tree of the two captives.

I shall not attempt to describe my feelings. I was dazed and overwhelmed with memories of the far-off past. Mr. Raizenne's pretty wife and old mother received us without embarrassment, and urged us to prolong our visit. We drank to the memory of the captives, and to the health and prosperity of their descendants, in wine made from vines originally planted by Ignace. We tasted water from his well; we ate apples from the sole survivor of his orchard. The climax of the afternoon's enjoyment for Jean Baptiste was reached when he presented to us his only son, a chubby boy of nine, named Riseing Raizenne. After taking a photograph of the place, and leaving little Guilhelmine in tears at our departure, we drove back to the village.

The peace and quiet of the convent were grateful after the exciting emotions of the afternoon. We begged Mother des Anges not to condemn us to another solitary meal, and after some hesitation, she kindly allowed us to take our tea with the nuns. Loyalty to our hostess forbids me to dwell on the spiritual and material delights of that repast.

In New England, the sunset hour is usually marked by an outburst of noise from the youth of the village. Not so at Oka. The whole place shows the sobering, orderly influence of the little Christian community in its midst. We sat on the doorsteps of the convent talking low with the Sisters. The soft air was redolent with the odors of heliotrope and mignonette from the garden below us. The river, still as the face of a mirror, reflected the splendor of the afterglow. Under the Lombardy poplars in the presbytery grounds, the aged mission priest walked slowly up and down, reading his breviary. Now and then, a blanketed figure stole silently past, on her way to say her evening prayer in the church. One by one the stars came out and the gleam of a brilliant planet left a silvery wake upon the water. The stillness of the midsummer night was broken only by the leaping of the fish at some swiftly skimming insect, the subdued voices of the Indian boys, and the sound of their paddles, as they glided by in their canoes.

The peaceful beauty of the whole scene; the absolute quiet of the village; the convent with its atmosphere of calm content; the serenity and repose of the low voiced nuns; the tranquillity of nature,—all conspired to make the hour a dream of Heaven.

But all things must have an end, and so this memorable day at Oka. We went over in the morning to say farewell to the reverend father and the *curé,* and as the presbytery was undergoing repairs and the grounds were necessarily open, they kindly gave us leave to stroll under the magnificent trees. As we stood with them for a moment under the cross, beneath which is a cannon, on the extreme point of their land, I rallied the *cure* on the incongruity of a cannon in the domain of apostles of the Prince of Peace. "It is to shoot Pagans" he replied quickly. "Since that is its use," said my companion, "It is lucky for us that we are on this side of it." "But mademoiselle," he answered with ready wit, "we do not shoot heretics, we pray for them." And so we said good-bye.

THANKFUL STEBBINS.

John Stebbins, son of John of Northampton, and grandson of Rowland Stebbins, founder of the family in America, was one of the earliest inhabitants of Deerfield, Mass., at its permanent settlement. He was a carpenter by trade; a soldier under Capt. Lothrop, through Philip's war, and, according to Mr. Sheldon, "the only man known to have come out whole from the massacre at Bloody Brook." His homestead in Deerfield was that known to the present generation as David Sheldon's. In the assault of Feb. 29, 1703-4, his house was burned, and he and his wife with their six children, ranging in age from five to nineteen, were carried captives to Canada, whence the father, mother and eldest child returned to Deerfield.

How Abigail, the girlish bride of Jacques de Noyon,—one of three Canadian bush-rangers unaccountably living in Deerfield at the time of the attack,—thus doubly a captive, went with him to his boyhood's home in Boucherville; how later, she sent her eldest child, René, a lad of ten, with a hunting party of French and Indians, to visit his grandparents in Deerfield; how, on the return of the hunters, René stayed behind, and grew up there as Aaron Denio, inheriting his mother's share of his grandfather's estate; how Abigail, his mother, after her father's death, probably accompanied by her brother Samuel, returned to keep the twenty-second anniversary of her marriage and her capture, with her widowed mother; how. though Deerfield records are silent concerning the interesting event, the parish priest of Boucherville, records the baptism there, of Marie Anne, her thirteenth child. All this is a twice told tale, and romantic enough to bear twice telling.

The following is a literal translation from the records at Boucherville, of the baptism of the little Marie Anne:

"On the 5th of November 1726. M. Meriel, Seminary Priest of Ville-Marie, in the presence of me the undersigned priest, *curé* of Boucherville, has baptized in the parish church of Sainte-Famille at
Boucherville, Marie Anne, daughter of Jacques Denoyons and Gabrielle Stebben married

and living at Boucherville, who was born on the 27th of February of the same year at Guerfil in New England. The godfather was Pierre Arrivée. . . . . .the godmother Gabrielle Denoyons wife of Nicolas Binet and sister of the infant. [Signed] Meriel Prêtre.

R. de la Saudraye,

Curé de Boucherville."

Samuel Stebbins probably remained in Deerfield. His name does not appear in Canada. Of his young brother Ebenezer, nothing has been found later than his baptism in Boucherville as Jacques Charles.

In General Hoyt's Antiquarian Researches we read that "A gentleman who recently resided in Montreal, stated that at the Lake of the Two Mountains, near the mouth of Grand River, he saw a French girl, who informed him that her grandmother was Thankful Stebbing, who was one of the captives taken from Deerfield in 1704."

Since the day of her capture we have had till now only this echo faintly sounding through the ages.

One October day, I had lingered long over the portrait of Bishop Plessis, in the sacristy of the parish church of Saint-Rochs, a suburb of Quebec. The sunset gun boomed from the citadel. Broad-hatted peasant women chattered noisily, as late from market they bumped along homeward in their quaint little carts. I was hurrying up the steep zigzags to the upper town, when I saw in a tailor's window, a pile of old pamphlets. Hoping to find among them some printed memorial of Plessis, I entered. "You are then a bibliophile?" was the eager question of the handsome young tailor in answer to my enquiry. Without waiting for my answer, he urged me to visit his private library, and I followed him to his dwelling above the shop, and was ushered into a long narrow room, with bare floor and no furniture but a common table and two wooden chairs. The back of the kitchen stove protruded through the wall at one end, the usual arrangement for heating two rooms in Canadian houses. At the opposite end a large window. The two long sides of the room, literally lined with the rarest books in choice editions, and elegant bindings. The pride of the young shopman in his books, and his delight at my surprise, were interesting. He flew from drawer to drawer, pulling out here a rare engraving, there an autograph. Finally he tossed me a ragged scrap of discolored paper. "What is it ?" I asked. "Oh, nothing much,—autographs," he said laconically. "Vaudreuil and Raudot, Governor-General and Intendant of Canada." The names were suggestive. The paper, dated Quebec, Oct. 30, 1706, proved to be the petition of certain English and Dutch in Canada for naturalization.   I ran my eye down the list:

Louis Marie Strafton, Pierre Augustin Litrefield Christine Otesse, Elizabet Price, Elizabeth Casse,

Mathias Claude Farnet, Madeline Ouarem, Thomas Hust, Marie Françoise French, Thérèse Stehen.

How many desolate homes these names recalled. Too well I knew them all, disguised as they were by their French names.

Amended the list would read: Charles Trafton of York, Me.

Matthew Farnsworth of Groton, Mass. Aaron Littlefield of Wells, Maine.

Grizel Warren and Margaret Otis, wife and child of Richard Otis, blacksmith, of Dover, N. H.

Thomas Hurst,	Elizabeth Price,
Freedom French,	Elizabeth Corse,
Thankful Stebbins.	

All of Deerfield.

Fancy these New England boys and girls, baby Otis and the rest of them, wrecked on a foreign strand by the storms of war, beseeching his Majesty, the High and Mighty Louis XIV, to be graciously pleased to grant them citizenship, declaring that they have established themselves in His colony of Canada, and that they wish to live and die in the Holy Roman Catholic faith. Much excited by my discovery, I sat there in the twilight and told the story of these captives to the little French tailor.

This was my first introduction to Thankful Stebbins, citi-zen of Canada, robbed of her Puritan name, member of the Apostolic church in good standing.

A year elapsed. I found her next at Boucherville in 1708, Thérèse already, and godmother to one of her sister Abigail's children. The record of her baptism not there, nor yet her marriage; neither at Boucherville, nor at Montreal, nor at

Quebec. Yet Thérèse she was, and a grandmother she was to be, (according to General Hoyt,) before my quest could cease.

On the parish register of Longueuil, the old Seigniory of Charles LeMoyne, stands the following:

February 4th, 1711, After the publication of the usual banns made at the mass in the church of La Sainte-Famille at Boucherville, on the 25th of January and the 1st and 2nd of February, to which no legal impediment has been found, I the undersigned, priest, *curé* of Boucherville, have married in the aforesaid parish church of Boucherville, Adrien grain, called La Vallée, inhabitant of chambly, aged 23 years, son of the deceased Charles le grain, and louyse la fortune living, inhabitant of Chambly to Thérèse louyse Stebens, aged 21 years, daughter of John Stebens and Dorothy Alexander his wife, inhabitants of the village of Guiervil in New England, and have given them the nuptial benediction in presence of Joseph Maillot, cousin of the groom, of Sieur Jacques de Noyon, brother-in- law of the bride, and others.

Thus at last Thankful Stebbins of Deerfield, our little pe-titioner for citizenship, having obtained her naturalization papers in 1710, under her new name of Thérèse Louise did "establish herself in His Majesty's colony of Canada," as the wife of Adrian le Grain, nicknamed La Vallée, *habitant* soldier of Chambly.

In my rambles among the records, there have been many red letter days, notably that at Chambly, in search of Thankful Stebbins, wife of Adrian Le Grain, bride in her 19th year and grandmother to be.

In the time schedules of suburban service on Canadian railways, the interest of the tourist is neglected. Properly enough, trains are run for the accommodation of the rustics, who must be in the city at early morn and out in the late afternoon. This prevents the student from looking up the parish records, even if he or she were bold enough to face the possibilities of a night in a Canadian village inn. However, the will makes the way, and one who is not too nice, may avail himself of a mixed train, heavy freight with a comfortless caboose attached, and crawl to his destination at the rate of six miles an hour, subject to tiresome waits at intervening stations.

However we go from village to village, up and down the noble river, we can never forget that we are treading the path once trodden by our footsore and sorrowing kinsfolk, listening to the same accents, that fell so strangely on the ears of the forlorn and homesick captives.

In 1665, the Marquis de Tracy arrived in Quebec as Lieutenant-General of Canada. The famous Carignan regiment had been given him by the king with orders to subdue or destroy the Iroquois. "The Mohawks and Oneidas were persistently hostile, making inroads into the colony by way of Lake Champlain and the Richelieu, murdering and scalping and then vanishing like ghosts."

Tracy immediately built a picket fort at the foot of the rapids of the Richelieu. Sorel, an officer of the Carignan, later built a second fort at the mouth of the river, where now is the town of Sorel ; and Salières, "colonel of the regiment, added a third fort two or three leagues above that at the rapids." No fort, however, could "bar the passage against the nimble and wily warriors who might pass them in the night, shouldering their canoes through the woods," and Tracy prepared to march in person against the Mohawks with all the force of Canada. This expedition against the Mohawks is the subject of one of Mr. Parkman's finest pictures, and, says that author, "was of all the French expeditions against the Iroquois the most productive of good." Tracy's work being done, four companies of the splendid regiment were left in garrison, and the Marquis with the rest of "the glittering *noblesse* in his train," went back to France. Many of the officers, however, weary of their life in the corrupt French court, and stimulated by promises and money from the king, who had the peopling of the colony much at heart, remained to marry and settle in Canada.

The lands along the Richelieu were allotted in large seigniorial grants among these officers, who in turn granted out the land to their soldiers. "The officer thus became a kind of feudal chief, and the whole settlement a permanent military cantonment.". . . . . ."The disbanded soldier was practically a soldier still, but he was also a farmer and a land-holder." Tracy's picketed fort below the rapids of the Richelieu, then known as Fort Pontchartrain, with the land adjacent, was awarded to Captain de Chambly. After his death the seigniory of Chambly passed to Marie de Thauvenet, his betrothed or his sister-in-law, through whom her husband, François Hertel "The Hero," father of Hertel de Rouville, became its owner, being known thereafter as Hertel de Chambly.

From that day to this, Chambly has been closely connected with our history. The fort was the point of departure and arrival for most of the expeditions against New England. Hardly a New England captive but was at some time sheltered within its walls.

On Saturday, probably March 25, 1704, Parson Williams'" of Deerfield says:

"We arrived near noon at Shamblee, a small village where is a garrison and fort of French soldiers. This village is about fifteen miles from Montreal. The French were very kind to me. A gentleman of the place took me into his house and to his table, and lodged me at night on a good feather bed. The Inhabitants and officers were very obliging to me the little time I stayed with them, and promised to write a letter to the governor in chief, to inform him of my passing down the river. Here I saw a girl taken from our town, and a young man, who informed me that the greater part of the captives were come in, and that two of my children were at Montreal."

Many of the Deerfield captives had reached Chambly three weeks before Mr. Williams's arrival. His son Stephen did not arrive there till the next August. There the French were kind to him. They gave him bread, which he had not tasted before .since his capture, and dressed his wounded feet;—and later, Hertel de Chambly tried to buy him from his savage master. Quentin Stockwell stayed four days at Chambly, and was kindly treated by the French, who gave him hasty pudding and milk with brandy, and bathed his frozen limbs with cold water. One young Frenchman gave the poor sufferer his own bed to lie on, tried to buy him, and went with him to Sorel, to protect him from abuse by the Indians.

Chambly was a village of but ten houses when Ben Waite and Stephen Jennings hurried through it, in agonizing search for their beloved ones, whom they found in the Indian lodges not far away.

I will not attempt to describe my feelings, as I walked alone through the village of Chambly on my way to the priest's. Aside from its associations, Chambly has a beauty of its own. A long line of Lombardy poplars defines the *côte* of Chambly, which with its low, red roofs and broadly overhanging eaves, goes straggling along the bend of the swift-flowing river. Opposite, two picturesque mountains, then gorgeous in their autumnal colors, complete the circle formed by the lake-like expanse, called Chambly Basin.

Half way round, the circle is broken by the river, which comes roaring and tumbling down, in a series of rapids, at the foot of which the ruins of the fort which in 1711 succeeded Tracy's palisade, advance boldly into the current.

The *curé* received me with a kindness which seems from the days of the captivity to have become habitual to the place, and I was soon absorbed in the records.

They begin in 1706, and on one of the first pages stands the baptism of Thankful Stebbins. The spelling and the grammar of the original would puzzle a schoolgirl of to-day. The following is a literal translation:

"This 23d of April 1707 I, Pierre Dublaron officiating in the parish of Chambly, certify that I have administered the rite of baptism to Louise Thérèse Stehen, English girl and baptized in England, (sic) Her godfather and godmother were Monsieur Hertel, Seigneur de Chambly and Madame de Perygny, wife of the commandant of the fort of Chambly."

[Signed]   Hertel de Chambly, Louise de Perygny.

As we have already seen, it was in February, 1711, that Thankful or Thérèse Louise Stebbins was married in the parish church of Boucherville to Adrian le Grain. In March, 1713, her first child Françoise Thérèse was baptized at Chambly. The child's godparents were Hertel de Beaulac and Thérèse, wife of Hertel de Niverville. In due succession follow William, Marie Jeanne, Marie, Charlotte, Isabelle, Antoine and Marie Thérèse. On the 4th of July, 1729, Véronique, the ninth and last child of Adrian le Grain and Louise Thérèse Stebbins, was born and baptized. Two children of Abigail Stebbins de Noyon[1] stood by their little cousin at her baptism, and just a week after followed Thankful Stebbins to her last resting place on earth. She was only thirty-eight years old when the end came.

My labors for her were finished. Listlessly turning the leaves of the register, I found the marriage of her brother, Joseph Stebbins, and learned from the *curé* that there are still in his parish descendants of Joseph, possibly also of Thankful. Fifty minutes to train time. Too little to prove my kinship to my new found cousins, if found. Enough perhaps to give me a nearer view of the old fort. Could I reach it ? Father Le Sage, glancing at the muddy road, at me, impeded by my weight, and my long skirts, prudently answers, "I have clone it in twenty minutes."

The cassock notwithstanding, thought I, and bade him a hasty adieu. The little children stared and the little dogs barked, as I flew through the town. Nor stopped I, nor stayed I. till trying a short cut to the fort, I crossed a swollen creek, on a shaky plank, and brought up breathless at a high picket fence, painted black and bearing the date 1707.

By a special Providence my. steps had been led to the ancient burying ground of the Seigniory. Wading through the wiry, brown grass, plunging into pitfalls, caught among the brambles and stumbling over hummocks and half buried fragments of old head-stones, I ran about the place. Would the grave give up its dead? Should I find here any of the lost ones of Deerfield?

No answer came to my eager question. Time and the annual overflow of the turbulent river, have levelled all the mounds. Here and there, a deeply furrowed slab of weathered oak, in form and color like the slates of our own old burying ground, totters to its fall, not a jot of its legend remaining.   Two gaunt wooden crosses, lately reared by the

reverent hand of the village antiquary, to whose zeal we owe also the preservation of the ruins of the fort, recall some noted names of the old Régime. Here lies Marie de Thauvenet, the fair devotee, who came with Mother Mary of the Incarnation to dedicate herself to the education of the Indian girls of Canada.

Turned from her purpose by the fascinations of a handsome young captain in the Carignan regiment, she became his betrothed. Bereft of her lover by death, so runs the tale, and inheriting his fortune, she became the lady of Chambly, which with her hand, she bestowed upon the hero, François Hertel.   Her romantic life ended here in 1708.

The other cross commemorates the death in 1740, of the wife of their son, Hertel de Beaulae.

Three or four small tablets of wood affixed above high water mark, to the fence posts of the enclosure, bear the names and date of death of French soldiers.

What gracious impulse had led the same kind hand to write there this name and date, unknown to fame:

Thérèse Stehen. 1729.

So I came to the last page of the story. Back and forth the shuttle flying had carried the thread weaving the web of her life. Deerfield to Chambly, Chambly to Boucherville and back again to Chambly. Warp and woof, in texture firm and colors bright and clear,—a tale so plain that the dullest might have followed it.

Carried in her thirteenth year by Hertel de Rouville, or one of his three young brothers, who marched with him to Deerfield, to the fort at Chambly in the Seigniory of their father, Thankful Stebbins was given in charge to one of the ladies of the Hertel family, and probably domiciled in the Hertel mansion.

Wr. J. F. Dion.

The seigniory was well stocked with sheep and cattle and the house was a good one. It brings us very near to the Old Régime in Canada, to remember that François Hertel the Hero, and Marie de Thauvenet, his wife, must have talked with the child and questioned her about her home and people. Unable to comprehend or pronounce her outlandish name, the family of the Seignior, perhaps induced by the similarity of the initial letters, called her Thérèse, after the wife of Hertel de Niverville. Becoming fond of the child, wishing to keep her in Canada and conscientiously believing that her salvation depended on her becoming a good Catholic, they put her name on the list of petitioners for naturalization in 1706.

The next year, Father Dublaron baptized her in the chapel of the fort, her godfather being either the Hero himself, or his son. Her godmother, Louise de Perygny, wife of the commandant of the fort, added her own name to that by which the girl was already well known in the neighborhood. We may fancy the feelings of the maiden of sixteen on that summer day of the same year, when she saw Mr. Sheldon, Nathaniel Brooks and Edward Allen of Deerfield, with seven more redeemed captives, escorted by young Hertel de Chambly and five French soldiers, set out from the fort for home. Standing on the very spot nearly two centuries later, I seemed to hear the plaintive voice of the girl pleading with the Captain, (Hertel de Chambly,) to let her go with them, and her bitter wailings when the boat put out from shore without her.

It was, perhaps, to spare her the recurrence of such scenes, that she was sent to Boucherville in 1708 to live with her sister Abigail. Here she gradually resigned herself to her lot.

Citizenship with all its privileges and penalties having been graciously accorded to her in 1710 by His Majesty, Louis XIV, she married the following year, Charles Adrian le Grain, *habitant* soldier of Chambly, returning there to live with him.

There I find her faithful friend Thérèse, wife of Hertel de Niverville, with Hertel de Beaulac[1] standing as sponsors to her first child, and there at the birth of her ninth child, she died in 1729. The spirit of the unredeemed captive, ransomed at last and safe in its eternal home, her dust lies there with that of the old *noblesse*, her friends and protectors.

Gentle breezes whisper softly among the grass that waves above the sod; the rapids of the Richelieu cease their angry roaring as they draw near the spot; and the beautiful river sings its sweetest cadence as it flows by the place where Thankful Stebbins sleeps.

'The frequent connection of the Hertel family with the Deerfield captives in Canada is interesting.

A SCION OF THE CHURCH IN DEERFIELD.JOSEPH-OCTAVE PLESSIS, FIRST ARCHBISHOP OF QUEBEC. Written for the Two Hundreth Anniversary of the founding of the Church in Deerfield.

The church in Deerfield, as in all our New England plantations, is coeval with the town. The plan of the eight thousand acre grant being laid before the General Court in 1665, was approved and allowed, "provided that they mayne-tayne ye ordinances of Christ there, once within five years. When in 1673, discouraged at the slow settlement of Pocumtuck, Samuel Hinsdell, Samson Frary and others, petitioned the General Court for liberty to cut loose from the mother town, and order all their own prudentiall affairs," permission was given them, "provided that an able and orthodox minister within three years be settled among them."

These requisites of ability and orthodoxy were easily found in the person of a Harvard graduate, young Samuel Mather of Dorchester, nephew of Increase, and cousin of Cotton Mather, the famous Boston preachers. "If God should

be provoked by the unthankfulness of men, to send the plague of an unlearned ministry on New England," writes Cotton Mather, "soon will the wild beasts of the desart live there, and the houses will be full of doleful creatures, and owls will dwell there."

This ancient town has never been stricken by the plague of an unlearned ministry. From Samuel Mather to the present day, her ministers have been able, and I venture to say, orthodox in the best sense of that word.

It is probable that the first gathering of the church in Deerfield was in the garrison house of Quentin Stockwell, where the boy-preacher boarded. This house stood on the site now occupied by the parsonage of the second church. Meeting-House Hill is named, in John Pynchon's account book, as early as 1673. From the same source, we learn that Worshipful John, who held much good land in Pocumtuck, paid there in 1675 a rate for the minister's house, and also for "ye little House for a Meeting house, that ya Meet in."

Years passed. Mr. John Williams, another youthful graduate of Harvard, was "encouraged" to turn his back upon the more alluring fields of the Bay settlements, and cast his lot among the pioneers of this frontier town, "to dispense the Blessed word of Truth unto them."

"Att a legall Town Meeting in Deerf^d, Oct. 30., 1694, Ensign John Sheldon Moderator that there shall be a meeting house Built in deerfield, upon the Town charge voted affirmatively: That there shal be a comitty chosen and impowered to agree with workmen to begin said building forthwith, and carry it on fast as may be: voted affirmatively

That ye meetinghouse shal be built ye bigness of Hatfield meeting house, only ye height to be left to ye judgment and determination of ye comitty voted affirmatively." . . . .We cannot too often rebuild the little hamlet as it was on that Sunday morning in February, when for the last time,

the faithful shepherd gathered his whole flock within the fold. North of Meeting-House Hill, on the west side of the street, lived Daniel Beldingon the old Stebbins place. John Stebbins's lot was the home of Lieut, and Deacon David Hoyt; I know not which of his titles to put first, as both were then of equal value to the little community. Ebenezer Brooks then held the homestead of the Deerfield Antiquary. On the east, John Stebbins and his good wife Dorothy, dwelt on what we know as the David Sheldon place. Martin Kellogg was their next neighbor. On the knoll now occupied by Mrs. Allen, lived Hannah Beaman, ever to be remembered as the good school dame of the early settlement, and a generous benefactor of the town. At the south, was the picketed house of Lieut. Jonathan Wells, the boy hero, whose valor in the Falls Fight made his name illustrious. Philip Mattoon's family lived on Airs. George Wells's lot, and the widow Smead, in the old house still standing opposite Mrs. Elizabeth W. Champney's. These, and many others equally worthy of remembrance, lived outside the stockade.

The fortification enclosed the whole of Meeting-House Hill, including the present sites of both churches. Towards the northwest corner of the palisade, was the well-built house of Ensign John Sheldon, the "Old Indian House" of our childhood.

Where Lincoln Wells's homestead is now, stood the dwelling of Benoni Stebbins, forever to be venerated as the spot where he, and six other brave men, nobly aided by the women, "stood stoutly to y'r armes. . . . . .with more than ordinary couridge," says an eye witness of that dreadful day.

As our school books mistake the old Indian House for the home of the Rev. John Williams, it is well that Deerfield children should be reminded that Parson Williams lived next south of Benoni Stebbins. The well that stood in his yard just west of the present Academy, is still in use. From the minister's to Mehuman Hinsdell's, there were no houses except perhaps a few rude structures, built for those families who, having homes outside, fled for shelter within the palisades in time of danger. The lot next south of Hinsdell's was held by Mr. John Richards, schoolmaster. Opposite, was old Godfrey Nims's; and next at the north, Samson Frary built the house in 1698 which is still standing. Nims and Frary were two of the first three settlers in Deerfield. Next north of Samson Frary lived Mr. John Catlin. His son-in-law, Thomas French, on the lot adjoining, now owned by the Second Church. In the northeast corner of the stockade, was Samuel Carter's house.

Equidistant from the houses of Benoni Stebbins and Ensign Sheldon, a few rods northwest of the soldiers' monument, stood the meeting house, a square, two-story building, with pyramidal roof surmounted by a turret, tipped with a weather-cock. In the front was a low, wide door, with a broad window on either side, and corresponding windows above from the galleries.

Sunday morning, Feb. 27, 1703-4 dawned bright and fair. One of those severe storms, which are so often the immediate forerunner of the breaking up of winter, had covered the ground with snow, to the depth of three feet on a level. A "sort of house" which Benjamin Munn had dug out and boarded over as a shelter for his family, in Mr. Richards's hillside, was hidden by the drifts. A little rain, and a gusty night had followed, a hard and glittering crust had formed, and the dead twigs lay scattered far and wide over its surface. Yet there was cheer in the air and sky, and though the mountain loomed black against the horizon, that tender

flush that shows the stir of the sap in every bush seemed to soften its outline. The brooks babbled joyously through the ice-bound swamps. The shrill crowing of cocks echoed from neighboring barn yards. The crows screamed noisily from the bare branches, as they wheeled from tree to tree in the meadows. There was spring in the air and in the hearts of the people as, at beat of drum, they slowly and decorously wended their way to meeting. Climbing the hill from both ends of the town plat, they passed through the gates of the palisade, and filing silently into the meeting house took their allotted places on the long wooden benches. At the right of the preacher are the men: first the town officers and aged men who have formerly served in that capacity; then those who hold any military rank. Behind them such as are known in the community as "Mr." or "Dr.," and finally all the rest of the men, with due regard to age, estate and place. Their wives occupy corresponding seats on the left of the broad aisle. The young men and maidens go quietly by separate stairs to the gallery, where a high railing separates them. They look down with curiosity, and perhaps envy, upon the three young couples lately joined in holy wedlock, who shyly pass up the broad aisle, to rear seats in the body of the meeting-house, to which marriage has promoted them. A sense of strangeness, and a half homesick longing for the old Chicopee meeting-house, lends a shade of sadness to the face of Hannah Chapin, but a glance from her manly husband, young John Sheldon, reassures her. Elizabeth Price shows a consciousness of having somewhat outraged public opinion by her marriage with "the Indian." Abigail Stebbins has a self-complacent air, mingled with pride and satisfaction, which stings the heart of many a youth in the gallery,—while her husband, Jacques de Noyon, bears himself with an air of saucy superiority and triumph, and evidently submits with ill grace to the tedious solemnities of the Puritan Sabbath. The boys are ranged on benches against the walls under the windows; the little children on the floor near their mothers. Below the pulpit and raised some steps above the floor, on a long bench facing the congregation, sit the two deacons, Lieut. David Hoyt and Ensign John Sheldon. The garrison soldiers are seated near the great door with bandoliers on shoulder and matchlocks close at hand. The seats were hard, the service long, the meetinghouse cold and gloomy, but the piety of our fathers was fervid,—and warmed and comforted, the people dispersed.

Among the dignitaries on the foremost seats of the meeting-house that day, were Mr. John Catlin and his daughter's husband, Thomas French, the town clerk.

Mr. John Catlin, born in Weathersfield, Conn., in 1643, and married there at the age of twenty-four, to Mary, daughter of Joseph Baldwin, had been an early settler at Branford, Conn., whence he removed to Newark, N. J. He was a leading man in church and town affairs in Branford and Newark. He stands on Newark records in 1678 as "Town's Attorney," and is spoken of as "an honest brother to take care that all town orders be executed, and if a breach occurs to punish the offender." He was one of the selectmen of Newark from 1676 to 1681. In 1683 he was in Hartford, where, the same year, his oldest daughter, Mary Catlin, married Thomas, son of John French, formerly of Rehoboth, Mass., but then of Northampton.

Thomas French and his father-in-law, John Catlin, probably came together to Deerfield in 1683, French settling on the Quentin Stockwell place which his father had bought some years before, and Catlin, on the next lot south. Catlin's dignity, services and influence, soon gave him the honorable title of "Mr." among his fellow-townsmen, and as before in Branford and Newark, he was in Deerfield a trusted leader in public affairs.

French, a blacksmith by trade, at once built a shop, and set up his anvil by the roadside in front of his house. The industry and morality of Thomas French gave him the respect of his neighbors, and from the beginning he served them in responsible positions. Sometimes as hayward, sometimes as corporal of the guard: on committees for building and seating the meeting-house, and for hiring a schoolmaster: for measuring the common fence, and laying out to every man his due proportion of the expense, and for fortifying Meeting-house Hill. His name appears in 1688, as one of the first selectmen chosen by the town. To this office he was repeatedly re-elected.

Encouraged by the news that the Prince of Orange had landed in England, the people rose in their might against Sir Edmund Andros. He was thrown into prison. A Council of Safety, headed by old Simon Bradstreet, was elected. A convention of delegates was summoned from the several towns of Massachusetts to assemble in Boston, on the 22d of May, 1689, to deliberate upon the future government of New England. There is no town record of any meeting in Deerfield in response to this summons. In the Massachusetts Archives the following paper may be found:

"Deerfield, May 17. 1689

John Sheldon,
Benj. Hastings,
Benoni Stebbins,   Selectmen."
Thomas French,

We, the Town of Deerfield, complying with the desire of the present Counsell of Safety, to choose one among us as a representa-tive to send down, to signify our minds and concurrance with the Counsell for establishing of the government, have chosen and deputed Lieutenant Thomas Wells, and signified to him our minds for the proceeding to the settlement of the government as hath been signified to us from the Honorable Counsell of Safety, and those other Representatives. [Signed]

The part played by Thomas French and his associates on this occasion, shows them to have been shrewd diploma-tists and fearless patriots. However justifiable, this was a revolution. If unsuccessful, the result would be for Thomas Wells, who held his commission from Andros, trial and punishment for treason. For John Sheldon, Benjamin Hastings, Benoni Stebbins and Thomas French, the severest penalties that a vindictive governor could inflict upon the leaders of a rebellion. The names of Thomas French and the others who did not hesitate to assume this grave responsibility for the town, must be forever honored.

At a Town meeting held "March ı 1694-5 Joseph Barnard was chosen Town Clerk for the year Ensuing"

"Sept. 17, 1695 Thomas ffrench was chosen Town Clerk"

Between these entries made by the two men respectively, he who runs may read the tragedy known in the annals of Deerfield as the Massacre at Indian Bridge. The births of a son and four daughters to Thomas and Mary Catlin French, had been duly registered by Joseph Barnard. When his hand was stilled in death by a shot from the skulking foe, Thomas French took up the pen and wrote the following:

"Abigail, daughter to Thomas and Mary ffrench was born ffeb. 28 1697-8"

"Jerusha and Jemima twins,—daughters To M^r Jn° and Mrs. Eunice Williams were Born Sept. 3, 1701.

Jerusha (2nd) Daughter To M^r Jn° and M^{r}s Eunice Williams, was Born January 15, 1703-4.

Jn° son to Thomas and Mary ffrench was born ffeb. 1 1703-4[1]

This is the last line of the town records written by Thomas French. Minutes of a town meeting held late in April instead of in March that year; the election of a few town officers,—notably of a new town clerk; the following and

'From the Town Records of Deerfield,

similar entries in a new handwriting- upon the town book,— these are all the record left by the afflicted people of Deerfield of the sorrows that befell them on the 29th of Feb., 1703-4.

"jerusha Williams Daughter to M^r Jn° & M^{r}s Eunice Williams was flain y° 29 of ffebruary 1703

Mrs Eunis Williams wife to M^r Jn° Williams head of y° Family was flain by ye enemi March 1 1704

Jn° ffrench fon to Thomas and Mary ffrench was fliyn by ye Enemy ffebruary 29, 1703-4

Mary ffrench Wife to Thomas ffrench head of this Family was flain by ye Enimie March 9 1703-4[1]

Our fathers were men of few words, and of stern endurance. They believed that their sufferings were the result of their sins, and that with wise and beneficent purpose, did God chastise them. To Him alone they poured forth their souls,—never in complaint, but ever in prayer that they "might be prepared to sanctify and honor Him in what way so ever He should come forth towards them"—and "have grace to glorify His name whether in life or death." More eloquent than speech is their silence in relation to the "awful desolations of that day."

Not long before break of day the enemy came in like a flood upon them. Pouring over the palisade the frightful tide swept on, overwhelming with destruction all that lay in its path. The morning dawned on a scene of horror. Sharing the fate of many of his neighbors, Mr. John Catlin with his son Jonathan lay dead among the smoking embers of their ruined home. The house of

Thomas French was gutted but not burned, and the town records escaped unharmed. The meeting-house that so lately had echoed with psalm and prayer, now resounded with groans of anguish. There lay the captives, ignorant of the fate of friends and kindred.

'From the Town Records of Deerfield.

There too, stretched upon the hard benches, were the enemy's wounded. There, Hertel de Rouville himself, smarting under his hurt, rushed in for a moment to cheer his wounded brother, to whom he whispered curses on the savage horde who had broken their promise to him that they would fight like civilized Frenchmen.

There were those whom we saw but late, so proud and happy. Hannah Chapin tense with anxiety, eagerly listening for every sound, while her husband, young John Sheldon, to whom love lent wings, was flying for aid to Hatfield. Elizabeth Price mute with woe, for Andrew, the Indian, had been slain at her side. Abigail Stebbins, not utterly cast down, for De Noyon, her father and mother, and sisters and brothers were all with her, and De Noyon had told her that his home was near Montreal, and that they would soon be released. There too, bound hand and foot was Thomas French with his wife, Mary Catlin, and their five eldest children. A few hours completed the devastation. The sun as it rose above the mountain, looked down on a dreadful sight. The main body of the enemy with their sorrowful captives had left the town. A few loth to cease their wanton pillage still lingered, and in the house of Benoni Stebbins, around his dead body, Lieutenant (Deacon) David Hoyt, and Joseph Catlin, with four other valiant men still kept at bay the Macqua chief and his followers.

Roused by the hoarse cries of young John Sheldon, as he sped on bare and bleeding feet through the hamlets below, thirty men on horseback, guided by the light of the burning village, were riding fast to the rescue. As they entered the stockade the foe fled precipitately from the north gate, across the frozen meadows to the northwest, reaching the river at the Red Rocks.

Capt. Wells at once took command of the rescuing party, reinforced by fifteen of his neighbors and five garrison soldiers, and instantly followed up the enemy. "Bravely but rashly and without order," I quote from Mr. Sheldon, "the pursuers rush on, intent only on avenging their slaughtered friends. As they warm up to the fight, they throw off gloves, coats, hats, waistcoats, neck cloths. Capt. Wells cannot control the headlong chase. He sees the danger and orders a halt, the order is unheeded, and the foe is followed recklessly into the inevitable ambuscade."

Meanwhile on Meeting-house Hill, the scanty remnant of the townsfolk, cautiously creep out from their hiding places, and gather in knots seeking for tidings. As the dreadful tale is told, they know not whether most to rejoice or to la-ment that they have been left behind. Among them is Mary Baldwin Catlin. While waiting with her children, and children's children, the order to march into captivity she had as was her habit, ministered to the needs, and soothed the sorrows of her friends and neighbors. Nor had she turned a deaf ear to the cry of her enemy for help. With the tender sympathy of a Christian woman, she had held the cup of cold water to the parched lips of the wounded French lieutenant, craving it with piteous appeal. In the hurry of departure, either by design, or by accident, none had claimed her as his captive. Her neighbors look upon her as one suddenly risen from the dead. They go with her to her desolated home, where she learns the fate of her husband, and of her second son. They find her little grandson, baby John French, dead on the threshold of his father's empty house. When someone says that Captain Wells has been repulsed, and that Joseph Catlin, her eldest son, has fallen in the meadow fight, her heart breaks. A Rachel, mourning for her children, and would not be comforted, she lingered a few weeks, and died from the shock of that day's horror.

On the 9th of March, Mary Catlin, wife of Thomas French, was killed on the retreat to Canada. Her husband with all

their surviving children, Mary aged seventeen, Thomas four-teen, Freedom eleven, Martha, eight and Abigail six, were carried to Montreal.

Mary French and her brother Thomas, with their father, were brought back to Deerfield in 1706 by Ensign John Sheldon, in his second expedition to Canada for the redemption of the captives. An interesting evidence of the proneness of Deerfield maidens to versifying, exists in a poem said to have been written by Mary French to a younger sister during their captivity, in the fear lest the latter might become a Romanist. Soon after his return, Thomas French was made Deacon of the church in Deerfield in place of Deacon David Hoyt, who had died of starvation at Coos on the march to Canada. In 1709, Deacon French married the widow of Benoni Stebbins. He died in 1733 at the age of seventy six, respected and regretted as an honest and useful man and a pillar of the church and state.

To his great grief all efforts for the redemption of his three daughters had failed. On her arrival in Canada, Freedom was placed in the family of a French merchant in Montreal, and in 1706 was baptized as Marie Françoise, the Puri-tanic name by which she had been known in Deerfield, being thus forever set aside. In 1713, she married Jean Daveluy of the village of St. Lambert, and thus became the ancestress of many French Canadian families of excellent repute.

Martha French was given by her Indian captors to the Sisters of the Congrégation de Notre Dame at Montreal. In 1707, she was baptized, *sous condition,* receiving from her god-mother the name of Marguerite. At the age of sixteen, she was married to Jacques Roi, also of St. Lambert. Marie Françoise French was present at her sister's wedding, and the autographs of the two sisters on the marriage register, are as clear to-day as when first written. The names of the bride's parents are given in full and Thomas French is called *"clerc ou notaire de Dicrfilde"* in New England.

BIOGRAPHICAL SKETCH OF JOSEPH-OCTAVE PLESSIS.

On the third of May, 1733, just one month from the day of her father's death in Deerfield, Martha Marguerite French, widow of Jacques Roi, signed her second marriage contract, and the following day married Jean Louis Ménard, at St. Laurent, a parish of Montreal. Nineteen years later, her daughter Louise Menard, was married at Montreal to Joseph-Amable Plessis called Belair.

The ancestor of Plessis, the first of the name in Canada, emigrating from Metz in Lorraine in the beginning of the eighteenth century, took up his abode in the outskirts of Montreal. There he, and his son after him, carried on the trade of tanning, and the place to this clay is known as "The Tanneries of Belair." At Montreal on the 3rd of March, 1763, Joseph-Octave, son of Joseph-

Amable Plessis and Louise Ménard, grandson of Martha and great-grandson of Deacon Thomas French, was born.

The boy was fortunate in his parentage. His father and mother cultivated the old fashioned virtues of simplicity, honesty and devoutness. His father was a blacksmith, so-called. Near one of the city gates, Joseph-Amable Plessis had a large shop, where he made axes, hammers, hinges, and all the iron implements in use in a new country. He had many apprentices and was chiefly occupied in making hatchets for trade with the savages. Discipline, industry and system reigned over his workshop. Irregularity, idleness and disorder he would not tolerate. The work of the forge for the year, was planned in advance, and the order never changed. A devout Catholic, determined to secure for himself and his *employes* a faithful observance of the fasts of his church, he humanely and with good business foresight, adapted his work to the conditions. In the Lenten season the heavy hammers of the forge were silent and the men took up the lighter labor of sharpening and polishing the axes that had been made in the autumn and winter and stored away unfinished. Once a month the father sent his sons and apprentices to the parish priest for confession. The mother took care that the religious duties of her daugh-ters and domestics were duly performed. On Sundays and *fete* days the whole household went together to the parish church. The children were taught reading and their first catechism by the mother, who also trained them in habits of economy and order.

From the teaching and example of such parents, Joseph Octave Plessis learned early to love labor, to be diligent, to be orderly and economical in the arrangement of his time and affairs, firm in self-discipline, and honest and upright in his dealings. Though by nature merry and gay, the boy was thoughtful and dignified beyond his years, and soon showed such a desire to learn that his parents put him in a primary school, founded by the gentlemen of the Seminary of Saint-Sulpice. Here, Joseph made such progress that he was soon promoted to a Latin School kept in the old Château Vaudreuil. Here he tried the patience of good father Curateau by his dulness in his Latin grammar which he hated, though he showed a fondness for Geography, History and Literature.

At the end of the first half of his course at the Latin school, he astonished his father one morning, by the announcement that he was disgusted with study, and that he would much rather stay at home than take up logic and metaphysics. The conduct of the father on this occasion, shows him to have been a remarkable man. Without the least intention
of permitting the shipwreck of the boy's intellectual career, he had too much sense to oppose or argue with him. "Very well, my son," he replied, "take off your scholar's gown, put on one of the boy's aprons, and go into the shop. There is work enough there to keep you busy. When you wish to go back to your books let me know." To the lad, his father's word was law, and with a heavy heart, he went his way to the shop, where he worked pluckily for a week, though every bone in his little body ached with the unusual fatigue. Then without a word of complaint he threw off his apron, donned his *capote* and marched back to school, a wiser and a happier boy.

At fifteen, with his brother and one or two comrades, he was sent to the Seminary in Quebec, which then offered greater advantages than that of Montreal. Communication between the two cities was difficult and infrequent. The choice lay between a schooner, which could not always be had, and a wagon, which was too expensive. Such was the delay and uncertainty, that it often happened that the little fellows would not reach their homes in Montreal till vacation was ended. Every year the Grand Vicar wrote from Montreal to the Bishop of Quebec, "The Montreal boys cannot be in Quebec at the opening of the course." Sometimes the more spirited boys took the matter into their own hands, and set out on foot for home at the beginning of the holidays. Picture Joseph-Octave and his friends ready for an early start on a fine summer morning. In the uniform of the Seminary boy, a long, black frock coat, many seamed and welted with white; a green sash ; a flat-topped cloth cap, with broad leather visor,—each boy with his little deerskin pack between his shoulders. First to the chapel for prayers to the protectress of pilgrims, thence to the court yard of the Seminary, where, surrounded by a crowd of their fellows, they cheer the time-honored walls.   Pouring through

the great gate, they run joyously down the steep hill, to the river, and following it to the west, singing gay *chansons* as they go, they soon reach the open country. At sunset they seek the nearest farmhouse, sure of a kindly welcome. The best room with its plain deal chairs and settle, its clumsy stove, and its bare floor with rag mats, is thrown open for them to rest in. Camping at night on the new-mown hay in the long barn, they rise at dawn to a breakfast of omelettes and black bread. The generous lads fling down a handful of coppers to the *habitant's* wife, but she is not to be outdone in courtesy, *"Non, non messieurs"* she is too glad to give her best to the young gentlemen of the Seminary, and off they start again followed by her blessing and her prayers.

The career of Joseph-Octave Plessis at the Seminary of Quebec, is thus summed up by one who knew him well : "Study had no difficulties that he did not level, nothing distasteful for which he did not conquer his disrelish, no obstacles that he did not overcome." Though this may be exaggerated praise, it is certain that Joseph was an intelligent, industrious and ambitious pupil, respected by his comrades and beloved by his teachers.

Born at the most critical period in the history of Canada, at the time of its cession to the English, this serious and thoughtful boy reflected much upon how he could best serve his country. Two careers were open to him ; the bar and the church. The former meant the delights of the world, a home, wife, children, wealth, the adulation of friends, office, success. The latter, a solitary life with its austerities, its poverty, and its possible compensations to an exalted nature.

At the age of seventeen Joseph decided to become a priest. It is not likely that the youth comprehended the greatness of the sacrifice, which, later, a man of his temperament must inevitably have realized. Having received the tonsure from Bishop Briand, who had watched his development with a fatherly interest, he was sent to the college of Montreal to teach till he could take orders. Though qualified in other respects for the place, young Plessis found to his great mortification, that two of his pupils were ahead of him in Latin. Nothing daunted, however, he set to work, and in two weeks mastered the Latin grammar so that forty years after he could repeat pages of it verbatim. We have here the key to his future success. Indomitable will, genuineness, willingness to work. His pupils soon learned to respect him. Such a teacher will always be respected. He became so fond of his profession, that to the last day of his life, in the midst of his most brilliant successes, he did not cease to regret that he had given it up. From this time he became fond of the. old Latin writers, and liked to recite many of the odes of Horace. In 1783, though still too young to take orders, he was called by Bishop Briand to be Secretary of the diocese of Quebec. The duties of this office, in a diocese extending from New Orleans to the coast of Labrador, were complicated and onerous. The Bishop himself was ill. His coadjutor, Mgr. D'Esgly, lived at a distance and was, moreover, aged and infirm. Plessis's prudence and good judgment, with the business-like habits to which he had been trained, made him equal to his task. He lived with the Bishop, venerated him as a father, and was beloved and trusted as a son. The Bishop had been a careful student of men and affairs. He talked earnestly with his secretary about the causes that had led to the fall of the French dominion in Canada and analyzed with him the character of the men who had held the reins of government at the time of the cession. It is safe to say, that the affectionate intercourse between the good Bishop and his secretary, was the foundation of the distinction finally attained by the latter.

At the age of twenty-three, Plessis was ordained priest, and six years later, while still fulfilling the duties of secretary, he was made *cure* of Quebec. Nothing is more trying than to become the successor in office of one who has been long considered as the embodiment of fitness and nobility in his position. Monsieur Hubert, the predecessor of Plessis, was the idol of his parish. His fine intellect and physical beauty, with the added charm of an affable manner, gentleness and consideration for others, had endeared him to all classes. Plessis, in these trying circumstances, behaved with credit to himself and to the satisfaction of all. His labors at this time were very severe. He rose at four in the morning, and rarely went to bed before midnight. This short rest was often disturbed by his duties as *curé*, which called him to the sick and dying. Eager in the pursuit of knowledge, he resolutely devoted one whole night of every week to study. His youth and good health at first upheld him, but after three or four months of it, he found himself so sleepy the next day that he gained nothing by the practice, and wisely gave it up.

The youth of his parish were his tender care. He never lost sight of them, but watched their conduct, and gave them good advice as they grew up. To those who were too fond of dancing, he liked to quote the words of Saint Francis de Sales,—"I say about balls, what the doctors say about mushrooms,—the best of them are good for nothing." Education occupied much of his thought, particularly that of the working classes. He founded schools in the suburbs of Quebec, chose the masters, and personally supervised the classes. When he found an especially bright child, he urged the parents to send it to college, and if poverty was pleaded as excuse, his own scanty purse supplied the means. He took one child into his own house and himself taught him for a year and a half. In a letter to a friend, he speaks of this boy with fond praise, and encloses with pride a *"rondeau* composed by my Rémi" as he affectionately calls him. He sent him to college, but after finishing his studies, the young man was unwilling to enter the church for which his benefactor had destined him, and the good *curé* generously made it easy for him to study law. He became afterwards Chief Justice of Lower Canada.

The first state paper of Plessis upholds parochial schools against a proposition by the government to establish a mixed college on equal terms for Protestants and Catholics. Plessis sees in this a blow aimed at the French language and religion; asks what place the Catholic Bishop of Quebec is to hold in the proposed institution; reminds the administration that the Jesuits had already a good college, where the boys are taught reading, writing and arithmetic,— and with keen satire, expresses his surprise that a government so zealous for the education of Canadian youth should have appropriated this building for its Bureau of Archives.

As a preacher Msgr. Plessis lacked that personal magnet-ism which touches and captivates an audience. His language was simple, his manner earnest. He was not a brill-iant orator, though in many of his occasional sermons he rises to eloquence, as in that on Nelson's Victory of the Nile. As an example of his energy, he mastered English in a few months, in order to keep within his fold some English Catholic families of his parish. He sometimes preached in English, but he never pronounced it well.

I will not detail the steps by which Martha French's grandson rose from being choir boy in the cathedral of Montreal, to become Bishop of the vast diocese of Quebec. In thanking a friend who wished him joy and peace in his new office, M. Plessis replied, "It remains to be seen whether the happiness of a Bishop on earth is anything but a series of difficulties and crosses by which he may be fitted for eternal glory." He saw the struggle that was before him. A weaker man would have shrunk from the contest. He nerved himself to meet it, and his foresight and prudence, his moderation and candor, his forbearance and self-control, his intelligence and his courage,—carried him safely and triumphantly through, and made him and his cause respected by all. To understand his position we must go back a little.

The treaty of 1763, nominally secured to the French Canadians the free exercise of their religion, and to the clergy, their customary dues and rights from the Catholic people of Canada. So long as both parties desired to maintain a good understanding and friendly relations with one another; so long as the French Catholic Bishop was moderate in his de-mands, and loyal to the king; so long as the English Protestant Governor was conciliatory, and disposed to allow the French reasonable freedom in the exercise of their religion, all was well. This had been the state of affairs between Bishop Briand and Sir Guy Carleton. Indeed the latter, in 1775, publicly declared that the preservation of the province of Quebec to Great Britain was due to the loyalty of the Roman Catholic clergy; and the Bishop was left undisturbed in his ancient prerogative of creating parishes and appointing *cures.* The two Bishops after Briand had enjoyed the same liberty unchallenged. On the election of Monseigneur Denaut as Bishop, Governor Prescott asked that a list of the *care's* appointed during the year should be annually sent him, in order that he might render an account to the minister, if necessary. In preferring this request, he assured the Bishop that he would be left free to act in all other matters. All the Bishops since the cession as before, in their private letters and public documents, had very properly signed themselves Bishops of Quebec. In the meantime, however, Dr. Mountain arrived in Quebec with his commission from the king as Bishop of the Anglican church of Quebec. Still the Catholic Bishop continued to issue his letters and circulars as Bishop of Quebec. The clouds began to gather. The anti-Catholic faction which had always existed in the colonial government, but had heretofore been held in abeyance by the harmony existing between the Governor and the Bishop, began to act more openly. We have seen the specious project of a mixed college, involving the right to seize the property of the Jesuits and Sulpitians, and to put all the educational interests of a Catholic population of two hundred thousand souls into the hands of a Protestant board of directors, with the Anglican Bishop at the head.

The most bitter of the anti-Catholic faction was Ryland, the Governor's secretary, who did not hesitate to avow his contempt and detestation of that religion. In a letter written in 1804, he declared his belief that Catholicism could be annihilated in Canada within ten years, and the king's supremacy established. In Plessis, as the defender of the rights of French Canadians, Ryland recognized a formidable antagonist, and tried by intrigue with the home government, to overthrow and degrade him. The Attorney-General Sewall shared Ryland's feeling, and pronounced a decision in the courts that the government had the sole right of creating parishes and of electing *cure's;* that all those created since 1763, were null and void, and that such a thing as a Roman Catholic bishop of Quebec did not exist. The Lord-Bishop, after tendering his resignation, on the plea that the right to elect curates was denied him, that the superintendent of the Romish church publicly assumed the title of Bishop of Quebec, while at the same time the said superintendent and his clergy took special care not to give him this title, set out for England to lay his complaints before the king.

This was the state of affairs when in 1806, Plessis became Bishop of Quebec. Fortunately the Lieutenant-Governor, then acting Governor and a devoted adherent of the English

church and its Bishop, was also in England, and though Ryland did all he could to prevent Plessis from being allowed to style himself Bishop of Quebec in taking the oath of fidel-ity to the king, the chief councillor in charge of affairs in the Governor's absence, admitted the oath. Plessis fully understood the situation. He had always seen, as few had, how easy it would be for a tyrannical colonial government to evade that clause of the treaty, permitting to the Canadians the free enjoyment of their religion. He felt, too, that that clause had been nullified by Parliament in the act of 1774. The destiny of the Catholic church in Canada was committed to his hands. There were rocks on either side. The helm must be firmly grasped, the ship steered straight. Single-handed he must fight against three of its most bitter enemies. Tact, caution, discretion, patience, self-control, firmness,—these must be his weapons. Towards the last of his life he said to one of his vicars involved in ecclesiastical strife, "Foolish speeches are for those who make them. Do not let their bad conduct vex you. Continue to act with charity and forbearance. In every contention, happy is he who knows how to keep good behavior on his side." This was the lesson he had learned in his long struggle.

During the ten years' contest between the officers of the crown and Plessis, he was often summoned to discussion with them concerning the king's prerogative. In his arguments, one hears now a Roger Williams, advocating obedience to the higher law,—and then the civil service reformer, opposing bribery and corruption in politics, and demanding the complete separation of church and state. Inflexible as Laval in maintaining the supremacy of the church, his methods were better. Laval was bigoted and imperious; Plessis, liberal and conciliatory. Aggression was the mission of the former, mediation of the latter. In these disputes with the Governor and Council, he never lost his temper, and only once does he allude to his personal feelings. At the end of a long discussion with Craig, he says, "It has been the principle of my life to support the government in every way that I can conscientiously do so. No one is more loyal, more obedient to the law of the land than I am, and having done as much as my predecessors for the service of the government, I hoped that the government would not treat me worse than it had treated them."

To efface the bad impression left by Craig upon the minds of the French Canadians, Sir George Prévost, a man of very different stamp, was made his successor. Doubtless instructed to adopt a conciliatory policy toward the French, educated by the mistakes of his predecessor in office, and perhaps believing that the time had come, when a slight concession from the Bishop would forever settle the vexed question of supremacy, the new Governor, as Plessis was about to depart for the missions of the Gulf, addressed him as follows: "I have received despatches from England. The govern-ment desires to place you on a more respectable footing, but it is expected that you yourself will name the conditions. Let me have your ideas on this subject before your depart-ure. We must provide for everything and have a good understanding."

Plessis had remained unmoved by the intrigues of Ryland and the threats of Craig. Temptation came to him now in a new form. It would have been easy for a man of weaker principles to have persuaded himself that he had borne and foregone enough; that he had stood long enough in the breach ; that with a Governor as well disposed as Sir George Prévost, a merely nominal surrender would secure to himself all the honors, privileges and emoluments of his position; that he had earned the right to ease and repose, and might now claim the reward of his services. But Bishop Plessis was not the man to shirk responsibility for the present upon the future. His fidelity to what he believed right was uncompromising. As if to fortify himself at the outset against the sophistry of such arguments, he wrote to the Governor: "I shall have the honor to send your Lordship a statement of my views, but I must declare in advance that no temporal offer will induce me to renounce any part of my spiritual jurisdiction. It is not mine to make way with. I hold it as a sacred trust of which I must render an account."

The memorial that follows defining the position and rights of the Catholic Bishops of Quebec, past, present and future, is a masterpiece of good sense, sound reasoning, candor and justice.

During the Bishop's absence at the missions of the gulf, the war of 1812 broke out. On his return to Quebec he found all Canada in a state of great excitement. The government had been forced to appeal to the Canadians, the same Canadians whom Ryland and his friends had chosen to represent as continually on the eve of revolt, for aid to resist the entrance into Canada of American troops. The French Canadians responded nobly to the Governor's appeal. This was Plessis' supreme moment; Mandements, addresses, circulars, pastoral letters fly fast from his pen. Letters to the people at home and in the ranks; letters of comfort to the women and children temporarily bereft of husbands and fathers in their country's service; letters to the militia, exhorting them to loyalty, patriotism and piety; letters to his *cure's,* thanking and encouraging them to stand by the government. Circulars and mandements providing not only for the immediate wants of those left behind, but for possible famine in the future in consequence of fields unfilled and harvests ungathered in time of war.

Full recognition of the Bishop's services was made by Sir George Prévost to the home government, and in 1813, the Prince Regent in the name of the king decreed to the Bishop of Quebec an allowance of £1000 per annum, as a testimony to his loyalty and good conduct. Plessis had his private satisfaction from his opponents if he desired it, when Ryland as clerk of the Executive Council had to name him as Bishop of Quebec.

His triumph was complete when in 1817, he was appointed by the crown a member of the Legislative Council of Canada.

To this hasty sketch of his public career let me add a glimpse of the private life of this remarkable man. Though short in stature, he was of commanding presence. His fine head was well set on his broad shoulders. His forehead was noble, his eyes dark and piercing. His mouth was firm and decided, but his expression was kindly. In his face, as in his character, are many traits of striking resemblance to some of his race whom we have known in Deerfield. Beneath his grave exterior was a fund of gayety that won him the love of children and youth. A clerical friend remembers having been carried when a child of five to see the great Bishop, who took him on his lap saying, "Come now, sing to me,—sing me all your little songs." On his visits to college and convent, the pupils gathered freely about him. He told them stories and taught them the games and songs of his boyhood. Affectionate and sensitive, he was equally suscep-tible to kindness and injury, and easily moved to tears or laughter. His- keen sense of the ridiculous came near be-traying him into untimely mirth on more than one occasion. In a small parish church, towards the close of one of his most serious discourses, his eye fell upon one of those crude paintings which at that period adorned the country churches. A purple sky, with sun, moon and stars. Saint-Michael in red coat, blue trousers and heavy riding boots, winging his way with flaming sword to earth and about to crush with heavy heel the big nose of Lucifer, while the latter parries

the blow with his horns. The preacher's gaze was riveted. Feeling that he must laugh outright he sat down; rose again, coughed,—abruptly wound up his sermon, and rushing to the sacristy burst into prolonged laughter.

The daily routine of the Bishop was much the same as when he was curate. He was in his office by half-past seven in the morning, and did not leave it, except for his devotions and the mid-day meal, till supper time. After that, he gave himself up for an hour to a pleasant chat with his priests. He was witty, with a fine appreciation of humor; a brilliant talker, told a good story, and liked a joke even though he himself was the victim. He used to tell with glee, how after giving an hour of good advice in English, to an old Irishwoman, she suddenly silenced him by saying that she didn't understand a word of French. His methodical business habits rendered possible his immense correspondence. He never let affairs accumulate on his hands. Volumes of his manuscript letters are carefully preserved. Letters to his clergy on every imaginable subject concerning the physical and spiritual welfare of his people; on education, moral and intellectual ; on vaccination, and the state of the crops. Letters to the Ursuline sisters, playful and affectionate like those of a father to his daughters. "In his very familiarity," says one, "there was something indefinable commanding respect. If we were entirely at our ease with Monseignieur Plessis, we never could forget that he was our Superior and our Bishop." Writing, on a voyage to the Gulf he says, "Your prayers have sustained me wonderfully up to this moment, though they have not prevented my having pretty strong doses of sea-sickness several times. So you have not besought Heaven to calm the waves and make the wind blow as softly as one of your lay sisters blows to kindle the fire in the morning. This breath of ocean is far mightier, and makes my poor little schooner roll so as to break dishes and bottles. All this, however, has no lasting effect on one's health. As soon as one lands the misery is over, and we will not speak of the inconveniences of life especially since we know we deserve so much worse things."

From the Magdalen Islands he writes, "Here there are no serpents, frogs, toads, rats or bugs. No grain grows, nor melons, nor flax, nor onions, nor turnips nor Indian corn. The women are as modest as nuns. They till the soil, while the men fish for a living. Bad faith, theft, quarrelling are unknown here; locks and keys unheard of. People would have a very bad opinion of anyone who bolted his door." Again he writes, "I am going to confess my ignorance. I can't succeed in making any good ink. . . . . . .I beg you to have one of your teachers make me some. I will pay for all the vinegar used. I will exchange empty bottles for full ones, and I will thank you very much into the bargain." From this time forth the nuns made all the ink he used, and if the consumption exceeded the supply he was sure to send a note written with bad ink and this postscript: "If you don't find my ink black enough you may send me some other." Though he kept two secretaries he replied promptly with his own hand to all who sought his help. He was generous to a fault, and reminds one of the Apostle Eliot in his lavish alms to the needy. He never could keep any money for himself. What was quaintly said of the patriarch White is as true of Plessis. "He absolutely commanded his own passions, and the purses of his parishioners, whom he could wind up to what height he pleased on important occasions."

The best summary of the life and character of Plessis, is to be found in his own eulogy on good Bishop Briand. "He had learned from Jesus Christ to render unto Caesar, the things that are Caesar's, and from Saint Paul, submission to the powers that be. . . . . . .No one was more upright more sincere,. . . . . . .more fearless and self-possessed amid untoward events. . . . . . .No one knew better than he,. . . . . . . how to reconcile what he owed to God with what he considered due to his fellow-men."

Three times during his Episcopate, Bishop Plessis visited every parish in Lower Canada, and so prodigious was his memory, that he knew the names of every family in each par-ish. If he heard of a black sheep in any nock, he hunted him up, talked to him like a father, set him on his feet and made him feel himself a man again. He used to relate that when he went to the Iroquois village near Montreal, he watched from the sacristy the Indians, as they stole noiselessly into the church and sat down, the men on one side and the women on the other. Though the women's faces were hidden by their blankets he could always recognize his aunt, by her tall figure and European gait. This was his grand-mother's sister, Abigail, daughter of Thomas French of Deerfield, taken captive at the age of six, and since lost sight of, until now found, among the Saint-Louis

Indians, where, adopting the language and habits of her captors, she lived and died unmarried. On his first visit to Montreal after his election, official announcement as usual was made, of the Bishop's readiness to receive his friends, and the public generally. His father receiving no special notice of his arrival, sent him the following: "My son, I am at home, and shall be glad to receive a visit from you, if you wish to see me." Remembering a former passage at arms between the self-respecting father, and the obedient son, we cannot doubt that Plessis was soon welcomed in the bosom of his family.

On the 2nd of July, 1819, he sailed for Europe on business of importance to the church. He had scarcely left the harbor when a Bull from the Pope arrived naming him Archbishop of Quebec.

The journal kept on this tour is extant. He jots down simple and loving thoughts of the friends left behind. He notices the birds that hover about the islands of the great river, and the gambols of the fish about the ship. The smoke and noise of Liverpool annoy him, but he is delighted with the public institutions of that city. He is especially impressed by the tender care and instruction given to the blind, and his heart is touched by their singing. He praises the smiling landscape, and good roads of England. "For two hundred miles, between Liverpool and London, I did not see a single rut," he says, but he misses the grand forests of his native land. His description of an English inn is capital. "The innkeeper and his wife meet you at the door, with as good grace as any Lord and Lady would receive their guests. That done, they disappear,—leaving you to the discretion of an intendant, who takes care of you with an air of grandeur and nobility that would do credit to the first gentleman of England. . . . . . .Nothing is spared. All your wants are anticipated. Only at your departure, the gentleman opens his hand, and besides the amount of his bill, he receives with gratitude the shilling which you give him." He does not relish English mutton, but speaks of the fine wool of the sheep. He remarks upon the large size of the horses, and the dexterity of the coachmen who use long whips, but never speak to their horses. He speaks with gratitude of the consideration of some English Protestants, with whom he travelled, who were careful not to disturb his devotions. He expresses admiration and respect for a good old Methodist with whom he lodged,—"Must we damn without mercy, those who live well, but do not believe?" he says; "No, charity forbids this." He believed that sooner or later, in some way, these good Protestant brethren would be brought to a knowledge of the true faith. His trust in the love of God and his own great love for his fellow-men, would not permit him to think that any could be lost.

Everywhere in Europe he was treated with distinction, George the Fourth in London, Louis the Eighteenth in Paris, and Pope Pius the Seventh in Rome, gave him flattering audience. Having accomplished his mission he returned to Canada, after a year's absence. Landing at Montreal, his passage down the river was a triumphal procession. After an ovation at Three Rivers, a frenzy of joy greeted his arrival at Quebec. The whole population turned out to meet him. He landed amid the firing of cannon, the clangor of bells, the music of the English band, and the shouts of the people. The multitude followed him to the cathedral, and filled the market place outside, while a Te Deum was sung. A flock of dove-like nuns fluttered on the mansard of the Ursuline convent, watching eagerly from afar the move-ments of the crowd, while others in their glad impulse, seizing the bell rope of the chapel, rang out a welcome to the Holy Father.

He had long been a sufferer from rheumatism. On the 4th of December, 1825, after a few days' illness, his busy and useful life ended suddenly at the hospital of the Hôtel-Dieu. On the 7th his body clad in his sacerdotal robes, a mitre on his head, a crucifix in his hand, was borne in an open coffin through the streets and followed to the Cathedral by an im-mense concourse of citizens,—the Governor-General and his Council, the Legislative Council, judges of the King's Bench and troops of the garrison. All the bells of the city were tolled, the shops shut and minute guns fired. A marble inscribed with an elaborate epitaph in Latin, marks his tomb, at the left of the altar, in the choir of the Basilica at Quebec, His heart in a crystal vase in a leaden box, was carried in procession to the church at Saint-Roch. The vault where it rests is covered by a mural tablet inscribed in French.

Lately I was present at one of the most imposing ceremonials of the Romish church, in the Basilica where Plessis was ordained, consecrated; and so long officiated at similar solemnities. It was the day, when from two hundred thousand altars all over the world, prayers arose for all the souls in Purgatory. A lofty catafalque, covered with a pall, symbolic of death, rose at the very entrance. Tall candles in silver candlesticks stood at its four corners and hundreds of tapers, row upon row ascending, flared and smoked about it. From ceiling to floor, the vast cathedral was draped in black and white. Its usual splendor was veiled by emblems of woe. Pictures and images, crystal chandeliers and silver lamps, were shrouded in black. Broad bands of black concealed the railing of the galleries, and thick folds of the same were wound about the pillars. Votive lamps burned before all the shrines. Colored lights illumined the recesses of the church. Thousands of people with chaplets, knelt in prayer that the souls of the dead might be released from the torture of Purgatory. From the organ loft came the wail of a solemn requiem. Odor of incense was wafted from the far away chancel, which was crowded with priests and boys. In fancy I saw the great Archbishop there, where he loved best to be, in his pontificals, and seated in his chair of state, attended by his clergy in vestments of black velvet embroidered with silver.

Then I thought of Thomas French in his leather apron, shaping ploughshares all the day long; in the evening, painfully recording in the town book the events of the every day life of the little plantation of which he was a leading member; on Sunday, in his homespun suit, sitting here in the deacons' seat below the pulpit, half-hidden from the congregation by the plain board hanging from the rail in front, and serving for a communion table when needed. Children and grandchildren watched by his deathbed, and finally, kindly hands of mourning neighbors bore him on a bier to his rest in the old burial ground. There the sun shines all day upon his grave, which is marked by an old red sandstone bearing the simple words,

"Blessed are the dead which die in the Lord."

Would it have shocked the old man more I wonder, to have known that one of his blood should become the most illustrious defender of the Roman Catholic faith in Canada,— or that a woman of the same stock should stand in this place on this anniversary, to ask you to honor this veritable scion of the church in Deerfield?

Who shall dare affirm or deny that to the drop of New England blood in his veins, Joseph-Octave Plessis, owes the grandest traits of his character ?

After all,—what matters it? Neither New England nor New France,—Puritan nor Catholic, holds a monopoly of virtue.

Sects perish. Nationalities blend. Character endures.

HERTEL DE ROUVILLE.COMMANDER OF THE FRENCH AND INDIANS IN MANY EXPEDITION'S AGAINST NEW ENGLAND.

"It is not far from New England to old France." One rushes by train at night across the fertile meadows of the Connecticut and Passumpsic rivers to wake in a wilderness of pines and hemlocks, alternating with forests of the more delicate larch. So, on to the valley of the Chaudière. Thence winding through picturesque hamlets bearing the names of the Virgin, and all the saints in the calendar,—each a dazzling row of stone cottages, built close by the river, with low walls and high pitched roofs, whose curved and broadly overhanging eaves are supported by brackets. The lofty gable ends are shingled and painted yellow, pink or dark red, in gay contrast to the white plastered walls. The massive cobblestone chimneys are built up from the ground outside, rudely daubed with clay, and encased in wood towards the top to protect them from wind and rain. Each cottage has its outdoor oven, its long, low barn with numerous bright red doors, always open, and barred by wicket gates. Behind the buildings the farm slopes gently upward to a high horizon line, a mile back from the river. While you are looking for Evangeline and wondering whether this is Acadia or Normandy, you find yourself towards sunset in the midst of a French-speaking crowd in the market-place of the Lower Town of Quebec,—on the very spot where in 1608 Champlain and his companions built their "habitation" and spent their first winter in Canada.

Above you, to the height of two hundred and fifty feet towers the magnificent cliff, so justly termed the Gibraltar of America. Clambering into a calèche, you crawl to the top by the zigzag road now known as Mountain Street. But you go not alone,—for this is holy ground, and your heart beats conscious of a procession from the past that silently goes with you up the narrow pathway.

Here is Jacques Cartier, hardy Breton mariner, first of white men who trod this winding way; Champlain, skillful seaman, brave soldier, restless, untiring adventurer,— cumbered with much care for the soul of the red man; and his gentle and beautiful young Huguenot wife, so far exceeding his efforts for her conversion that she learned to look even upon her love for him as disloyalty to God. Here are mendicant friars in gray cloth robes, girt up with knotted cord, and naked feet shod in wooden sandals; black-gowned Jesuits for whom Indian tortures have no terrors, their emaciated faces looking more ghastly beneath their looped-up hats; and dark-eyed nuns, whose woe-begone faces, pale and weary with weeping and sea-sickness, are yet radiant with unabated zeal for their mission. Here, too, are splendid regiments of soldiers, whose valor has been proved on many an old world battle field; and a long line of viceroys, governors and intendants, surrounded by liveried guards and followed by a throng of young nobles from the most corrupt of European courts gorgeous in lace and ribbons and "majestic in leonine wigs."

Gaining the summit of the rock you look off upon a landscape of incomparable beauty. Below, the noble river with white-winged vessels and drifting smoke of many steamers. Midway between its banks lies the beauteous island of Orleans like an emerald set in silver. The long, white côte of Beauport, with its glittering twin spires, stretches away toward the gleaming cataract of Montmorenci. Across the river, russet fields of waving grain slope in billowy uplands to the blue horizon. Far away are the rounded summits of the grand old Laurentian mountains, the land first lifted above the waste of waters, nucleus of a world as yet unborn. Imperial in the splendor of their autumnal robes, wrapped about in the purple haze of the September afternoon, tranquil and serene as befits their dignity, solemn and impressive in their sublimity, they stand there as they have stood since time began.

Halting on the rampart of this walled town that seems like a dream of the middle ages, you hear the muffled drums beating the funeral march of a soldier. The Angelus peals from the cathedral spire. You listen to the low, sweet chanting of cloistered nuns at their vespers. Surely this is a bit of old France.

But again it is not far to New England from Old France, for, to the thoughtful student of our colonial history who stands for the first time beneath the Lombardy poplars on the esplanade at Quebec, especially to one reared under the elms of Massachusetts, no place is so near to the impregnable fortress of the St. Lawrence as the frontier town of Deerfield on the Connecticut. Instinctively he peoples the streets of the old French city with the shadowy forms of those, who, driven from their burning homes on the night of the 29th of February, 1703-4, dragged out a miserable captivity on this very spot. Yonder, tended by Hospital nuns, Zebediah Williams, that pious, hopeful youth, breathed his last. Not far away are the dilapidated walls of the Intendants palace, over whose threshold many a New England captive has passed. Between this and the Governor's council chamber Ensign John Sheldon must have walked daily while besieging these officers with petitions for the release of the Deerfield captives.

Here, in this now deserted market-place young Jonathan Hoit sat with the vegetables which he was sent to sell in the city, when Major Dudley saw him and bought him of his Indian master with twenty bright, silver dollars. Facing this square were the Jesuit buildings where the Deerfield pastor so often dined and argued with the Father Superior; and within sight, stood the Ursuline convent where the little New England girls were bribed and beaten by those as piously bent on the salvation of their souls as ever was good Parson Williams himself.

With all these names, that of Hertel de Rouville must be forever associated. We have hitherto thought of him but as a Popish bigot, a leader of murdering savages. It seems to me that the time has come when we can afford to honor him and his ancestry as we do our own for their patriotic and brave defence of their country and their faith.

In that part of Normandy, known as the Pays de Caux in the picturesque town of Fécamps by the sea, lived Nicholas Hertel and his wife Jeanne. Early in the seventeenth century we find the name of their son, Jacques Hertel in Canada, where the rank of a lieutenant gave him the entree to the best society. Here he devoted himself to the study of the Indian language and became known as one of the most skillful interpreters. The interpreter was then a man of high consideration and authority in intercolonial affairs. His position as mediator between the savage and the white man required the possession of unusual courage and intelligence. Mr. Parkman mentions Hertel as one of the four most famous interpreters of New France in the decade following 1636, and says of the class, "From hatred of restraint and love of a wild and adventurous independence they encountered privation and dangers scarcely less than those to which the Jesuit exposed himself from motives widely different,— he from religious zeal, charity and the hope of Paradise; they, simply because they liked it. Some of the best families of Canada claim descent from this vigorous and hardy stock."

On the 23d of August, 1641, Jacques Hertel married at Three Rivers, the daughter of Francois Marguérie, another of the quartette of renowned interpreters. Three Rivers was then a fur-trading hamlet surrounded by a square palisade. Between it and Montreal, on both shores of the St. Lawrence were clearings, marking the sites of future seigniories. Among the early settlers of Three Rivers, are names connected with some of the most romantic episodes in the history of Canada.

One of the neighbors of Jacques Hertel and François Marguérie was Christophe Crévier, whose eldest daughter later married Pierre Boucher, Governor of Three Rivers. Their daughter, when but twelve and a half years of age married René Gaultier de la Varennes, a lieutenant of the Carignan regiment, and became the mother of La Verendrye, the discoverer of the Rocky Mountains.

Jacques Hertel, at his death, left two daughters and a son. The son, Francois Hertel, was born at Three Rivers about 1643, and early distinguished himself as a soldier. Charlevoix calls him "one of the most valiant warriors of his time." A later French writer says, "By his boldness and success he deserves to be called the most intrepid champion of New France against its eternal enemies, the Iroquois and the colonists of New England."

One summer afternoon in the year 1661, François Hertel, then a youth of eighteen, was made prisoner by the Mohawks, and with two of his comrades carried to one of their towns, where they were cruelly tortured with his poor, mutilated hand the brave boy wrote on birch bark and cartridge wrappers a letter to his mother and two to Father Le Moyne, a Jesuit priest, who had been sent a little before to Onondaga on a political mission during a truce with the Iroquois. In them not one word of complaint of his own sufferings escapes the heroic youth, but elsewhere he thus speaks of his little fourteen years old friend, Antoine Crévier, who had been captured with him : "Poor little fellow, I pitied him so ! These savages made a slave of him, and then while hunting they stuck their knives into him and killed him."

Hertel's other comrade in misfortune wrote home to Three Rivers as follows: "There are three of us Frenchmen here who have been tortured together, and while they were tor-menting one the other two were permitted to pray to God for him, which we did continually; and they let the one they were tormenting chant the Litanies of the Virgin or the Ave Maria, which he did while the others prayed. The savages mocked us and made a great hue and cry when they heard us singing, but that did not keep us from doing it. They made us dance around a great fire to make us fall into it. There were more than forty of them round the fire, and they kicked us from one to another like tennis balls, and after they had burned us well they put us out in the rain and cold. I never felt such dreadful pain, but they only laughed at us. We prayed with all our might, and if you ask me whether I did not hate the Iroquois who were hurting us so, and curse them, I tell you, no, that I prayed for them,. . . . . . . and I must tell you about Pierre Rencontre whom you knew well. He died like a saint. I saw them torture him. He never said a word but "My God have pity on me.". . . . . ..

'Mr. Parkman gives us these letters on p. 67 of the Old Régime.

The youthful captive describes more suffering's endured at the hands of the merciless Mohawks, and at the close of his letter, as if overwhelmed with the horror of it all, he says, "I can't help weeping in saying good-bye." What a picture this is of the constancy and fortitude of these lads! The lapse of two centuries cannot deaden our sympathy with those distressed mothers at Three Rivers as they read these agonizing letters from their beloved boys.

Thus early did François Hertel begin to deserve the title of "Le Heros" by which he is later known in the annals of New France.

On Sept. 2nd, 1664, three years after his captivity among the Mohawks, François Hertel married at Montreal, Mdlle. Marguerite Thauvenet. She had come to Canada with Madame de la Peltrie, intending to consecrate herself to the education of Indian girls, but became betrothed to M. de Chambly, a captain in the Carignan regiment, whose seigniory she inherited at his death, becoming later the wife of François Hertel and the mother of his nine sons. Mr. Benjamin Suite, an eminent historian of Canada, gives a new version of this story in his history of Saint-Francis. He says that Marie Thauvenet's sister married Captain de Chambly and died without children; that De Chambly was killed in the wars with Italy and that his Canadian fief passed to his wife's sister's husband, François Hertel, who thereupon assumed the title of Seigneur de Chambly. Be this as it may, François Hertel's title was Hertel de la Frésnière. From his inheritance of the seigniory of Chambly through his wife or her sister, he became Sieur de Chambly. I find a letter from François Hertel, dated at Three Rivers, July 28, 1666, to the surgeon at Orange, [Albany] thanking him

'François Hertel's title was Hertel de la Frésnière. He gave up this to take that of "Seigneur de Chambly," and is thereafter known as Hertel de Chambly.

for his good treatment while a captive, and regretting that another Mohawk invasion has prevented his being sent by the governor on an embassy to Albany. He adds: "As for news regarding myself I will inform you that I've got married since I was with you, and have a big boy who will soon be able to go and see you; only let him be fourteen or fifteen years older than he is now ; that will make him about sixteen."

On the 28th of March, 1690, we find François Hertel leading the attack at Salmon Falls1 and performing prodigies of valor at Wooster River. He had with him his three eldest sons, of whom our Hertel de Rouville was the third. He was also accompanied by his nephew, Louis Crévier, (the son of his sister Marguerite,) and by Nicolas Gatineau, son of Marie Crévier. These were all gallant and spirited young officers.

Retreating to the Kennebec, he left his eldest son, Hertel de la Frésnière, who had been severely wounded in the action, among the Abenakis, and joining a war party under Portneuf, whose soldiers clamored to be led by Hertel, he shared in the triumph at Fort Loyal on Casco Bay.

We get an interesting glimpse of Hertel's home life at this period. One little daughter had been born to him to whose education the pious mother devoted herself, although, says the Ursuline Superior who tells the tale, "She did not neglect her nine sons, as is proved by the fact that though they were somewhat gay and tremendously brave, they made it a principle to be as faithful to God as to their king." While the husband was fighting for the king at Salmon Falls, his wife was presenting their little ten years old girl for her first communion. This was the first step in a remarkable religious career in which the daughter of "The Hero" "displayed the same heroism which her father had shown on the field of battle."

From the time of her first communion, Marie Françoise Hertel's life was regulated by herself with the sole view to her eternal salvation. She showed thereafter no looseness, idleness nor inconstancy in her tasks at the pension. Delighted with her progress, her parents took her home intending to arrange for her a marriage suitable to their position, but her heart was fixed on becoming a nun. Though this was a great disappointment to her father, who had counted upon her companionship in his declining years, he loved her so tenderly that he would not sadden her by remonstrating against her chosen vocation, and rarely spoke to her on the subject. Her brother, De Rouville, however, was not so considerate. He importuned her incessantly to marry one of his companions in arms who was greatly admired by all. "What nonsense in you, Fanchette," he would say, "at your age to think of shutting yourself up in a convent. Leave your place among the Ursuline sisters to some old maid whom nobody wants, and who is good for nothing but to say her prayers. Why need you put yourself behind a grating to serve God? Look at our mother. Isn't she a good, true Christian ?"

All this did not prevent the young religieuse from fulfilling her intention. In September, 1700, she became a novice under the name of Soeur Marie Françoise de Saint-Exupère, taking the white veil, in the convent then newly founded in her native town.

When in 1713 it became necessary to elect a Mother Superior for the convent at Three Rivers, the minds of all his friends and neighbors naturally turned to the daughter of "The Hero." The matter being decided otherwise by the Ursulines at Quebec, a crowd of his tenants, who believed that everything belonging to the name of Hertel must of necessity hold the highest position, assembled at the convent doors showering invectives upon the authorities at Quebec. The uproar reached such a height that poor little Sister St. Exupère was driven by her humility to leave her native town and seek entrance to the Ursuline convent at Quebec, where she took at once the black veil. There on the 4th of March, 1770, she died at the advanced age of ninety, after a retirement from the world of seventy-one years, which she spent in active service for the church, showing an especial aptitude for teaching young girls.

"About this time," says Mr. Parkman, "Canada became infatuated with noblesse. . . . . . Merchant and seignior vied with each other for the quality of gentilhomme. . . . .'Every-body here,' writes the Intendant Meules, 'calls himself esquire and ends with thinking himself a gentleman.' " The exploits of François Hertel entitled him to letters of nobility from his king. These, according to Canadian Archives, though promised in 1690, were not granted till a quarter of a century later.

In 1712, probably despairing of a proper recognition of his services, and ambitious for his sons, François Hertel, wrote a memorial recapitulating their military exploits. In this he sets forth in detail the expedition of his third son, Hertel de Rouville, to Deerfield.

The following extracts are literally translated:

"The Sieur Hertel is **76** years old.. . . . . . . He has ten sons all in the troops. . . . . . . The Sieur Hertel *père* began to bear arms in 1657, in the beginning of the war against the Iroquois. He was wounded and made prisoner by these Savages in 1659, and was about two years a slave among them. He is maimed in one hand by the bad treatment of these barbarians. . . . . . .

In all the wars there has been no party or expedition in which
the father or some of his children have not been. M. the governor
general. . . . . . . in 1703 honored the Sieur de Rouville with the command of a party of
200 men among the number of whom were three of his brothers. He took by storm at
daybreak the fort guerfil where there were a hundred and twenty-seven armed men. He
killed in this assault, and in a combat which he sustained while retreating with his rear-
guard of thirty men against more than a hundred, one hundred and fifty persons, took one
hundred and seventy
prisoners, his lieutenant was killed and eleven others of his men.
He was wounded and twenty-two others, among which number
were three officers and one of his brothers who was serving as adjutant."

The long-deferred patent of nobility was granted to François Hertel in April, 1716, he
being then seventy-four years old. It appears in Canadian Archives as follows:

[Translation.]

"Services which the Seignieur Hertel Lieutenant of our troops in
Canada has rendered to the late King, ... in the different expeditions in which he
has been against the savages, have led us to give him proof of our satisfaction, which
may descend to his posterity. We resolve upon this the more willingly, as the valor of the
father is hereditary in his children, two of whom have been killed
in the service, and the seven others who still serve in our troops in
Canada and Isle Royale, have given on all occasions proofs of their
good conduct and bravery. And since the father and his children still continue to serve
us, with the same zeal and the same affection, we have been pleased to grant to the head
of this family our letters of nobility. . . . . "

We find Francois Hertel until his death constantly employed in the service of his
government: a man useful in its councils and idolized by the whole colony. Charlevoix,
who saw him at the age of eighty full of health and strength says that "All the colony
bore witness to his virtue and his merits."

The head of the younger branch of François Hertel's family was Jean Baptiste Hertel
de Rouville, so intimately connected with the history of New England.

He was the third "big boy" that rejoiced the heart of his youthful father and was
probably born about 1668. His father procured for him a grant of land on the river
Chambly near his own seigniory, which, it will be remembered, came into his
possession through a romantic episode in the life of his wife, Marguerite de Thauvenet.
Embracing, as did all his brothers, a soldier's career, "he became," says the Canadian
Chronicler, "the rival of all those intrepid warriors who made the English colonies
repent of their unjust attacks." He held the rank of lieutenant, and was accompanied in
his expedition against Deerfield by three of his brothers. For his exploits on that

occasion he was recommended for promotion by De Vaudreuil in a letter to the Minister as follows:

"Quebec, 16th ober 1704.

.... I had the honor to write to you, My Lord.......... and to inform you of the success of a party I sent this winter on the ice as far as the Boston government at the request of the Abenakis Indians whom the English attacked since Sieur de Beaubassin's return last autumn, and at the same time took the liberty to speak to you of Sieur de Rouville who commanded on that occasion: he desires, My Lord, that you would have the goodness to think of his promotion, having been invariably, in all the expeditions that presented themselves, and being still actually with the Abenakis..........

Sieur de Rouville's party, My Lord, has accomplished everything expected of it, for independent of the capture of a fort, it showed the Abenakis that they could truly rely on our promises, and this is what they told me at Montreal on the 13th of June when they came to thank me."

"At a meeting of the Commissioners for managing the Indian affairs at Albany the 21 of June, 1709. Intelligence given by an Indian called Ticonnondadiha, deserted from a French party gone to New England, says that it is now 24 days ago since that party went out from Canada wch he left three days ago at the head of the Otter Creek at a place called Oneyade; and to goe over a long carrying place before they came to the New England river. This party consists of 180 men, 40 Christians and 140 Indians; they are designed for Dearfeild and intended to post themselfes near the fort and then send out a skulking party to draw out the English, thinking by that meanes to take the place. That by another Indian come latter from Canada, confirms that this party is out, and that two New England captives deserted from thence 14 dayes ago. Albany 22th June 1709. Hereupon the Com" for the Indian affairs have sent Danl Ketelhuyn expresse with a letter to Col. Partridge to give an acc^t thereof."

The origin of this expedition was as follows: Having been worsted in an attack by the English under Captain Wright, "a party of Indians," says De Vaudreuil, "feeling piqued, asked me to let them go on an excursion with some fifty of the most active Frenchmen, and to allow the Sieur de Rouville and another to command. I immediately assented the force went to Guerrefille [Deerfield] where, having prepared an ambush they caught two alive.

Hertel de Rouville appears to have made many little "excursions" of this sort into New England and New York. On the 29th of August, 1708, he commanded the attack on Haverhill. Here his brother, Hertel de Chambly, and Louis de Verchères, the friend whom he had ardently desired as his brother-in-law, were slain.

Joseph Bradley, the same who accompanied John Sheldon to Canada, secured the medicine chest and packs of the party which they had thrown aside on going into battle and had not time to gather up in their hasty retreat with their captives.

De Rouville was sent by the governor on an important embassy to Boston. Of this De Vaudreuil writes to Pontchartrain that he "had been fortunate in his choice of two officers, the most capable of all Canada of reconnoitring a country which at any moment they might be called upon to attack."

Amidst his severer duties De Rouville found time to marry twice. By his second wife he had five children. The names of his daughters appear on the convent lists of pupils, and in their records the holy sisters mention with pride Hertel de Rouville and his brothers as defenders of the church. He was finally sent to Cape Breton where he spent some years, and died June 30th, 1722, at Fort Dauphin, of which he was commandant. Among the prisoners huddled together in Ensign John Sheldon's house in Deerfield on that dreadful night in February, 1703-4, waiting with her weeping children, grandchildren and neighbors, the order to inarch into captivity, was Mary Baldwin Catlin, wife of Mr. John Catlin. A wounded French officer was brought in and laid upon the floor. In his agony he called piteously for water. Mrs. Catlin raised his head and tenderly moistened his fevered lips. Reproached by a neighbor for this kindness to their enemy, she answered, "If thine enemy hunger feed him; if he thirst, give him drink." When the captives were gathered together for the march Mrs. Catlin was left behind, — tradition says in return for her compassion. One touch of nature makes the whole world kin. I like to think that the wounded officer may have been Hertel de Rouville's young brother, and that that humane act, distilled through the blood of succeeding generations, has inspired me with the wish to present the Hertels in a more favorable light than that in which we of New England are accustomed to view them.

The Canadian heroine, Madeleine de Verchères, at the age of fourteen, defended her father's house for a week against the Iroquois, while he was on duty at Quebec. Putting a gun into the hands of her younger brother she said, "Remember that our father has taught you that gentlemen must be ready to shed their blood if need be in the service of their God and their king."

In our estimate of the character of Jean Baptiste Hertel de Rouville, we must not forget that this was the creed on which he was nurtured.

FATHER MERIEL—MARY SILVER.INTRODUCTION.

"In 1657," says Mr. Parkman, "the association of pious enthusiasts who had founded Montreal, was reduced to a remnant of five or six persons, whose ebbing zeal and overtaxed purses were no longer equal to the devout but arduous enterprise. They begged the Seminary of Saint-Sulpice to take it off their hands. The priests consented, and though the conveyance of the island of Montreal to these, its new proprietors, did not take effect till some years later, four of the Sulpitian fathers came out to the colony and took it in charge.

Thus far, Canada had had no bishop, and the Sulpitians now aspired to give it one from their own brotherhood. This roused the jealousy of the Jesuits, who, for thirty years had borne the heat and burden of the day,—the toils, privations and martyrdoms, while as yet the Sulpitians had done nothing and endured nothing;—and under the leadership of the great Laval, the long quarrel between the two orders began." It ended in the triumph of Laval and the Jesuits.

From the earliest period of their history, the labors of the three religious communities.—Sulpitian priests, nuns of the Congregation de Notre-Dame, and Hospital nuns, have supplemented each other: the Seminary priests serving as teachers of the boys and as directors and chaplains of the other two orders; the Congrégation nuns teaching the girls; and the Hospital nuns doing duty as nurses to them all.

The most pious friendship unites the three orders, and together they are regarded in the eyes of the people of Montreal as an image and embodiment of the Holy Family, Jesus, Mary and Joseph.

FATHER MERIEL.

In 1690 or 91, M. Henri-Antoine de Meriel of Meulan in the Diocese of Chartres, France, was sent by M. Tronson, Superior-General of the Sulpitian Order in Canada, to succeed M. Barthélémy as chaplain at the Hôtel-Dieu in Montreal.

At the age of thirty, M. Meriel bade farewell to riches, honors and the congenial associations of his native land, to devote himself to the poor and unfortunate.

Though his birth, education and talents made him a leading spirit in the best society of New France, his life was one of arduous labor and self-sacrifice. In addition to his duties at the Hôtel-Dieu he ministered with great success to the parish of Notre-Dame in Montreal, and was director and confessor to the pupils of the Sisters of the Congrégation.

On Canadian records, Father Meriel is everywhere present as a part of the personal history of the New England captives, and to those familiar with their story, the priest's name is as well-known as that of the Puritan preacher, Rev. John Williams. The latter found in him a foeman worthy of his steel.

To Father Meriel's knowledge of the English language, "and his facility in its use, an accomplishment rare at that
time in Canada, we owe the marvellously exact records by which we are able to identify so many of our captives. The name, age, parentage, the date and place of capture, are given with minute detail, in his exquisite handwriting, which is like an oasis in the desert to one groping among the dry and almost illegible records of two hundred years ago.

By his ability and zeal, many were converted to the Romish church. Not content with devoting himself soul and body to this work, he spent his patrimony in the cause.

Shortly before his death the Intendant and the Governor-General wrote to the home government asking that in consideration of his services he might be re-imbursed by the crown.

The French minister replied as follows:

"His Majesty has been informed that M. Meriel, priest at Montreal, has spent his fortune on the conversion of the English of the colony, and that he is so impoverished as to be unable to continue the good work.

As His Majesty is very glad to give him proof of his satisfaction with his zeal, he desires M. M. de Vaudreuil and Bégon to inform him how much money they think should be annually awarded to M. Meriel."

Father Meriel could not profit by the good intentions of his sovereign. He died in the odor of sanctity while ministering to the sick at the Hôtel-Dieu, on the 12th of January, 1713, at the age of fifty-two.

MARY SILVER.

One of the fruits of Father Meriel's labors among the captives was Mary (Adelaide) Silver. She was the eldest child of Thomas Silver of Newbury, Mass., and his wife Mary Williams.

Thomas Silver died in 1695, and his widow married Cap-tain Simon Wainwright.

On the 29th of August, 1708, [Sept. 9, N. S.] a party of French and Indians attacked Haverhill, Mass., then a village of about thirty houses, with a meeting-house and a picketed fort or garrison house. The following account is by Joseph Bartlett, a soldier in the garrison house under Capt. Wainwright.

"In the year 1707, in November, I, Joseph Bartlett was pressed, and sent to Haverhill. My quarters were at the house of a captain Waindret. August 29, 1708, there came about 160 French and 50 Indians, and beset the town of Haverhill—set fire to several houses; among which was that of captain Waindret. The family at this time were all reposing in sleep; but Mrs. Waindret waking, came and awaked and told me that the Indians had come. I was in bed in a chamber, having my gun and ammunition by my bed-side. I arose, put on my small clothes, took my gun, and looking out at a window, saw a company of the enemy lying upon the ground just before the house, with their guns presented at the windows, that on discovering any person they might fire at them. I put my gun to the window very still, and shot down upon them, and bowed down under the window; at which they fired, but I received no harm. I went into the other chamber, in which was Mrs. Waindret, who told me we had better call for quarter or we should all be burnt alive. I told her we had better not; for I had shot, and believed I had killed half a dozen, and thought we should soon have help.

After reloading my gun, I was again preparing for its discharge, when I met with a Mr. Newmarsh, who was a soldier in that place.

He questioned me. . . . . .I answered that I was going to shoot. He told me if I did shoot, we should all be killed, as captain Waindret had asked for quarter, and was gone to open the door. . . . . .He said we must go and call for quarter; and, setting our guns in the chamber chimney, we went down and asked for quarters. The entry was filled with the enemy, who took and bound us, and plundered the house.

They killed no one but captain Waindret. When they had done plundering the house, they marched off, and at no great distance, coming into a body, I had a good view of them, so that I could give a pretty correct account of their number expecting to escape."

A rare volume, entitled "Incidents in the Early History of New England," gives substantially the following account of the attack on Haverhill:

"One party rifled and burned Mr. Silver's house. Another attacked the garrison house of Capt. Samuel Wainwright, killing him at the first fire. To the surprise of the garrison who were bravely preparing to resist, Mrs. Wainwright herself unbarred the door," spoke kindly to the enemy as they entered, served them and offered to get for them whatever they wanted. The invaders, bewildered by this unexpected reception, demanded money. Promising to get it, Mrs. Wainwright left the room, and fled from the house, "with all of her children, except one daughter who was taken captive, and was not afterwards discovered."

The rage of the enemy on discovering that they had been duped by a woman, may be imagined. They attacked the garrison with great violence, at the same time attempting to fire the house. They were forced to retreat with three captives, one of whom was Joseph Bartlett, quoted above,—another was Mrs. Wainwright's daughter by her first marriage, Mary Silver, then about fourteen years old. The route of the captives may be traced by Bartlett's narrative. In February he became the servant of a rich Frenchman afflicted with gout. In his leisure moments he "Wrought at shoe-making." He describes his religious experiences in Canada, with charming naïveté. His mistress asked him why he did not "attend meeting." "I answered that I could not understand what they said. She said she could not. I asked her what she went for. She answered, to say her prayers."

In his quaint New England dialect he gives us this glimpse of Father Meriel's work among the captives:

"On my coming to reside with the French, Mr. Meriel, a French priest, came and brought me an English bible. As I sat at shoe-making, he came and sat down beside me, and questioned me concerning my health, and whether I had been to their meetings. I told him I had not. On his asking the cause I answered (as I had done before) that I could not understand what they said. He said he wished to have me come and witness their carryings on. I told him it was not worth my while. But he was very earnest that I should come to his meeting; and advised me to try all things, holding fast that which is good. Who knows, said he, but that God hath sent you here to know the true way of worship. I told him I believed ours was the right way. Says he we hold to nothing but what we can prove by your own Bible. After considerable conversation I told him I did not know but that I should come to their meetings and see how they carried on: which after a little while I did. Now in their meeting-house there stood a large stone pot of their holy water, into which everyone that came in dipped their finger making a sign of a cross, putting their fingers first to their foreheads, then to their stomachs, afterwards to their left shoulder, then to their right shoulder, saying, 'Father, Son, and Holy Ghost —amen,' and kneeling down, they say a short prayer to themselves. They have pulpits in their houses for public worship; in which the priests sometimes preach.

After a short time the priest came again to visit me, and asked me how I liked their manner of worship. I told him it seemed strange to me. He said this was generally the case at first, but after a while it would appear otherwise."

The simple cobbler at his last, disputing doctrines with the educated priest, is an interesting picture of the sturdy New England character. Bartlett gives us much more of his theological discussion with Father Meriel,—but the priest's efforts to convert him were unavailing. Bartlett was redeemed and returned to Newbury after a captivity of four years, two months and nine days.

On arriving at Montreal Mary Silver was probably given at once in charge of the "Sisters of the Congregation." Her name appears in our Archives on a "Roll of English Prisoners in the hands of the French and Indians at Canada Given to Mr. Vaudruille's Messengers," dated 1710-11. This roll was probably sent to Canada by the French officers who had come to Albany with Dutch prisoners, bringing also John Arms of Deerfield to exchange for Sieur de Verchères, who had been taken prisoner in the attack on Haverhill.

In Canada the usual agitation follows this demand of our Government for the return of the captives. The records are teeming with their baptism and marriage. Here is one:

"On Sunday, the 2nd of February 1710, the rite of baptism was administered by me the undersigned priest, to an English girl named Mary Silver, who born at Haverhill in New England on Wednesday, March 10th, 1694, [28 Feb. 1693-4] of the marriage of Thomas Silver, deceased, and Dame Mary Williams now Widow, by her second marriage, of Mr. Simon Wainwright, ludge, Captain and Commandant of the said place; which girl having been captured on Sunday, the 9th of September, 1708, by Monsieur Contrecoeur Esquire, officer in the troops of Canada, and brought to this country, lives as a pupil in the house of the Soeurs de la Congrégation de Notre-Dame, at Villemarie.

Her godfather was the High and Mighty Seigneur Messire Philippe de Rigaud, Marquis de Vaudreuil, Chevalier of the military order of Saint-Louis, and Governor General of New France; her god-mother, Madame Charlotte Denis, wife of M. Claude de Ramezay, Chevalier of the order of Saint-Louis, Seigneur de Lageste Boisfleurant, and Governor of the Island of Montreal and its dependencies,—all of whom signed with me according to the ordinance."

The autographs of Mary Silver, her godparents, and Father Meriel follow.

She was probably confirmed soon after her baptism. The precise date is unknown, as no records of this rite were then kept. As it was the custom at confirmation to add another name to that given at baptism, she then received the name of Adelaide. Thenceforth, on Canadian records, she appears as Adelaide Silver.

Her Puritan mother, distressed by the rumor that her child was about to become a Romanist, addressed to the General Court the following petition

"Haverhill, April 29. 1710

To His Excellency Joseph Dudley Esq

Capt Generall and Governor in Chief, and to yᵉ Honorable Council and General Assembly Now Mett the petition of Widow Mary Wainwright humbly showeth that Whereas my Daughter hath been for a long time in Captivity with yᵉ French in Canada and I have late reason to fear that her soul is in great Dainger if not all redy captivated and she brought to their ways theirefore I would humbly Intreat your Excelency that some care may be taken for her Redemption before Canada be so Endeared to her that I shall never have my Daughter anymore; Some are ready to say that there are so few captives in Canada that it is not worthwhile to poot yᵉ Cuntry to ye charges to send for them but I hoope your Excelency no [r] No other Judichous men will thinck so for St. James hath Instructed us as you may see Chap. 5 v 20 Let him know that he which converteth the sinner from the errour of his way, shall save a soul from Death and shall hide a multitude of sins this is all I can do at present but I desire humbly to Begg of God that he would Direct the hearts of our Rulers to do that which may be most for his Glory and for the good of his poor Distressed Creatures and so I take leave to subscribe myself your most Humble petitioner

Mary Wainwright Widow

In the House of Representatives June 9. 1710.

Read yᵉ 12ᵗʰ read and recomended

In Council

June 12. 1710   Read & concurred in."

This petition was of no avail. It was not long before her friends in New England learned that Mary (Adelaide) Silver had made public abjuration of the Protestant faith, and before the close of the year 1710 in her eighteenth year she entered the convent of the "Hospital Nuns of St. Joseph," usually known as the "Soeurs de l'Hôtel-Dieu:' Her desertion of the convent in which she had been protected and educated, to enter a different order, seems strange and capricious. It is, however, explained by the fact that she preferred the duties of a nurse to those of a teacher.

Teaching is the vocation of the Sisters of the Congregation; nursing, that of the nuns of the Hôtel-Dieu. From the earliest period of their history in Canada the two orders have been closely united in affection and intercourse, so that to use their own words they have always regarded themselves as one and the same community.

In the early days, the two convents were near neighbors, their court yards adjoining, and they made each other frequent visits. The nuns of both convents love to tell how in the olden time, they used to sit at sunset on their respective balconies, responding to each other with hymns and canticles of gratitude and of pious joy.

The New England girl of to-day will find it hard to understand how a young girl, free to choose, should have elected the arduous duties of a nurse in a cloister in preference to the more agreeable occupation of teaching, with greater freedom and variety in her life. It is evident that her training and surroundings, at the most impressible period of a young girl's life, had made of her a devotee.

At the Hôtel-Dieu she came again under the influence of Father Meriel.

The treaty of Utrecht in 1713, while stipulating for a general exchange of prisoners, included a clause whereby the English converted to Catholicism during their captivity should have entire liberty to remain in Canada. This apparent freedom of will was greatly hampered by their training and naturalization in Canada, and comparatively few converts returned to New England. Mary Adelaide Sil-ver's mother wrote entreating her to return, and sent money with an urgent appeal to the Governor of Canada, to send her home.

"But," says the annalist of the convent, "the generous girl preferring the treasures of the faith to all worldly advantages replied to the Governor as follows: 'Monsieur, I tenderly love my dear mother, but before everything, I am bound to obey God, and I declare to you that I am resolved to live in the holy religion which I have embraced, and to die a nun of Saint-Joseph. My dearest wish is, that before my death, I may see my mother embrace the holy Catholic faith, with the light of which it has pleased God to enlighten me.' "

Mary Adelaide Silver adhered to her resolution to remain in Canada. Her zeal was as fervent, her industry as untiring as that of Father Meriel. At his death she took his place as catechist and apostle to the captives. After thirty years of convent life, she died at the Hôtel-Dieu on the 2nd of April, 1740. Two days later she was buried in the vault of the old convent church, then standing at the corner of St. Paul and St. Sulpice streets in Montreal.

In 1860, those there interred were removed to the crypt of the church of the new convent on the Avenue des Pins, where the mortal remains of Mary Adelaide Silver now rest.

APPENDIX.

A.CHRISTINE OTIS.

Grizel [or Grizet] Warren, wife of Richard Otis of Dover, N. H., was captured in the attack on that town, June 28, 1689, with her infant Margaret, and two older children. In Rev. John Williams's "Redeemed Captive," Grizel Otis figures as "Madam Grizalem." Captured earlier than those of Deerfield and other towns, she seems to have become reconciled to her fate before their arrival in Canada, and to have befriended them, while serving as a valuable assistant to Father Meriel in his ministrations among them.

The following is a copy, verbatim et literatim of the record of her baptism in Canada. Evidently "avec trois de ses enfants" is omitted before *"duquel"* &c.:

> *"Le Samedi neuvième jour de Mai veille de la Pentecôte de l'an mil six cents quatre vingts treize a été solenellement batisée une femme Angloise cy-devant nommée Madame Kresek Laquelle née à Barwic en la Nouvelle Angleterre le vingt quatrième jour de Février [vieux stile ou 6 mars nouveau stile] de l'an mil six cens soixante et deux du mariage de Jacques Waren Ecossois Protestant et de Marguerite Irlandoise Catholique et mariée à défunt Richard 0theys Habitant de Douvres en la Nouvelle Angleterre ayant été prise en guerre le vingthuitième jour de Juin de l'an mil six cens quatre-vingt neuf (duquel ne lui est resté qu'une petite fille agée de quatre ans comme etant née le 15 Mars 1689) nommée au batême Christine aiant été prise en guerre le vingt huitième jour de Juin vieux stile [ou 8 Juillet nouveau stile] de Van mil six cens quatre vingts neuf demeure au service de Monsieur de Maricour. Elle a été nommée Marie-Madeleine. Son Darrein a été Monsieur Jaques Le Ber Marchand. Sa marraine, Dame Marie-Madelaine Dupont épouse de Monsieur le moine Ecuyer Sieur de Maricour, Capitaine de détachement de la Marine*
>
> [Signed]   Le Ber.

> Fran: Dollier de Casson, Gr. vic.

> M. M. Dupont:'

Marie-Madeleine Hotesse is on a list of persons confirmed Sept. 8, 1693.

The following is an exact copy of the record of her marriage in Canada:

> *"L'an de grace mil six cent nonante et trois le quinzième d' Octobre apyrès les fiançailles et la publicaon d'un ban faite en la grand Messe d'Onzième jour dud mois et an, d'entres Philipe Robitaille fils de Jean Robitaille et d'Martine Cormon, ses père et mère de la Paroisse de Bronroux en Artois et Marie Madeleine oiiaren veuve de défunt Richard Otheys habitant de Douvres en la Nouvelle-Angleterre tous deux de ce paroiffe Monsieur Dollier grand vicaire [illegible] ayant donné la despense des deux autres bans et ne s'étant découvert aucune empechmt M. Meriel prêtre du consentement de moi soussigné curé de la paroiffe de Villemarie les a mariée selon la forme préscrite par la Ste Eglise en présence de Charles Le Moyne Ecuyer Sieur de Maricour capitaine réforme dans les troupes de la marine qui sont présent de Dame Marie Madeleine Dupont son épouse, de Monsieur Jaques Le Ber Marchand de M^r forestier et plusieurs autres amies."*

Philippe Robitaille, son of the above, was baptized in Montreal, Feb. 5, 1695.

On a list of persons to whom naturalization is granted in May, 1710, are:

"Mag^{dne} Ooarin Englishwoman, married to Philippe Robitaille cooper, established at Ville-Marie, by whom she has four children."

"Christine Otis, Englishwoman, brought with her mother to Canada, married to Louis Le Beau, carpenter established at Ville-Marie."

B. ESTHER WHEELWRIGHT.

Note. Capt. Phineas Stevens was born in Sudbury, Massachusetts, whence his father removed to Rutland, Vt. At the age of sixteen he was carried captive to Canada. On his return he settled in what is now Charlestown, N. H., then known as "Number Four."

He was an active partisan officer during the French and Indian war, and died in public service in 1756. He was often employed by the Massachusetts Government as ambassador to Canada for the exchange of captives. His name appears frequently in our Archives.

Note. Major Nathaniel Wheelwright, son of Colonel John, grandson of Colonel Samuel, and great-grandson of the celebrated Reverend John Wheelwright, was born in Boston in 1721. He married there in 1755, the daughter of Charles Apthorp, his distinguished fellow-citizen.

Major Wheelwright was a merchant and banker of Boston and London. His character and his social position gave him great influence in public affairs, and he was employed by the Massachusetts government in diplomatic positions, requiring tact, judgment and personal dignity. He served twice at least as ambassador from New England to Canada for the redemption of captives taken in the old French and Indian wars. Major Wheelwright died in 1766, on the island of Guadaloupe.

In the summer of 1752, Phineas Stevens and Major Nathaniel Wheelwright, (nephew of the captive Esther Wheelwright,) were sent to Canada by our government, to demand the rendition of New England captives. The history of their embassy appears in the records as follows:

"Jan. 30, 1752

In the House of Representatives it was Voted that his Honour the Lieut. Governor with advice of the Council be desired to take speedy and effectual Care for the Redemption of the Captives now in Canada at the charge of the Government."

"At a Council held at Harvard College in Cambridge upon Friday the third of April 1752, sitting the General Court. It was Advised that his H0n^r: the Lieutenant Govr: appoint Capt. Phineas Stevens & Mr Nathaniel Wheelwright to negotiate the affair of Redeeming the Captives in Canada in pursuance of a vote of the General Court pass'd the 29th of January last, and that His Honour direct them to proceed to Canada with his Despatches as soon as the Season of the Year will permit."

"At a Meeting of a Number of the members of Her Majesty's Council held at the Court House in Charlestown, April 17, 1752, It was advised and consented that a warrant be made out to the Treasurer to pay unto John Wheelwright Esq. for the Use of the Gentlemen going to Canada in the Service of the Governmen^t; sum of ninety Pounds towards the defraying their charges on the affair, they to be accountable therefor at their Return. The Secretary laid before the Council the Draught of a Letter his Honour proposed to send to the Governor of Canada for demanding the Release of the captives. Which letters being considered were advised by the Council. The Secretary also laid before the Council a Draught of Instructions His Honour proposed to give to the Gentlemen going to Canada on the affair of the Captives, to which the Council ad-vised."

"At a Council held at the Court House in Concord upon Thursday the Fourth of June, 1752 it was Advised and Consented that a Warrant be made out to the Treasurer to pay to Jacob Wendell Esqr the Sum of Fifty Four Pounds six shillings to discharge a Bill of Exchange drawn on the said Treasurer by Messrs Stevens and Wheelwright Messengers to Canada for Moneys taken up for the Public service."

"At a Council held at the Lieut.-Governor's House in Cambridge on Thursday Aug. 13. 1752 His Honour communicated to the Council Letters he had received from Monsieur Longueil Commander in Chief in Canada & Messrs Stevens & Wheelwright Messengers sent from this Government on the affair of the Captives and the Copy of a Conference between the said Gentlemen and some of the St. Francois Indians, with a List of the English captives ransomed by them with other papers relating to their Negotiation."

The following are the official documents above-mentioned: "Speech of the Abenakis of Saint-François to Captain Stevens, deputy from the Governor of Boston, in presence of M. le Baron de Longueuil, Governor of Canada, and of Iroquois from the Sault Saint-Louis, and from the Lake of the Two Mountains, on the 5th of July, 1752. Arti8aneto, Chief Orator:

"Brother,

We shall talk to you as if we were speaking to your Governor in Boston. We hear on all sides that this Governor and the Bastonnais say the Abenakis are bad people. It is in vain that you charge us with bad hearts; it is always you, our brothers, who have attacked us; you have a sweet tongue, but a heart of gall. I admit, that when you begin it we can defend ourselves.

We tell you, brother, that we are not anxious for war. We like nothing better than to be at peace, and it needs only that our English brothers keep peace with us......We wish to keep possession of the lands on which we live......We will not give up an inch of the land which we inhabit, beyond that long ago decided upon by our brothers......We forbid you absolutely from killing a single beaver or taking one bit of wood on our lands. If you want wood we will sell it to you, but you shall not have it without our permission. Who has authorized you to have our lands measured? We pray the Governor of Baston to have these surveyors punished, for we cannot believe they are acting under his orders. You are then the arbiters of peace between us. As soon as you cease to encroach upon these lands, we shall be at peace."

HE PRESENTS A B E LT.

"I repeat, by this belt, it belongs to you only, to keep peace with us Abenakis.

Our father here present has nothing to do with what we are saying to you. It is on our own behalf and for our allies that we speak.

We regard our father simply as a witness of our words......Under no pretext whatever must you pass beyond your limits......

We are a free people; allies of the French King from whom we have received our Religion, and help in time of need. We love him and we will serve his interests. Answer this speech as soon as possible. Report it in writing to your Governor. ' We shall keep a copy of it. It will not be difficult for your Governor to send us his reply. He can address it to our Father who will kindly send it to us."

STEVENS'S REPLY.

"I shall report to my Governor, your words, my brothers, and I will carry it to him in writing that nothing in it may be altered.

1 ask you, my Abenaki brothers, if your attacks upon the English during the past two years have been because of their encroachments upon your lands. Are you satisfied with the death of your people by means of the blows you have struck against the English? I know that we must not encroach on your lands. Those who have done so are stupid, lawless people."

ABENAKIS CONTINUE.

"When peace was made we expected to enjoy it with the French, but at the same moment we learned that you, our English brothers, had killed one of our men and had hidden him in the ice. When we demanded why you had killed him, you promised us satisfaction, but your ill-will towards us has been shown by your inaction during seven months, and we resolved to defend ourselves, and have destroyed a house. Since that a man and a woman of our village are missing. We have learned their sad fate by an English-woman who is now with us, who affirms that this man and woman were killed by the English in her presence, and as positive proof of this she has brought us a bag which we recognize as having belonged to these unfortunates. We were touched by this murder as we ought to be, and we avenged ourselves last year. The English that we have killed this year. . . . . . .and the two others taken prisoners, may attribute their hard fate to the fact that they have been caught hunting on our lands, and we repeat with all the firmness of which we are capable, that we will kill all the English that we find on our lands,. . . . . . . .if any of you are caught on our lands you will be killed."

THE IROQUOIS TO THE ABENAKIS.

"We have heard with pleasure your speech to the Englishman. We are delighted that you have defended your rights with spirit. We beg you to make your words good, if need be, and we promise to help you."

"Procés-Verbal," or official report of their embassy dated July 25, 1752, signed by Stevens and Wheelwright with their Interpreter Daniel Joseph Maddox:

"Nous soufsignés Phineas Stevens et Nataniel Weerlight deputes par ordre de Monsieur S. Phips Lieutenant Gouverneur et Commandant en chef à Baston auprès de Monsieur le Baron de Longueuil Gouverneur de Montréal et Commandant en Canada à l'effet de traitter *(sic)* de la liberté des prisonniers Anglois qui sont detenus en Canada certifions que mon dit Sieur Le Baron de Longueuil dès le six de Juin que nous sommes arrivés à Montreal, a donné ses ordres et nous a donné une entière liberté pour parler aux dits prisonniers, et les rapeller auprès de nous pour les ramener dans la nouvelle Angleterre.

Qu'en conséquence nous Nathaniel Wierlierlight nous fommes transportés aux trois

Rivières et à Quebec, et avons conferé aux trois Rivierés en présence de Mr Rigaud de Vaudreuil Gouverneur, avec les Anglois faits prisonniers par les sauvages, et qui sont au pouvoir tant les dits savages que des François qui les ont rachetés.

Que la même facilité nous a été donnée à Quebec où nous nous sommes aussi transporté par M. le Chevalier de Longueüil Lieutenant de Roy Com^dt en la ditte *[sic]* Place.

Qu'à notre retour à Montreal nous avons rejoint le d'Sr Phinehas Stevens qui de son côté a travaillé à rapeller les dits Prisonniers qui sont dans le Gouvernement de Montreal. Et après avoir fait le séjour que nous avons jugé nécessaire en Canada, nous nous fommes determinés à partir pour aller rendre compte de notre mission à Mr S. Phips notre Com^dt en chef et en conséquence nous declarons et affirmons Premièrement que les nommés cy après nous ont été delivrés, et que nous les ramenons avec nous Sçavoir

Thomas Stannard racheté ci devant à Quebec par un françois des
               mains d'un Sauvage lequel françois lui a donné
sa liberté gratuiteusement.

Samuel Lumbart retirés de chez le Sr Cadet à Quebec en lui pay-
Edouard Hinkley ant cent livres, dont il s'est tenu content, quoy
qu'il eût payé davantage aux Sauvages.

Amos Eastman retirés de ches le Sr Gamelin à St François, en
Seth Webb lui remboursant pour chacun trois cens livres
          qu'il avoit payeés aux Sauvages.

Oner Hancock retiré de ches la dame Hertel de St François, en payant trois cens Livres
qu'elle
          avoit payeés aux Sauvages.

Thimoty Mackerty qui avoit resté malade à l'hôpital à Montreal,
fait prisonnier pendant la guerre.

Joseph fortner pris aux Miamis s'est retiré volontairement.

En second lieu qu'il ne nous a pas été possible de ravoir les nommés cy après quelques ordres que M. le Baron de Longueuil ait pu donner, Scavoir

Berney Gradey a voulu rester à Quebec.
          Rachel Quaenbouts rachetée des sauvages par Mr De Rigaud, ou elle
          veut absolument rester, s'y trouvant parfaitement bien.

Jean Starkes le d'Starkes vient d'être rendu sous promesse
          d'être remplacé par un esclave pris par les Abenakis de St François
          qui se sont obstinés à les garder quelques instances que Mr de Rigaud
          ait faites, les ayant adoptés.

Abigail Noble pris et resté au pouvoir des Abenakis de Bequancourt qui l'ont adopté.
          Salomon Mitchel âgé d'environ douze ans a voulu absolument rester à
          Montreal ches le Sr Des Pins, et Mr Le Baron de Longueuil n'a par cru

devoir le forçer à partir, malgré luy.

    Elizabeth schinner a voulu rester ches M^r de St Ange Charly, qui l'a rachetée des sauvages il y a quelques années, elle a fait abjuration.

    Samuel freeman Indien au pouvoir de Mr de la Corne St Luc a été pris à Sarastau par les françois. M^r de St Luc le rendera pourvû qu'on le remplace quoy qu'il ait été décédé par feu M. le Marquis de la Jonquière qu'il était de bonne prise, et qu'il estoit esclave.

William --	Nègre pris à Chibouctou, au pouvoir de Mr Le Ch^{er} De La Corne qui le garde par les mêmes raisons que M^r de St Luc, et offre de le remettre aux mêmes conditions.
Thomas Neal	a voulu rester à Montreal.
Saras Davids	pris par les Iroquois du Sault Saint-Louis qui

l'ont adopté et n'a pas voulu les quitter.

"En troisième lieu, nous déclarons et affirmons, que toutes perquisitions par nous faites, et quelques facilités que M^r Le Baron De Longueuil nous ait donné, nous n'avons point trouvé d'autres prisonniers Anglois en Canada. En foy de quoy nous nous sommes signés avec mon dit Sieur Baron de Longueuil et le Sr Maddox interprête en langue Angloise fait double à Montreal le vingt cinq juillet mil sept cens cinquante deux.

    [Signed] Longueuil,
          Phineas Stevens,
          Nat. Wheelwright,
          Dan^{ll} Joseph maddox."

"A List of the English Prisoners which the Abenakis Indians have brought to Quebec. The Saint-François Indians to the Number of Forty have struck near Richmond Fort to revenge the Death of an Abenakis Chief which the English have killed near Boston, & have Brought in this City, the Prisoners following which they have sold to the French who was willing to buy them, viz:

The Sieur Chalour has bought		
named Lazarus Noble for		£200
For Cloathes furnish'd	40.	
		£240.
Le S^r: Rivolt has bought		
Jabez Chub for		£200
For Cloathes furnish'd		80.
	£280.	
The S: Turpine has bought		
John Rofs for		£150·
For Cloaths furnish'd		50.

	£200.
Mr Decouagne has bought	
Abigail Noble for	£200
For Cloaths Furnish'd	122 — 15ˢ

£282 – 15

Mrs Duperé has bought	
Anna Homes for	£200·
For Cloaths Furnish'd	50.

£250

The S: Bazin has bought	
Phillipps Jenkins for	£150
For Cloaths Furnish'd	100

£250

This man died at the Hospital 28. Oct. 1750.

Those which follows have been taken by the Becancourt Indians and bought of them.
The Cadet Bought John Marten he has Obtain'd permission of the Governor General to Return to New England and pafs'd his Note

to the Sr: Cadet for	£260.
Mrs Fornel has bought	
William Rofs for	£124. — 10ˢ
John Noble	150.
Marie Noble	184. — 10
For Cloaths Furnish'd	100.

£559

Ten Algonkins of the same party has bought & sold to the Sr: Amiot

Mathew Noble for	£86.
For Cloaths Furnish'd	130. — 15ˢ

£216 — 15

One named Solomon Whitney[1] made his Escape from amongst the Indians to whom the Governor General was not willing to give him back again, he died at the Hospital 18th Novᵐ 1750.

Seth Webb ⎫
⎬ are [at] St François
⎭

Joseph Noble
    Frances Noble   at Montreal with
    Mr Strange
Bought for   £300

Benj Noble   is at La Prairie
with Du May Bought   £200
Abigail Noble   at Becancourt.
Timothy Whitney Bought and Paid   £315
This Account taken from Capt. Stevens's List Feby 1, 1752 Pr J. Wheelwright."

The embassy of Stevens and Wheelwright ends with the following letter5 from the Governor of Canada of the same date as their Procès-Verbal. It is addressed to "Mr S. Phips

    L^{nt} Gouverneur et Com^{dt}: en chef à Baston."

                    "Montréal le 25. Juillet. 1752.

  Monsieur

En qualité de Commandant Du Canada par la mort de M^r Le Marquis De La Jonquiére j'ay l'honneur de répondre a la Lettre que votre Excellence a écrite a ce Général le 14 Avril dernier Les ordres respectifs qui ont été donnés par Les Roys De France et De La Grande Bretagne, pour l'Echange mutuel des Prisonniers, récût son Execution dés l'année 1750, et Mr Stouder^1 votre Deputé du Gouvernement De New York ramena tous les prisonniers Anglois qui étoiént depuis la Guerre dans ce Gouvernement, ce dont feu De la Jonquiére rendit compte a la Com De france quoy que ces Echanges fuffent entièrement terminés, et que le dit Sr Stouder en eût, donné sa declaration par écrit, néanmoins j'ay reçû avec plaisir Mr Phineas Stevens, et Nathaniel Weerliwright, Deputés De votre Excellence pour la délivrance des mêmes Prisonniers vous verrés, *[sic]* Monsieur, par le Procés-verbal cy joint qu'ils ont eû une entière liberté pour travailler à leur recherche, et que je leur ai accordé mon authorité, pour avoir ceux qui sont dans cette colonie au pouvoir des sauvages, ou des françois qui les ont rachetés, ils en ramenent neuf avec eux et a l'égard de ceux qui ont resté vous verrés *[sic]* par le dit Procés-verbal les raisons qui n ont point permises a M^{rs} vos Deputés de les ramener.

Ce qu'il y a de bien certain, c'est qu'il ne resté par un seul prisonnier Anglois fait par les françois pendant la Guerre, dans cette Colonie; ils furent tous renvoyés en 1750 comme je viens d'avoir l'honneur de l'observer à votre Excellence, ils furent très bien traittés pendant leur séjour dans ce Pays et l'ors *[sic]* de leur délivrance *[sic]* on n'eût garde d'exiger aucune rançon Les Prisonniers dont il s'agit aujourd'huy, n'ont point été pris par les françois, ils l'ont été depuis la guerre par les sauvages, et si les instances De feu M^r Le Marquis de la Jonquière et les miennes auprès de ces nations avoient pû leur faire quelque impression elles ne se feraient point portées à faire les dits Prisoniers quelques fondées qu'elles pretendent avoir étees *[sic]* ou du moins elles n'auroient point hésité à les mettre en liberté mais vous savés *[sic]* Monsieur que les sauvages de Canada comme ceux de partout ailleurs sont entièrement libres, et qu'ils ne sont point comptables de leurs actions envers de qui que ce soit aussy ne m'a t'il pas été possible de leur faire rendre les Anglois qu'ils ont adoptés dans leurs villages ce que M^{rs} vos Deputés ramenent avec Eux auroient vraisemblablement subi le même sort, si des françois par des sentiments d'humanité ne les avoient retirés des mains de ces sauvages, en leur payant une rançon que M^{rs} vos Deputés leur ont remboursé avec justice et connoissance de cause.

Il n'y a aucune sauvage Prisonnier dans cette Colonie, j'ay toujours ignoré qu'il y eût des sauvages sujets au Gouvernement Anglois; ce seroit une nouveauté merveilleuse dont les françois n'oseroient jamais se flatter, les sauvages de cette colonie ne reconnoissant aucune authorité [sic] et n'ayant d'autre Loy que leur passion et leur caprice.

Les Abenakis de St François ont parlés a Mr Stevens[1] votre deputé de façon a ne laisser aucun doûte à cet égard, je n'ai eû aucune part à leurs paroles, j'en ay seulement été témoin et j'ay bien voulu, pour faire plaisir à M^{rs} vos Deputés, faire transcrire ces paroles, et leur en donner une copie que j'ay certifiée.

Si vous souhaittés [sic] Monsieur, y repondre vous pourrés [sic] me les adresser, et je les ferai parvenir aux dits Abenakis Je supplie, votre Excellence d'etre persuadée pendant que J'auray le Commandemant de ce Pays et dans tous autre tems [sic] je feray toujours mon possible pour correspondre à la Bonne intelligence qui doit régner entre nous, et vous prouver que je suis avec un profond respect
Monsieur,
Votre très humble et très obéissant serviteur,
Longueuil."

The occasion of Major Wheelwright's next embassy to Canada was as follows:

During the summer of 1753, Lazarus Noble and Benjamin Mitchell had been sent to Canada by Lieut. Gov. Phips, then acting as governor of Massachusetts, with a passport and official letters demanding the release of their children, who with others had been captured at Swan Island. This mission had been futile, and Noble and Mitchell had been badly treated in Canada.

Indignant at the treatment of its envoys, the General Court of Massachusetts, upon the return of Governor Shirley from England, desired him to demand restitution of all the captives in Canada. The story is thus told in the records:

At a Council held at the Council Chamber in Boston upon Tuesday, Oct. 23, 1753. Present His Excellency William Shirley, Esq. Gov. His Excellency laid Before the Board the Draught of a Letter he proposed to send to the Governour of Canada agreeable to the Desire of the General Assembly to demand the Restitution of the Captives in his Government—Which being read and considered was approved of.

At a Council held at the Council Chamber in Boston upon Wednesday, October 31, 1753. . . . . .

His Excellency asked the advice of the Council respecting the manner of Sending his Letter to the Governour of Canada for demanding the Restitution of the English captives—Which Matter being fully considered it was Advised that His Excellency send the said Letter by some suitable Person to be by him Commifsionated to make the

Demand of the said Captives—and His Excellency having accordingly appointed Mr Nathaniel Wheelwright for that Service: Advised and Consented that a Warrant be made out to the Treasurer to advance & Pay unto the said Nathaniel Wheelwright the sum of Ninety Pounds towards his Charges in his proposed journey to Canada, he to be accountable for the same; and it was further Advised and Consented that a Warrant be made out to the Treasurer to pay unto Mr Nathaniel Wheelwright the Sum of Thirty-four Pounds one shilling and eleven Pence to discharge his Accompt of Expenses in his late Journey to Canada in Company with Capt. Phineas Stevens in the service of this Government.

Gov. Shirley's letter to the governor of Canada, sent by Nathaniel Wheelwright, dated Boston, October 22, 1753, is a most interesting document. In it he complains of the insult to the ambassadors as a "violation of the Amity between the two nations," as "contrary to the Laws of Humanity," and "an Infringement of the Natural Rights of Mankind."

In closing he says "I now send Mr. Nathaniel Wheelwright   to Demand of you the Restitution. . . . . .of any other English Captives belonging to this Government which may be found in the hands of the French in Canada, and desire that Your Exc^y: would Use Your Influence and Power

over the Indians in whose hands the. . . . . . .before mentioned Children may now be found for the Immediate Delivery of them, likewise of any other English of this Province whom they have made Captive, to the said Mr Nathaniel Wheelwright.

I have the Honour to be wth very great Regard, Sir, Your Excys most Humble and most

Obedient Servant."

[no signature.]

" --November, 1753.

Instructions to Mr. Nathaniel Wheelwright who is commissioned to transact affairs with the gover^r of Canada for the Release of English captives. Having appointed & Commissioned you to proceed in the Service of this Government to Canada for the Redemption of English Captives belonging to this Province. You are hereby directed to set out on your journey as soon as may be The Season of the Year not admitting of Delay, Taking with you such Persons either English or Indians as you shall find necessary for your Guidance & safe Conduct thither and as soon as you shall arrive at the French Fort at Crown Point you must apply to the Commanding officer there for a safe & speedy Conveyance to the Place where the Governor Genl shall then reside. Upon your Arrival at the Place of the Governor's Residence you must immediately wait upon him with my Letter & after Delivery thereof acquaint him that you are appointed by me to solicit the affairs contained in the said Letter, (and if need be to shew him your Commission for that Purpose) and desire that he would appoint you some proper time to treat with him about these Matters. When the ^{sd} Governor shall admit you to a Conference on that subject, you must Signify to him that you do by my Order in the name of His Majesty the King of Great Britain demand that he would cause to be Delivered up to you the English Captives belonging to this Province who are detained by the French in his Governm[l] contrary to the Peace and Amity now subsisting between Great Britain & France. If he should consent to the Delivery of them either with or without Ransom, you must take care of their Speedy & safe conveyance to Boston. If he should insist upon the Ransomes as they were Purchas'd out of the Hands of the Indians you must shew him the Unreasonableness of such a Demand considering that their Fathers with great Expence & Loss of Time had made a Journey to Canada with Credentials from this Governm[t], with Money in their Hands for Procuring their Release, but were violently driven out of the Country before they had Time to effect it. If finally you shall not be able to get off the Ransom Money, you must draw upon the Treasurer of this Province to pay the Same.

You must likewise Request the Governor of Canada to use his Endeavor to get any other Captives now in the hands of the Indians to be delivered up to you; and you are upon such Encouragement to treat with the Indians for their Ransom & agree with them upon any reasonable Sum or Sums & draw upon the Treasurer for Payment thereof as aforesaid. When you shall have accomplished your Mitchell.

business as far as you are able & the Season will admit of your Travel, you must return back to Boston first waiting on the Govern[r] of Canada for his answer to my Letter which if he should decline to do by Writing & do it by a Verbal Message have such Message or Reply down in Writing as Soon as you can that there may be no Mistake in it thro Forgetfulness: You must ask the Govern[rs] Passes for your Safe Conduct thro the French Territory.

Given under my hand at Boston the ⸻ Day of Novem[br] Anno Domini 1753 in the 27th Year of his Majes[tys] Reign.

W. Shirley."

Letter from Major Nathaniel Wheelwright to Governor Shirley:

"Montreal, Nov. 30, 1753.

Sir,

I had the honour the nth of November past to acquaint your Excellency of my arrival at Albany which place I left as soon as possible, and made all the Despatch I could on my journey and voyage to Canada. Permit me to advise Your Excellency by this opportunity that I arrived with Mr. Lydius and my servant yesterday noon at Montreal we were immediately conducted by the officer who was sent with us from Fort St. Frederic, and introduced by him to the General, Monsieur le Marquis Du Quesne who asked me my business I acquainted him that I was sent by Your Excellency to have the Honour to deliver him a letter which he received and immediately retired into his cabinet. He soon returned saying the letter was in English and that he would send for some person to translate it. Then very genteelly told me as I was not a stranger I might go and repose myself and procure Lodgings where I pleased. After dinner he sent an officer, Monsieur

St. Luc la Corne, who is my particular friend, and much in favor with the General, this gentleman surprised me with a message from his Excellency, that he had been informed that the last time 1 came into the country, I had with me an Engineer who passed for my Domestick, and that 1 had with his assistance taken a plan of this City, Quebec, and the River I assured the Gentleman it was false, and that some ill-minded busy person must have raised the report, to prevent my having an opportunity to execute the Commifsion I had the Honour to receive from your Excellency, and desired he would afsure the General the truth of this. He did and was kind enough to acquaint me in the evening that the General had your Excellency's letter translated, and would see me in the morning, when he sent for me, as soon as I paid my respects to him, he desired me to withdraw with him into his cabinet where I had the Honour to converse with him more than an hour without Interruption. He very genteelly told me he was charmed to have an Opportunity of a Correspondence with your Excellency and that he would answer your Excellency's letter very particularly: he was surprised at your Excellency's mentioning his not answering Mr. Phipps his letter which he assured me he never received. He then said he had been informed that I came into the Country the last time with some other design than for prisoners, but he was now persuaded to the contrary and did me the Honour to say I might stay a convenient time to accomplish my affairs, that I should be at Liberty, and should want no assistance he could give me; that I should go when it was agreeable to me to three Rivers, St. Francis & Becancourt with an Interpreter to endeavour to get those captives. He also gave orders to Monsieur St. Luc to go with me to Monsieur DePain, and acquaint him that it was his orders that I should have liberty to see and converse with the English boy, Mitchell's son at all times and as often as I pleased. I saw the Boy but had not time to say much to him. Permit me to assure your Excellency that I shall omit no opportunity to endeavour to reconcile him to return to his Parents. Mr Noble's child which Monsieur St. Ange Charly has the care of, and which he assured me with great grief the last time I was in the country was dead, is now at three Rivers at the Convent. I hope your Excellency will be satisfied with my Conduct and permit me to assure you that I shall be very circumspect in my behaviour, and shall punctually observe your Excellency's Instructions: Should your Excellency have any further commands during my stay in Canada and should send your letters to Col. Lydius at Albany he may have an oppertunity in the winter of conveying your Letters to this Place. The Inclos^d letter I had the Honour to receive from the General in answer to that I had the Honour to receive of Your Excellency and Delivered Him. Your Excellency will I hope Forgive the Liberty I take to inclose a letter for my Good Father.

Your Excellency will excuse my giving you a particular account of the Country. They have had a plentiful summer and a very fine Harvest in this part of the Country. Permit me that I have the Honour to be with the utmost Respect Your Excellency's most Obedient and most Humble Servant

Nat: Wheelwright."

Letter from M. Du Quesne, Governor General of Canada to Governor Shirley of Massachusetts enclosed in that of Major Wheelwright:

"Mountroyal Decr 1st: 1753

S^r: I have had the Honour of a Letter from your Excellency dated the 22d of Oct": last Jn which J was surpriz'd to find a circumstantial Proof of my Being honour'd with a Letter from M^r: Phips On Occasion of a Journey undertaken to this Place by Benjamin Mitchel & Lazarus Noble to recover their Children.

Tho J have not the Honour to be known to your Excellency J flatter myself you will readily believe this Letter could never have reach'd me, since J had not answer m^r: Phipp's Civility, who merits all Respect as well on his own Account, as of the Post he sustain'd, and it would be a heinous piece of Jncivility of which a man of Rank cannot be thought capable.

With regard to the ill succefs the above mentioned Persons met with, your Excellency will give me leave to observe, that if J sent them away sooner than J might have design'd, they must look upon it as wholly occasioned by the Interpreter, whom they had chosen who was a Person that Return'd here of a very suspected Character, and who besides began to behave in so insolent a manner, that J determined to cause him to depart immediately, rather than to be forc'd to put him into Prison.

But to convince your Excellency how sensibly J was touch'd with the lively Sorrow these Fathers felt at returning home without carrying their Children with them. I sent for the Child that is with one Despin and before all the Officers of this Government reproached him with his bad temper in not being willing to follow his Father. He told me for answer, bursting into tears, that absolutely he would not leave his Master.

As it is Evident they are Slaves fairly sold J did not think proper to oblige their masters to give them up, which would have been done without any Difficulty, if they had been Prisoners of war.

Your Excellency will now be Sensible of what Importance it is on such an Occasion to make choice of such a Person as Mr Wheelwright for Negotiatour. Since he will have the Honour to Jnform you that as He was the Bearer of your Excellency's Letter J gave him a very Suitable Reception & promis'd him Protection in everything his Commifsion related to.

I depend upon Your Excellency's being perfectly convinced of my Earnestnefs in concurring to maintain the Friendship that subsists between the two Crowns, when you are Inform'd that, at your Jnstance J have interposed my authority to cause the two Children, that are in the hands of ye French to be restor'd and have given Mr Wheelwright an Interpreter to signify to the Abenakis of S^l François & Becancourt, that they cannot do me so great a Pleasure as by releasing the three other Children that are with them.

Your Excellency will have the Goodnefs to look upon it in this Case, as an unavailing thing to lay my Commands on the Jndians, and that it is to be done only by Treaty, which can be Concluded by nothing but a Ransom to influence them because they are extremely attached to their Slaves; This I leave to the Prudence with which I think m^r Wheelwright capable of conducting & J very Readily give him all the assistance in my Power.

J am very far from pretending to Deprive the Children of your Excellency's Nation, which were taken during a profound Peace, of their Liberty and Religion, when they are Happy enough to have fallen into the Hands of the French, over whom I have an Absolute Power, but J repeat it to your Excellency, that J cannot Answer for the Inclinations of the Jndians in this Case, for there is nothing so difficult as to get their Slaves from them, especially when they have distributed them among their Wigwams to make up for their Dead J hasten to inform your Excellency that J have the honour to afsure you, that in whatever depends immediately upon me, you will receive intire Satisfaction, as no one is more desirous than J am of corresponding with you as frequently as J do with Mr Hopson: J assure you every Thing ingages me to it: Your Excellency's Reputation which is known to me: your distinguished Merit in all Respects, and the Desire J have to maintain & augment the good Understanding and harmonie which ought to subsist between the respective Governours of the two Provinces in Amity, must be to you a sure Pledge that J shall keep these objects in view with as much Alacrity & Earnestnefs as J am desirous of proving personally the infinite Respect with which J have the Honour to be S^r

      Your Excellency's
most humble & most

                obedient Servant
                Du Quesne.

J take the Liberty to pray your Excellency the favour with your leave the Packett directed by me to the Duke de Mirepoix Embassadour to his Britannic Majesty."

That Mr. Wheelwright's despatches were duly received in Boston, appears by the following:

"In the House of Representatives Jan. 8, 1754, It was Ordered that Mr. Speaker, Col. Partridge & Mr Lyman with such as the Honble Board shall join be a Committee to take under Consideration the Letters of the Governor of Canada & Mr Nathaniel Wheelwright to his Excellency the Governor communicated to the Court this Day, & Report what it may be proper for the Court to do.

                Sent up for Concurrence.
                T. Hubbard, Speak'."

           "Wednesday, January 9. 1754.
      Present in Council.

The Secretary by Order of his Excellency laid before the two Houses a Letter His Excellency had received from the Governor of Canada and another from Mr Nathaniel Wheelwright respecting the English Captives in the hands of the French & Indians there

In the House of Representatives Ordered that Mr Speaker, Col. Patridge & Mr Lyman with such as the Honble Board shall join be a Comm^tee to take under Consideration the Letters of the Governor of Canada & Mr Wheelwright to His Excellency the Governor and Report what may be proper to be done thereon—

In Council Read & Concurr'd and Jacob Wendell & Eleazer Porter Esq^rs are joined in the affair."

While the Governor and Council in Boston were considering the despatches received from Wheelwright, he was eagerly prosecuting his search for the captives in Canada. Having got possession of Elinor Noble and others, he left them at Three Rivers and proceeded on his memorable visit to his aunt Esther at the Ursuline convent in Quebec.

I find no mention in our Archives of his return to Boston, or of his employment later in the service of the government. I therefore conclude that Nathaniel Wheelwright went only twice to Canada; his second embassy extending from the early autumn of 1793, into the late spring of 1794, having misled me at first into the statement [see ante,] that he went three times as ambassador to Canada. Proof of this conclusion seems to me to be also given as follows:

"In the House, of Representatives, Dec. 27, 1754.

Inasmuch as Sundry persons belonging to this Province, some of whom were Soldiers & taken from the fort on Kennebec River are now in Captivity in Canada—and as this Court have been Informed that there are also divers Persons in Captivity at Canada belonging to the Government of New Hampshire. Therefore, voted that the Governor of Massachusetts, write to the Governor of New Hampshire & Inform him that this Court proposes to employ Capt. Phinehas Stevens of N° 4, to go to Canada to Redeem the captives of Massachusetts provided that New Hampshire joins and pays its proportion of the expence of the Same."

A letter of the same date as the above vote was at once sent by Governor Shirley of Massachusetts to Governor Benning Wentworth of N. H. asking his co-operation in sending Phineas Stevens of N. H. on this joint embassy, the expenses of the journey to be proportionately paid by both governments. Governor Wentworth replies:

"Portsmouth, Jan. 4, 1755. Sir, Haveing with great difficulty at last prevailed with the Assembly to unite with your Excy^s Government in Employing Cap. Stevens of Charlestown to proceed to Canada in order to redeem the Captives belonging to this Government now in the hands of the French & Inds. I must Desire your favour in Despatching him here as soon as possible, the Sec. having wrote him by my order to that purpose. The Sum already voted is £150. Stirling, but I am hoping to get it Enlarged by Capt. Stevens arrival. I am with great Esteem

Sr Your Excellency^s most Obedient
humble Servant,

B. Wentworth"

While this embassy is pending one Johnson arrives in Boston, empowered by the government of New Hampshire to go to Canada for the redemption of captives and desires to be employed by Massachusetts for the same purpose. There arriving "Just upon his Departure some Intelligence that made it appear not convenient that he should proceed at this time," he was called back by Shirley and detained in Boston.

"Feb. 8, 1755.

In the House of Representatives: Ordered that Col. Hale, Mr. Welles & Mr. Quincy with such as the Honble Board shall join, be a Committee to Consider of some Proper Method for the Redemption of the Captives now in Canada, belonging to this Province. In Council Read & Concurred and Samuell Watts & Thomas Hutchinson Esq^s are joined in the affair."

"At a Council held Tuesday, Feb. 11, 1755. I" Council Read a first &: second time & passed a Concurrence.

A Report referring to the Redemption of Captives in Canada Pursuant to the above Directions the Committee have attended the Service assigned them; and are humbly of the opinion that it is not Convenient at this time for the Court to Employ any Person in Purchasing Captives belonging to this Province; now in Canada. It appearing to the Committee that the Indians have by Means of such Purchases been encouraged to continue their Depredations upon our Frontiers, and the Committee are further of the opinion that no Effectual way can be Projected to put an End to their Depredations but by Revenging the Injury upon the Indians themselves or upon those by whom they were imployed. Which is Humbly submitted.

Per Samuel Watts per Order.

In Council read and Ordered that the Report be accepted."

The last mention of Wheelwright's services as ambassador is the following:

"Att a Council held at the Council Chamber in Boston upon Thursday, the 27 of February 1755:

Advised & Consented that a warrant be made out to the Treasurer to pay unto the Persons herein after mentioned the following sums to discharge the Accounts by them respectively exhibited viz:

To Mr. Nathaniel Wheelwright the Sum of Three Hundred & Seventy three Pounds & Six pence, being the Ballance of his Accompt of Charges in his late Negotiations in Canada for the Redeeming of Captives."

Later, Governor Shirley writes to explain to Governor Wentworth, his action in not permitting Johnson to proceed to Canada.

C. EUNICE WILLIAMS.

THE SIEURS DE LA PERLÈRE AND DUPUIS, AMBASSADORS FROM CANADA TO LEARN THE CONDITION OF THINGS IN ORANGE "PRETEXTING AN EXCHANGE" OF BARENT STAATS, NEPHEW OF PETER SCHUYLER FOR FATHER MAREUIL, THREE OTHER DUTCHMEN FOR THREE FRENCHMEN, AND JOHN ARMES OF DEERFIELD

ON PAROLE FOR ENSIGN DE VERCHÈRES ("BOVENEY.")

By a letter from the Intendant, M. de Ramezay to the Marquis de Vaudreuil written at Montreal the 19th of October, 1709, we learn that Lieut. Barent Staats, the husband of Peter Schuyler's niece, was captured Oct. 12, 1709, near Fort Nicholson and carried to Canada, arriving in Montreal, Oct. 18th.

May 1st, 1710, M. de Vaudreuil writes to M. de Pontchartrain:

"The Onnontagué........request me not to harm Peter, that is the government of Orange, protesting that Peter and the Dutch had been forced by the English to take up arms against us. As
these Indians requested me, My Lord, to be pleased to permit them to untie the cords of Peter's nephews—that is of the Dutch prisoners—whom I held in my hands, I embraced that opportunity to learn distinctly the condition of things in the government of Orange, and pretexting an exchange with Peter Schuyler, of his nephew for Father de Mareuil, the Jesuit missionary of Onnontagué, and of three other Dutchmen for three Frenchmen, and of an officer belonging
to the Boston government whom I have here for Ensign de Verchères, I sent Sieurs de la Perière and Dupuis and six other Frenchmen and an Indian to Orange,"..............I go up to Montreal, My Lord..............to be in a better position for learning what is transpiring within the government of Orange and among the Iroquois, either by the return of Messrs de la Perière and Dupuis or from letters they will find an opportunity to write me.".................De Vaudreuil's despatches to the Minister, in June, 1710, and his letter of Oct. 31 of the same year give us the following: "Sieurs de la Perière and Dupuis having left Orange so as to arrive at Montreal at the opening of the navigation. I found them there at my arrival together with Father Mareuil, Jesuit, whom the English carried off last year from Onnontagué, where he was on the mission. This Jesuit and these two officers.......informed me that Boston was not disarming and even was expecting a reinforcement from Europe to make an attack by sea either on this country or on Acadia."

The story of "Boveney" and John Arms and Johnson Harmon is thus continued in our Archives:

"At a Council held at the Council Chamber, Boston, upon Tuesday Ult° [28th] February, 1709, Present His Excellency Joseph Dudley Esq Gov. &c, &c, &c. His Excellency communicated A letter from Col. Partridge received by an Express the night past accompanying letters to him from the Commissioners at Albany and copy of a letter from Mr Vaudreuil to Col. Peter Schuyler sent by his messengers from Mont Real now attend[g] at Albany who brought in with them some Dutch prisoners & one John Armes of Deerfield upon their parole to return back with them in case they could not obtain their release by exchange for French Prisoners at New Yorke and some in the hands of this Government And the heads of a Letter to Col. Partridge were agreed upon to be Signed by the Secretary."

"Letter to Col. Partridge relating to m^r Vaudrueil' messeng^{rs} at Albany,—and French Prison".

Boston February ult: [28th] 1709-10.

S^r

His Excellency has this day communicated in Council your Letters to himselfe accompanying those from the Magistrates of Albany with the Copy of a Letter from m^r Vaudreuil directed to Col. Peter Schuyler by the hand of his Mefsengers there attending from Mont-Real on pretence of negotiating an Exchange of Dutch Prisoners & one Armes of Deerfield brought thither with them, for some French Prisoners at New Yorke & Beuvenire taken at Haverhill and Leffever, two of theirs in our hands, the latter proposed to be Exchanged for Armes with a great Demand upon him for his redemption out of the hands of the Indians. It's no hard thing to penetrate into their Intreagues, the Designe being to conciliate a new friendship and neutrality with the Albanians as they have lately had; to gain Intelligence of the motions and preparations of the English and leave this and other Her Majesty^s Colonys to take care for themselves. Mr Vaudreuil takes no notice of his Excellency, neglects to write to him, thinking to obtain his Prisoners from hence by the Interposition of the Gent^s at Albany; well knowing how false he has been and Violated his promises made Once & again to return all the English Prisoners, and that long since, upon which all the French Prisoners on his side were sent home by way of Port-Royal. Knowing also his Excy^s Resolution never to set up an Algiers trade to Purchase the Prisoners out of his hands and Direction not to have them sent to Albany but to have them brought in a Vessell by water from Canada or down Kennebec River to Casco Bay or Piscataqua. In which Resolution he continues and it is agreeable to the mind of the Council.

So that Armes must go back with the Messengers, unlets he can otherwise obtain his Liberty; you will further Examin him particularly referring to the State of Quebeck and Mont-Real how they are as to Provisions and Clothing, what store-ships arrived there the last Summer and other Shipping and what are there now? what new Fortification they raysed in the Summer past and where ?

And by the next Post from Albany you must send for Beuvenire from thence and write to the Major and Magistrate to adjust the Accompt of the Demand for his Keeping, which as is Intimated is very Extravagant beyond what is usually allowed for Prisoners and Let draw upon the Governm^t here for payment and It shall be Done. In case the Hunting Mohawks attend you Its thought advisable that Major Stoddard joyne a Serg^t & six Centinels of his best Hunters wth them who will take care to observe them and they will be a good out scout for which you have his Excellency Letter & Order wth this.

You may Adjust the Post as is propos^d from Albany. If the service will be as well Perform'd & the Charge of the Province be thereby Eased but the Albanians must not think to make a Purse from us and to Exact more than it would be done for by our own People It being much better that they have ye Advantage of what must be necessarily

Expended.

This by the Order of his Exce^{5'} with the Advice of the Council from Sr
Your very humble Servant
J^s Addington Secy. The Letter to M^{1'} Vaudreuil must be sent to Albany by ye Post &
forwarded from thence by an Ind wthout Charge or otherwise by ye french Messengers
there now attending."

"At a Council held &c. upon Monday, the 6th of March, 1709, [1709-10]
Present His Excellency Joseph Dudley, Esq., Governor. &c, &c.

John Armes of Deerfield, a prisoner with the French in Mount Real & permitted to
come with the French messengers to Albany upon his parole, attended bringing a letter
from Col. Partridge & another from Mr. Williams, and gave some further account of
affairs there and was dismissed, the Governor and Council not seeing reason to alter
anything of their direction to Col. Partridge by their letters the last week."

"Tuesday 30th, March, 1710, His Excellency communicated to the Council a letter
from Col. Partridge and another from Mr. Williams, Minister of Deerfield,
accompanying some letters from Albany referring to Bovenee a French Prisoner of War
sent by His Excellency the year past to Albany with intent to be exchanged for Mr.
Williams' daughter, prisoner in the hands of the enemy."

As we have seen by De Vaudreuil's dispatches to the French minister, the Sieurs de la
Perière and Dupuis returned to Montreal before the opening of navigation;
unaccompanied, however, by John Arms, their prisoner on parole.
THE FOLLOWING IS FROM JOHN ARMS TO COL. PARTRIDGE. PETITION OF
JOHN ARMES, ON PAROLE AS EXCHANGE FOR SIEUR DE VERCHÈRES.
["BOVENEY."]

"Deerfield, May ye 27, 1710.
Worthy & Reverant Si^r Thes Lins are to inform yourself of ye account of my Charges
Both for my time & expences, sence I Came into this Contrey ye time that I spent in
waiting on ye french Gentleman at Albany & in ye marching in ye woods Contains ten 10
wekes whic at 12 pence par day is   03—00—00
ye charges for my Diyat & Lodging was   02—06—00
& my charge for 2 horses jorny to Allbany
at 10 shilens par jorney   01—00—00
having giving yourself an account only for my time & my diat &
my lodging & my horses jorney all amounts to six pounds
          six shlens.   06—06—o
pray s present my humble Duty to his Excelency and inform him of my Dificult
surcumstance both in Canada, being then a wounded prisener & stript of all my clothes I
could get none out of ther magesend but was fourst to by them with my one money
having Credit with a gentleman there & allso of my oblagasion that I am now under

which I supose that ye french Cap^{tn} has informed his exelency abought & intreat his Excelency to helpe me in so Dificult A cas as I am under: j shall not ade but Remain your humble saurvuent Joh Arms."

"To His Excellency Joseph Dudley Esq^s Captaine Generalle in Cheife &c to ye Honourable Counsell & Representatives in Generall Corte assembled this 31 May 1710.

J Humbly Move in behalf of John Armes now at Derefield a prisoner to the Frentch being taken by the enemy in June was twelve month & Carried to Canada & since he came hither hath been at great Charges at Albany as per account annexed prays it may be allowed & payd him out of the treasury of this province as alsoe Such other allowances for his Losses of his tyme & Cloathing his wounds & c as this Corte may judge meete & just & for yor Excellency & Honors Shall ever Pray Samll Partridge in behalfe

of John Armes afores^d In Council ist June 1710. Read and Recommended In House of representatives June 16: Read and Comitted

" 17 Read & In Answer to the above Petition Resolved That the Sum of Six Pounds and Six Shillings be Allowed & paid out of the publick Treasury to the Hon$^{1'10}$ Samuel Partridge Esq for the use of the s^d Armes Sent up for Concurrence John Park Speaker, 17 June, 1710. Read & concurred Js^a Addington Sec^y"

PETITION OF JOHNSON HARMON, OF YORK, SENT ON PAROLE AS EXCHANGE FOR SIEUR DE VERCHÈRES. ["BOYENEY."]

"To his Excellency Joseph Dudley Esqr Cap^n Gen^{11} & Govr in Chief of her Maj^{ties} Province of the Massachusetts Bay &c and The Honble: Councill and House of Representatives The Humble Petition of Johnson Harman of the Town of York in the Province of Main Sheweth

That Yo^r Petitioner being about his Lawfull Occations at winter Harbour on the 8th day of October last, was taken captive by a party of Penobscot & Kennebeck Indians & by them Carried to Quebecq in Canada, where he continued a Prisoner untill the 22nd day of may following, Having Borrowed some money of Maj Levingston & other friends, by it prevailed on Maj Parotte to come home to see his family & settle his affairs, Providence favouring this good humour of Monsr De Vaudrieull, and his Excellency's Goodnefs to Return A Prisoner from here in his Room, (which Favour is for Ever to be Acknowledged) But now he is Commanded away in the Present Expedition (wherein he hopes & Designs to do Some Signall Service) But his Misfortunes are such by this imprisonm^t and his affairs are such that all that is Dear & good to him lies at stake & his family Suffers Extreamly for want of his being at home &c

Therefore he humbly prays this Honble: afsembly to Consider the Great fateigue & Expence he hath been at & the poor Circumstances of his family and affairs, & to afford them Some Support & help to fit himself out in his Station this Expedition as in yor Wisdom Shall seem meet

And yor Pet. as in Duty bound shall
ever pray &c   Johnson Harmon"

July 24th 1711 In the House of Representatives
"In answer to this petition Voted that Twenty Pounds be paid the petitionr out of the province Treasury
Sent up for Concurrence[1]   John Burrill Speaker"

July 24. 1711.
"Upon Reading the Petition of Johnson Harman of York late Prisoner of Quebec, Praying Consideration of the great Fatigue & Expence he has been at & the poor Circumftance of his Family & Affairs Voted in Concurrence with the House of Representatives, That the Sum of Twenty Pounds be paid to the Petitioner out of the Treasury of this Province:—   Consented to. J. Dudley."

While Johnson Harmon of York, Me., a captive in Canada, was at Chambly fort on his return to New England on parole, to be exchanged for "Boveney," he received the following interesting letter from Father Meriel. I give it to show Father Meriel's knowledge of the English language and his facility in its use. The original is in Mass. Archives, Vol. 51, pp. 212-213:
"To Mr Johnson Harmon
at Shamblee.
Sir,
Since you are gone, a Squaw of the nation of the Abnakis is come in from Boston. She has a pass from your Governour. She go's about getting a little girl, daughter of Mr John Williams. The Lord Marquess of Vaudreuil helps her as he can. The business is very hard because the girl belongs to Indians of another sort and the master of the English girl is now at Albany. You may tell your Governour that the squaw can't be at Boston at the time appointed and that she desires him not to be impatient for her return, and meantime to take good care of her two papows. The same Lord Chief Governour of Canada has insured me in case she may not prevail with the Mohoggs for Eunice Williams, he shall send home four English persons in his power for an exchange in the Room of the two Indian children. You see well, Sir, your Governor must not disregard such a generous proffer as according to his noble birth and obliging genious ours makes. Else he would betray little affection to his own people. The Lord Marquess of Vaudreuil has got a letter for Madam Vetch which he's very glad to see safely convey'd unto her. I pray Sir you with all my heart to present unto her my most humble respects. We have at Kebeck two vessels by means whereof we have had this information. In Spain the King and under him the Duke of Vendôme have upon the 9 and 10 of December Last fought a great battle wherein an army of 25,000 men has been routed. General Stanhope and 5,000 others taken prisoners at Brihuega. General Staremburg with 4,000 men only made their escape and retired to Barcelona whither before him the Archduke of Austria repaired. The Duke of Vendome was in March to besiege that city. So Ships with 6,000 men sent from England and Holland to relieve it have all of them been destroyed by a storm. The King

of Sweeden with 200,000 Tartars invade Moscovy and Poland. At his approach the Northern & German crowns withdraw their troops from the Netherlands. The Parliament of England consisting of Presbyterians has been dissolved, and another called, whereof all members are Episcopalians. At Brest in Little Britain, there is a great navy preparing for a design that is kept very secret. The gallion of *[illegible]* are come in safe. The people of France are very *[illegible]* their King for the prosecution of the war. The paper money has been taken away and rent assigned for the ready paiement thereof. The Duke of Noailles who has taken Girona is to joyn the Duke of Vendôme for the siege at Barcelona with 25,000 men. The English and Hollanders having sent to the Most Christian King sueing for peace his Majesty won't yield to their proposition. A French squadron under the command of Mr DuClerc had landed 800 men at Rio Janeiro in the river of the Amazon and had taken the town. But 15000 Portuguese having fain upon them have made them prisoners of war. The ships are come safe. There is also a flying report that there is in old England a navy of 3,000 men fitting out for an expedition against New France. Our army in Flanders is of 130,000 men under Marshal Villars. Some say the King will be at the head thereof. That of the Allies commanded by the Duke of Marlborough is far inferior. There is no mention of Prince Eugene. We do hourly expect two other French vessels from Rochel. If they bring freshe tidings and I find an opportunity to make them known to you I shall. Write, I pray, to me from Albany and afterwards from New England. I have sent your letters to Kebeck. Do my commendations to my acquaintance at Wells, and at Boston, namely to Mr Hern a Lawyer to Mrs. Rawlings and her father and to Mrs. Mary Pleisted to Catharine Leatherby to Lieutenant Josiah Littlefield to Mr Sam-uel Emery, to Lieutenant Thomas Baker &c I remain

Out of Acadia we have the   Sir
confirmation of the news we   Your Most
    had already had that most of   Humble Servant
    the souldiers of the garrison   Meriel Prieft.
    at Port Royal were dead of the scurvy.
    Ville-Marie in the Island of Montreal June 25.
1711"

Letter from Governor Dudley of Mass. to Governor Hunter of N. Y.:

"Boston 31 Decem^r, 1711,

    S^r

This last post I troubled you with a letter referring to a Letter J sent to Albany directed to Mr Voderil for the Exchange of prisoners which I have holden with him these nine years past and since I sent Mr Boveney a french ensign who J have had in my hands these two yeares (in exchange for whom mr voderil the last spring sent me Captain Harmon an English officer) with a passport to returne home by way of Albany by whom J further acquainted Mr Voderil that I had in my hands forty french prisoners which J offered him in Exchange for as many of mine Jn his hands both my said Letters & Boveney are stayed by the Gentlemen at Albany for your Excellencys allowance as they write, I pray of you s^r that the said french prisoner & the Letters may be allowed to pass that I may have her majestys subjects return & may be quit of the frenchmen in my hands which J judge is for her Majesty's service & very well accepted at all times by her majesty's government, if the sending by Albany be a trouble J will avoyd it for the future he the said Mr Boveney was sent with General Hill into Canada river to be sent home and is now in Albany at his own desire & will find the way home with my letter with a couple of straggling Indians if he may be allowed which is what J Desire of your Excellency if it may consist with your own good opinion 1 am ^{sr}

Your Excellency

most faithful
humble servant
J. D."

"To his Ex^{ey}
     Joseph Dudley Esqr Govr
and Capt. Gen^{11} of her Maty^s Province of New Hampshire and
Massachusetts. S^r
I am honor'd with two of yours relateing to the Gentleman upon his returne to Canada. Upon advice from the Commissioners at Albany of that persons being arrivd there I consulted her Majesty's council here, who were of opinion that as matters stood it was neither safe nor expedient to let him proceed at this time, considering our own ill posture and the advices he might give as to the state of the Roads and Lakes by which he was to passe. Upon which I sent to detain him till further orders; the Roads are such at present as he could not possibly wade through So soon as they are more practicable, I shall Send orders to let him goe and accommodate him with what may be necessary, But I must Intreat you for the future to give me notice of all such as you send that way, there being a strict prohibition on the frontiers of Suffering any to goe that way without leave of ye Government not without Good cause. I Shall In all my best Indeavour to approve myself Your Ex^{eys} most obedt

Humble Servant
Ro. Hunter.

    N. York ye 15 Jan. 1711-12."

On the above letter of Gov. Hunter is endorsed, the following, which is evidently a copy of Dudley's answer:

"Boston, 29th January, 1711.

    S:
There are eight years past since J have had Exchanges of prisoners with M^r. Vodruelle which has Occafioned many Letters and Mefsages between M^r. Vaudruelle and myself and J have Generally Sent them by Albany and have had from Canada by Several Ways

by Sea and Land some hundreds of priſoners and have Sent more to him and have now Forty that J Keep at great Charge to Exchange for as many and More that are in French hands of Her Majesty's good Subjects. The Letters that Accompany Mr. Boveney the Frenchman are to procure this Exchange at the Earnest Desire of the Assembly & Council of this Province at all times to whom J Communicate always what J write to that Side, and would be Glad J could Communicate with you at all times in this and Everything Else Jmporting Her Majesty's Service. Boveney now at Albany is a poor Country Boy for whome J Recd Captain Harmon a very Good Officer and must Returne again if J cannot Get Boveney home he was in the Fleet going to Canada with the General to have returned that way and being unfortunate there J thought this the best way J could be Glad while he Stays those Letters might go forward otherwise J shall have no Exchange the Spring coining and if Boveney may not go home Soon J must Send Some other way to Acquaint Mr Vaudruelle That I have Captain Harmon and That Boveney Shall come as soon as J can Tho if sould be Stayed till News from Great Britain it will be worse to Send him then, then it is now

> I am Sr
> Your Excellencys most
> ffaithfull Humble Servant
> J Dudley."

Letter to Col. Samuel Partridge of Hatfield, Mass., from Jonas [or Jona] Douw:

"Albany ye 15th Desembr 1 7 1 2
Sr   this gives Occation to me to write to You Since J did
Some time ago Give mr Sam Aſhley a power of attorney to Receive Such Sumse of money Due to me for Keeping of mr Bouene de Verſhare J find Your promiſe for the payment when J should Send a power of atterney to Receive the same but J at Constant
Trouble Giveing power to Receive Such Demands as proposed by Your Selfe and as Yet Nothing Comes to Perfection Sr J Earnestly Desire of You to lett me know the Reaſon my Moneys is Detained from me and you will Verry much obleadge me Sr Your Verry humble

> Servant
> Jona Douw"

Letter from Col. Samuel Partridge to Governor Dudley:

> "Hatfield, dec: 31 1712

May it pleaſe yor Excellency
I have this day the Return of the poſt from Albany who have reacht the Frentch Meſsengers & the Letters J Recd of mr Williams are ſent by them for Canada as J suppoſe yor Selfe is Enform'd by the Encloſsed from Albany to yor Self & by mr Robt Levinftons Letter here Encloſsed alsoe, Capt. Jonas Dowe follows me with Letters for to be payd for

his Keeping Monf.ʳ Bovenee de Versher 13 or 14 Months at *21£ os od* or thereabouts he never had any Engagem.ᵗ from me Jn the day of it J fent the s.ᵈ de Versher to Col. Shuyler according to directions he s.ᵈ Dowe infifts on the paym.ᵗ of the Money or the Reason why it is not done J have Enclofed his Letter & Wee have No Occurent hath happened & are in quiett at p.ᵉfent J am informed by the poft that an Jndian from Canada s.ᵗʰ there is no Motion of Warr goeing forward there with my Humble Service p.ᵉsented to yo.ʳ Self Madame Dudley & yo.ʳ whole family. Rendering my Selfe Much oblidged in Obeydience & am yo.ʳ verry Humble Serv.ᵗ

Sam Partridge."

P. S ......"

DAGEUILLE, AMBASSADOR FROM CANADA TO ALBANY, MAY, 1711.

In the correspondence between the Governors of Canada and New England quoted in the story of Eunice Williams, p. 146, ante.

De Vaudreuil writes:

"Your Interpreter has ill-explained my Letter. . .in that you did not furnish Mr Dagueille with anything. . .I complain with reason that in sending me three prisoners by him you obliged him to furnish them out of his own money with provisions and other necessaries for the return of those three men,. . . .contenting yourself as he and they inform me, with wishing them a good journey."

To this charge Dudley replies:

"I dare appeal to any disinterested and competent judges as to my invariable conduct in regard to supplies and provisions for the French captives returned by Mr Lesguilles [Dagueille]. . . . It has exceeded and never fallen short of what has been done for my poor people elsewhere."

Letter from General Nicholson and others to M. de Vaudreiul.

"Annapolis Royal, 11. oct. 1710.

Monsieur,

It having pleased God to bless with success, the just and royal enterprise of Her Majesty Anne,. . . . Queen of England, France and Ireland, defender of the faith, by reducing to her subjection the Fort of Port-Royal and the country adjacent,. . . . .we think it proper to inform you that, since you have made several attacks upon her Majesty's frontiers, your cruel and barbarous Savages and Frenchmen having inhumanly massacred many poor people and children, in case the French after your receipt of this letter, shall commit any hostilities and barbarities, immediately upon information of such acts, we will avenge ourselves by similar atrocities upon your people in Acadia. But as we abhor the cruelty of your Savages in war, we hope that you will give us no occasion to imitate them. . . . . you have a great number of prisoners under your jurisdiction, especially a young girl, the daughter of the Rev. Mr. Williams, Minister of Deerfield, we hope that you will have all the Said prisoners ready to be delivered up, at the first flag of truce that we shall send, in the month of May next; otherwise you may expect that an equal number of the inhabitants of this country will be enslaved among our savages until there shall be a complete restitution of the subjects of Her Majesty, whether they be in the possession of the French or Indians. . . . . .

[Signed] F. Nicholson,
Sam Vetch,
Charles F. Ebbey,
Robert Reading,
G. Martin,
Thomas Mathew,
William Bidele,
George Gordon."

De Vaudreuil speaks as follows of the above letter, and of his action thereupon in a letter to the French Minister dated 25th April, 1711:

"M. de Subercase having surrendered on the 13th of October, he and Mr Nicholson, General and Commander-in-Chief of the Queen of England's forces on this Continent, have both sent Baron de St Castine and Major Levingston to me through the forest. I annex hereunto, My Lord, the letter Mr Nicholson has written me and my answer to him, which I have sent by Messrs de Rouville and Depuis, being very glad to employ these two officers on this occasion in order to obtain information through them of the movements of our enemies, and at the Same time to make them acquainted with the Country and the most favorable routes to send parties thither."

On the 15th of June, 1711, Costebello, Commandant at Plaisance, writes that he has "sent the Sieur de la Ronde-Denis to Boston concerning an exchange of prisoners. He will reclaim Pore Justinian and bring him back to Plaisance." Father Justinian was a Recollet priest, missionary and curé of Port-Royal, who in January, 1710, while celebrating mass, had been captured with five of his flock, carried to Boston and imprisoned there, where one had died. That Father Justinian was not released appears probable from the following:

"At a Council held Munday 2nd of April, 1711. The Honourable Governour Vetch Commander-in-Chief of Her Majesty's Fort of Annapolis Royall and the Country of Nova Scotia &^{ca}, representing that Father Justinian a French Priest a lawfull Prisoner of War taken within the Government under his Care was brought hither by his order with design to obtain Mr. Williams' daughter in exchange for him having hitherto been supported at his charge, and that being now about to return to his Government, he shall otherwise dispose of him; unless the Government be willing to take him into their care to be exchanged for Mr. William's daughter or some other valuable Prisoner.

Advised that the said Priest be kept to be exchanged accordingly."

Sieur de la Ronde-Denis came several times to Boston, as ambassador from Bonaventure, Governor of Port-Royal.

"At a Council held at the Council Chamber in Boston, 22nd of February, 1705. His Excellency [Dudley.] communicated to the Council a Letter from Mr. Bonaventure Commander at Port Royal received by the hand of a French Gentleman whom he sent hither with Capt. Rouse who arrived two days since and brought seventeen English prisoners, and all appeared at the Board."

"At a Council held at the Council Chamber in Boston upon Wednesday the 17th of April 1706. His Excellency acquainted the Council that Mr L'Ronde Messenger from Mr. Bonaventure Commander at Port-Royal is very desirous to return the time for his stay here being pafs'd and there being several French prisoners to be sent thither and of ours there to be brought from thence.

Ordered, That Mr Commissary General do take up and dispatch a suitable Vessel for the transporting of the s^d Mr L'Ronde with the French prisoners, and for bringing home ours from thence accordingly.

J. Dudley.

His Excellency communicated the Draft of his letter to Mr. Bonaventure to be sent by Mr. L'Ronde."

The real purpose of De la Ronde's mission appears in the following resume of a letter from Bonaventure to the French Minister, dated Port-Royal, Dec. 24, 1706:

"He had sent the Sieur de la Ronde-Denis to Boston, under pretext of informing himself of what had been done between M. de Vaudreuil, and the governor of Boston about an exchange, in order that he might examine the harbors, ports, and forces of the colony— This he has done so that he (Bonaventure) is in a condition to attack this colony (Boston) if he had a sufficient force."

Concerning this embassy the Minister writes to the Sieur de la Ronde-Denis:

À Versailles 30th June 1707

"I am satisfied with your account of your journey to Baston and to Quebec for the exchange of prisoners, and I am very glad that you have taken cognizance of the ports of the coast from Port-Royal to Baston. . . . . You have only to follow the orders of M. de Subercase, and devote yourself especially to interrupting the commerce of Baston"

Writing on the same date to De Subercase, the Minister says:

"I am very glad that the Governor of Baston has sent back the man named Baptiste who has been a prisoner there for four years.

You can employ him in teaching navigation to the young men of the country, since they prefer this trade, rather than to work on the land."

An account of an "Enterprize des Bastonnias sur l'Acadie" dated July 6, 1707, mentions Subercase "accompanied by the Sieurs de la Ronde, Faillant, and Baptiste, and about 200 men," attempting to defend the mouth of the Gaspereau against the Bastonnais.

Here we have evidence of Baptiste's return to Port-Royal previous to June 30, 1707.

The Sieur de la Ronde came twice, at least, to Boston after this: in June, 1711, when he demanded Father Justinian, and again in October, 1723.

What tales the Council Chamber of the old State House in Boston might tell.

At a meeting of the Council Munday 2nd of April 1711. "His Excellency proposed the sending of the Indian Woman lately taken by the troops under Colonel Walton with a Letter directed to Moxis the Eastern Indian Sagamore importing that if he will procure Mr Williams daughter from her Indian Master at Canada &: send her hither that then this squaw & her son &: daughter (who are to be detained as hostages for her return again) shall be sett at liberty & returned home."

The return of Maj. Livingston and his French escort appears as follows in our Archives:4

"At a Council held at the Council Chamber in Boston upon Saturday the 24th of February, 1710

Present His Excellency Joseph Dudley Esqre Governor

Wait Winthrop

Elisha Hutchinson Esq^{res}	Penn Townsend
Samuel Sewall	Andrew Belcher Esqre
Peter Sergeant	Edwd Bromfield
John Walley Esq^{res}	

Wm Hutchinson

Isaac Addington Esqre

Major Livingston arriving here yesterday from Canada accompanied with some French Gent^n who brought Letters from Mr Vaudreuille to his excellency to the Honble Col Vetch &c

His Excellency communicated his letter to the Council it chiefly referring to an exchange of Prisoners as also did Col Vetch his

And his Excellency gave directions in writing to Mr Commissary General and Mr Sheriff Dyer to visit the said French Gent" now at the George Tavern & offer their service to them in settling their quarters where they are & at the houses adjoining and to acquaint them that the sherriffe will attend them to the Town House in Boston on Monday next three o'clock afternoon where the Governor will see them in Council to receive their Credentials and withall to let them understand the Governor has assigned that House where they are for their entertainment and will take care that they be not imposed upon by excessive rates for their expences. "

"At a Council held at the Council Chamber in Boston upon Monday the 26th of February 1710.

Present [as above.] Pursuant to the intimation given on Saturday last to Messrs D'Rouville and Dupuix Messengers from M. Vaudreuille Governor of Canada they were admitted to attend the Governor in Council, and shew^d forth their credentials; His Excellency assured them, the accompt depending betwixt this government and Mr Vaudreuille for money by him advanced to Messrs Appleton & Sheldon in their respective negotiations at Quebeck should be forthwith adjusted and the Ballance paid and that he will confer with them upon the proposal for the exchange of prisoners on both sides, if they can come to a mutual agreement thereabout; so as to dispatch them this week without being detained longer agreeable to Mr Vaudruille's desire in his letter and return before the Ice begone."

Sewall, the omniscient, has the following:

"Feb 26. 1710-11

This day p. m. the Govr has the French Messengers from Canada in Council; Had the Councillors on his Left hand, Col. Vetch and them on his right; on the right also were Mr. Secretary and Mr. Commissary. Read their Credentials by Mr Weaver the Interpreter. Reprimanded one Anthony Oliver[1] forgoing to them at Meers's and to the Frier without leave; made him take the Oaths, and subscribe to the Declaration. Told the Messengers they should depart that day sennight as had told the Council with some Spirit, last Satterday: at which time Col. Vetch said the people of N. E. were generally given to Lying; to which the Govr said not a word."

"At a Council held at the Council Chamber in Boston upon Saturday ye 3rd March, T710.

Ordered that Messrs Rouville & Dupuix Commissioners from Mons D'Voudruille Governor of Canada to negotiate an exchange of Prisoners on both sides be allowed twenty shillings pr Diem for their Table during their stay in this Government

And that Mr Commissary General make up the account of the charge of the two men and the Horses that attended 'em from Rehoboth to Boston and have been detained to accompany them back as far as New London and pay the men for their service at the rate of eighteen pence per man and twelve pence for a horse pr Diem over & above men & horses subsistence until the return back to Rehoboth Articles for the Exchange of prisoners proposed and concerted between His Excellency & the said Messrs Rouville & Dupuix on the part of Governour Vaudruille were read & approved"

"An Accompt presented by Andrew Belcher Esqr Commissary General of twenty-eight pounds sixteen shills paid to Messrs Rouville and Dupuix Messingers from Mr Vaudruille Governour of Canada being the Ballance of the account of money Mr Vaudriulle supplyed to Messr3 Appleton & Shelden in their respective Attendances on him from this Government and for exchange of the money paid them

And the further sum of Sixty two pounds four shillings & two pence paid charges of men & horses & coach hire attending the said Messrs Rouville & Dupuix in their way thither [hither?] and return as far as New London & for their entertainment whitest they remained here, the whole amounting to ninety one pounds and two pence, read accepted and Advised. & Consented That a Warrant be made out thereupon to the Treasurer to reimburse & pay the said Andrew Belcher Esqr the aforesaid sum of ninety one pounds."

The date of the return of the Frenchmen is given us in a letter to the Minister from De Vaudreuil, dated Quebec, 25th of April, 1711. He says "Sieurs de Rouville and Dupuis arrived at Chambly eight or ten days ago. The English had not received any news from Europe up to the 17th of March, the date of their departure from Boston."

They carried a "Roll of English Prisoners in the Hands of the French and Indians at Canada" 1710-11.

A duplicate of this list is in our Archives. It contains the names of 113 New England captives with a few repetitions. Among them are "The Minister's Daughter, Deerfield," Johnson Harmon, Mary Sawyerd, Hester Sawyard, all of York. Mary Silver, Haverhill, Hester Wheelwright, Wells. On the back of the list is the following letter:

"Boston 5th March 1710.

Sir,

This comes to your hand by Messrs D'Rouville & Depuis Messengers from Mr D'Voudruille I have to thank your kind Discreation in sending them the Round Way that they might not know our Albany Road, upon the Same Consideration I have Returned them the same way & am Glad we have had no News from Europe dureing their stay here & hope to have them Dispatch before anything Arrive. They have shewed themselves good men here have signed Articles with me for the Rendition of all Prisoners in June next. I pray you to speed them away as soon as possible.

I am Sir your very humble Servt J.

Dudley.

To. Col. Schuyler."

EUNICE WILLIAMS AND HER DESCENDANTS.

FROM THE RECORDS AT CAUGHNAWAGA.

Since John Schuyler's Memorial, little has been known of Eunice Williams. It is hoped that the following may throw light upon her later history.

Baptismal records at the mission of Sault Saint-Louis, (Caughnawaga) exist from March 1, 1735, to March 10, 1745. From this to March 25, 1753, they are wanting. After that to the present date they are complete.

Marriage records exist from Sept. 30, 1743, to June, 24, 1747, and from Jan. 29, 1763, forward to this day.

Records of deaths begin January, 1762.

From this it will be seen that the baptism of Eunice Williams as Margaret, and her marriage, both previous to Schuyler's visit (about 1713) do not appear on Caughnawaga records, nor does her English name.

Nehemiah Howe in his narrative of his own captivity, says that at Crown Point he saw an "Indian named Amrusus, husband to her who was Eunice Williams."

Mr. Edward W. Williams, Jr., quotes the name Amrusus from Mr. Sheldon, and says that it was "roughly civilized into Toroso." It is with diffidence that I have declined to accept the name Amrusus, and prefer to await further knowledge. Nehemiah How saw and talked with Eunice's husband, but he cannot be taken as authority on either French or Indian proper names. Possibly Amrusus is a corruption of Ambroise, a favorite

French name in Canada. Rev. J. G. L. Forbes, a scholarly man, an adept in the Iroquois language, curé of Caughnawaga and a diligent student of its records, says that the name Amrusus does not appear there.

"Toroso and Amrusus," writes Mr. Forbes, "are certainly corrupt names. They are not Iroquois at all. They remind one of "Arosen" and "Tekentarosen," which are Iroquois, and proper names for men." The records of Caughnawaga have been carefully studied in the hope of finding a name suggestive of Amrusus or Toroso. Arosen and Tekentarosen occur as masculine names, but nowhere in connection with Eunice Williams or her children. The impartial research and patient labor of Mr. Forbes, with his knowledge of the Iroquois language has furnished me with authenticated ex-tracts from the registers, otherwise impossible to me. From these, and what I have been able to supply from the New England end of the story of Eunice, I am able to collate what follows:

On Caughnawaga records a certain Marguerite with an Indian name of four variations, was four times godmother.

On one of these occasions, she was godmother to the child of an Indian named Karenhisen.

A Catharine was also godmother to one of Karenhisen's children. It is now and always has been a custom of the Caughnawaga Indians for kinswomen of the father to stand for his children. Therefore, Mr. Forbes concludes that Marguerite and Catharine were kinswomen of Karenhisen, and probably related to each other.

We know that Eunice (Marguerite) had a daughter Catharine. Why may we not assume that this Marguerite was Eunice, and this Catharine her daughter? Admitting this, we get here Eunice's Indian name, given in these four baptismal records with four variations, viz.: Marguerite 8aon'got, Marguerite Gon'aongote, Marguerite 8aongote and Marguerite Aongote.

"This name," says Mr. Forbes, "may be translated 'They took her and placed her as a member of their tribe.' " It thus appears, that whoever this godmother was, she did not belong by birth to the tribe: "they took her and placed her as a member of their tribe." If this be Eunice Williams, as I believe, what more touching and appropriate name could have been given her?

The order and the dates of the births of Eunice's children are unknown. Rev. James Dean, missionary to the Indians at Caughnawaga and Saint-Francis in 1773 and 1774, knew Eunice well. He wrote to her brother Stephen Nov. 12, 1774. "She has two daughters & one grandson which are all the Descendants she has."

John, son of Eunice, died childless at Lake George, in 17583. Catharine, daughter of Eunice, [see ante] appears on Caughnawaga records as Catharine Asonnontie and Catharine Kassinontie. (Flying leg.)

There is no record of her marriage. Her husband was Francois Xavier Onasategen. They had no children, but adopted two. Onasategen died in 1805. Catharine (Flying leg) his wife, in 1807.

"Le douze septembre mil huit cent sept par moi prêtre soussigné a été inhumée dans le cimitière de cette mission Catherine Kasinontie, sauvagesse de ce village, décédée l'avant veille, agée d'environ quatre vingts ans, veuve de François-Xavier Onasategen. Présents Charles Sa8enno8ane et Simon Tagaratensera, qui n'ont su signer.

(Signed) A: Van Felson ptre."

"Le vingt six Juin mil huit cent cinq par moi prêtre soussigné, a été inhumé dans l'Eglise de cette Mission, François Xavier Onasategen, Grand Chef de ce Village, décédé la veille, âgé de près de Quatre vingts ans, epoux de Catherine Gassinontie. présents Messieurs Jean Baptiste Bruguier, Curé de Chateaugai, Pierre Consigny de la Chine, et autres, soussignés

(Signed)   A: 8anFelson ptre

Bruguier ptre

Pierre Consigny ptre

Chs De Lorimier Le clerc miss."

It is through Onasategen, Catharine's husband, that we recognize the following as the record of Eunice's (Marguerite's) burial:

"1785. Le vingt six novembre j ai inhumé Marguerite belle-mère dannasategen elle était ageé de quatre vingt quinze ans.

(Signed) L. Ducharme. miss:"

Translation. "On the twenty-sixth of Novembre, 1785, I have buried Marguerite, mother-in-law of Onasategen. She was ninety-five years old."

Signed,   L. Ducharme, Mission priest."

So after all the vicissitudes of her life, it is only as the mother-in-law of the "Grand Chef Onasategen," that Eunice Williams's death is noticed. Doubtless these vicissitudes had made her look older than she was. She was born in September, 1696, and would therefore have been eighty-nine at her death.

We have seen that two out of Eunice's three children died without issue. Mary is the only child of Eunice through whom we can trace the descent. The name of her husband, the father of her children, has hitherto eluded search. Mr. Wight quoting Eleazer's statement on this point, leaves it without a shadow of credibility and says, "The fact is that the husband of Sarah, [meaning Mary] was an Indian of unknown, mayhap of unpossessed name."

The following extracts from the records at Caughnawaga, establish the fact that Eunice's daughters were Catharine, who died without children, and Mary, [not Sarah] who became the mother of Thomas.

Mary appears on the records of Caughnawaga as Marie Skentsiese. (New fish.)

There is no record of her marriage. Her husband's name heretofore unknown, was Louis Satagaienton. (Equally sown.) The only child of this marriage was Thomas, baptized as follows:

"1759 Die 6. jan: ego idem [J. B. Denonville S. J.] Baptizavi cum ecclesiae ceremoniis puerum recens natum ex pat re Ludovico Sateguienton et matre Maria Skentsiese conjugibus quern Thomam nominavit Thomas Taronhiagannere."

Translation. "On the sixth day of January, 1759, I, the same [the priest here refers to his own name J. B. Denonville of the Society of Jesus,] have baptized with the rites of the church, a newborn boy, the father Louis Sataguienton, the mother Marie Skentsiese, husband and wife, whom Thomas Taronhiagannere named Thomas."

Thomas Thorakwanneken or Tehorakwanneken, (Two suns together,) of whose Indian name there are several variations, was the only child of Louis Sataguienton and Marie Skentsiese. His mother's death is thus recorded:

"Mai le 14. 1779 a été enterrée Marie femme de Satagaienton, agée d'environ 40 ans. G. S. [grand service] sur le corps.

Jos Huguet ptre. S. J."

Out of respect to his wife's ancestry, Louis Sataguienton had taken the name of Williams. He married a second time, Jan. 29, 1780, still keeping the name of Williams, which his children by his second wife also assumed.

His first child by his second wife was born Oct. 27, 1780. Louis Satagaienton died in 1803. His widow died in 1812. Thomas Tehorakwenneken, the only child of Louis Satagaienton by his first wife, Marie Skentsiese, the daughter of Eunice Williams, married in 1779.

"Janvier le 7, 1779 Thomas teHorak8annegen a épousé Marie Anne, fille de Haronkio8annen.

"7. 7bre 1780 idem [i. e. Jos Huguet priest S. J.] supplevi ceremonias baptismi in puerum pridie natum ex patre Thoma Tehorakwannegen et ex matre Maria Anna Gonate8enteton, conjugibus, quem Joannem Baptistam nominavit Catharina honnasategen conjux."

Translation. "On the seventh of September, 1780, I, Jos Huguet priest S. J. have administered the rite of baptism to a boy born the day before, son of Thomas Tehorakwannegen and Mary Anne Gonate8enteton, husband and wife, whom Catharine the wife of Onosategen, has named Jean Baptiste."

The above is interesting because the godmother was Thomas's aunt Catharine, daughter of Eunice, and granddaughter of Rev. John Williams,—who gave to the baby the name of John.

Catharine was godmother also to Thomas's second child, a girl whom she named for herself. Catharine's adopted daughter Louise was godmother to Thomas's third child, whom she named Louise. Catharine, daughter of Eunice and wife of Onosategen, died in 1807.

The records at Caughnawaga give the births of eleven children to Thomas. We have plenty of evidence that Eleazer also was his son. There are now in Caughnawaga several grandchildren and great-grandchildren of Thomas Tehorak8anneken.

CHILDREN OF REV. JOHN AND EUNICE MATHER WILLIAMS.

Rev. John Williams married successively two cousins, granddaughters of Rev. John Warham of Windsor, Conn. His first wife and all their children except Eleazer, the eldest, who was away at school, and two who died previously, were either killed or captured, Feb. 29, 1703-4.

Eleazer became the minister of Mansfield, Conn.

Samuel died unmarried in 1713.

Esther married Rev. Joseph Meacham of Coventry, Conn. Stephen became the minister of Longmeadow, Mass. Eunice remained in Canada.

Warham became the minister of Watertown, West Precinct, now Waltham, Mass. Rev. Stephen Williams of Longmeadow, kept a diary for many years. It consists of eleven Mss. volumes, very closely written scarcely punctuated and with many abbreviations peculiar to himself. One volume was burned in the lire which destroyed the old parsonage in 1846. The part covering the period between 1738 and 1742 inclusive, consists of 591 pages. The narrative of his captivity, carefully edited by Mr. Sheldon, has been published by the P. V. M. Association of Deerfield. Through the generous courtesy of the custodians of the diary, that part which relates to the first two visits of Eunice Williams to New England are here published for the first time. The name of her husband has not yet been found in this diary, though careful search has been made for it.

EXTRACTS FROM THE DIARY OF REV. STEPHEN WILLIAMS OF LONGMEADOW.

"1740.   Aug. 9.   Saturday this day I have a letter [from] Albany informing me yᵗ my sister Eunice is expected at Albany next week & I am desired to go thither.

Monday

11   I have wrote to my br at M Giueing him an accᵗ of whᵗ I have heard o [from] Albany & wait this day to see whether he'll come & oh yt God wᵈ direct & help us all in this weighty affair

12.   This day I set out to Albany accompanieᵈ by my br w of m & my brother Meacham we had a comfortable journey and got to Albany on yᵉ 15ᵗʰ yᵉ particulars of w'h I met with till yᵉ

27 [I have wrᵗᵉ in my travailing journal w'h I propose to keep] when we had (ye joyfull Sorrowfull meeting of oʳ poor Sister yᵗ we had been separated [from] for above 36 years) Ye next day [28th] we got her and her Husband' promise to go with us to my house & tarry wth us 4 days, we prepar'd for our journey & set out from Albany Aug 29, & thro ye Good hand of God upon us Got safely to my house on ye 2ⁿᵈ Tuesday of Sepᵗ: at n'ᵗ [night] & (ye whole place Seemed to be greatly moved at our coming) Yt Evening Capt K (Kellogue) came to us

Sept.

3   Wed this m [morning] my Brother R. W. & Br m[l] went home Capt.
Kellogue' sister came to us and y[e] neighbours came in & shew[d] Great kindness &
Mr Edwards of N. H. came to visitt us

Thurs
4   This m [morning] we gain'd a promise o [from] my Sister & Husband to
tarry with us untill Monday night Capt K left us but his sister tarry[d] B[r] Elijah
W[rinsâ] & Aunt W[rms] of Hatf[d] and Sister Meacham come to us.

Friday
5   Clutter[d] & full of care & company joy & sorrow hope & fear.
This day came Hither cosen Jn[a]th[n] Hunt Mr Estabrook an two of Brother
W[ins] daugters.

Sat 6
This day Aunt Hawley came hither & went along Colen Stoddard, Cozen J. S.
Hunt & Sister Hinsdell. Uncle Park W[inss] and his xdren came hither & I sent to
Capt. Kellogue neighbors & friends show great kindness affection & respect
7 Sabbath   my poor sister Attend[d] y[e] publick worship with us both parts of ye day oh
yt this
might be as a pledge y[t] she may return to the house & ordinances of God o
[from]
wch she has been so long separated In y[e] Evening we (Col. S. assisting †
directing) had a Set discourse with my Sister † her husband and thô we
could not obtain of y[m] to tarry wth us yet [they] have promis'd us y[t] now the
way is open [they] will certainly come & make a visit & spend a winter in y[e]
country among y[r] Friends [they] seem in earnest & say [they] wont be
divert'[d] unless it be something very extraordinary

Sept 8
Monday   Uncle & Aunt Edwards Er W & Br m & many friends & neighbors come to
visit us o[r]
neighbors sent in plentifully to us and come & assist us so y[t] we had Even a
Feast,
o[l'] Sister & Family Din' in ye room wth y[m] Company Sister M & I sat at y[e] table
wth y[m]
At evening o[r] young people sang melodiously y[t] was very Gratefull to my Sister
and
company & I hope we are something endeared to her. She says twill hurt her to
part
wth us.
Tuesday
9   my Sister & company left my house I accompany[d] y[m] beyond Westfield about a

mile &

when I took leave of her (I do think her affections were mov^d) she repeated
her

promise of coming & spending a long time wth us if God spared y^r lives

19   This day my son John return^d from Allbany & gives
            acc$^{.t}$ he got on safely with his company he tells me y^t his Aunt & Husband
            were well pleas'^{d} with their visitt and went away cheerfull"

"1741   July 26.   Sunday I preach'^{d} at Suffield in y^e evening
            came a messenger to me [from] Westfield bringing me an acc^t my Sister was
            come to Westf^d [from] Canada upon it I went to Capt Kellogue and got his son
            to go on to Westfield & I myself lodg^d at ye captains

Monday 27   I return^d home & Find my Sister & her Husband & two xdren here I
am glad

            to see them & pray God to bless them. . . .I am in concern lest
they take y^e

            infection of ye measells.

Tuesday 28 my Sister & Family seem Easy & I rejoice at it   my brother w' ham & his
son went

            over to Capt Kellogue who has sent me an acct what their sentiments
are I hope

            [they] maybe prevail with to come & tarry in ye country

Wed.
29   my sister & company are gone to Coventry ye L^d be pleas'^{d} to go wth y^{ml}

Friday
31   my xdren came home from M & C^a having been wth their Aunt [Eunice]
whom the^y left

            at m I praise God for his smiles respecting this journey

       Ye Sabbath
Aug ı. . . . .
" 2
" 4

13. Last n^t Br W W & cosen W came hither to see Sister E. I am glad to see them ye B
W preached a very agreeable Sermon to us
       14.   This day the^y set away to Coventry .... B^r H &
            E came hither & lodged here
       15.   they went away to Coventry ye L^d be pleas'^{d} to Grant y^l the meeting of so
many Friends

may be for ye benefit of y^{m}selves & of o^r Sister my wife is poorly of it

16.   ye Sabbath

17.   This day my Brethren and Sisters come here [from] Below the Ld Grant o^r being

        together may be comfortable & beneficiall

Tuesday

18.   My Br of m. preached a sermon

Sept 3   This day I went to Westf^{ld} to meet my Sister and Family who are upon y^r Return to

        Canada tis pleasant to See her but Grievous to part with her ye L^d mercifully overrule

        y she may yet Return & dwell wth us Oh God thou hast ye hearts of all in thine hand &

        canst turn y^m as pleaseth thee &c the L^d go wth y^m & preserve y^m & be pleas'^{d} to be wth

        & preserve my Son John who is gone wth them to Albany.

Sat

Sept **5**   Oh God bless my poor Sister Eunice & graciously bring her & hers home to thy Self &

        preserve her on her journey & cause that she may long to return to us again

15   this day John return'^{d} home in safety [from] Albany having had a difficult journey."

The volume of the Diary from October, 1742, to March, 1748, is missing, having been burned with the parsonage in 1846. We have, therefore, no details of the visit said to have been made by Eunice in October, 1743. She arrived again in Longmeadow on June 30, 1761, accompanied by more of

        1761 June 30 This day my Sister Eunice, her Husband her daughter Katharine and others come hither from Canada. Y^e L^d grant it may be in mercy to her y she makes this visit. We have no interpreter and So can't say what her intentions and pretensions are.

July ι   I have been seeking for an interpreter—have sent to Deerfield. Thus I am in concern

        Y^e L^d be pleased to direct and bless me—Grant I may take prudent measures

2   We attended ye meeting before ye Sacrament and after meeting people came in Great numbers to see my Sister I am fearful that it may not be agreeable to be gazed upon I am sending hither and thither to my children & friends, & I pray God to bring them together

that we may have a comfortable & profitable meeting. My cares increase I have an Interpreter come from Sunderland—sent by Sister Williams of Deerfield— but I fear he does not understand ye Language very well—but I hope will be somewhat serviceable
4 Sabbath & Sacrament My Daughters Eunice & Martha are now here with me upon ye joyfull sorrowfull occasion of my poor Sister Eunice who is now with me—also her Husband, Katharine and her Husband and a little son of Mary I beg God to Direct me what to do for my Sister, be pleased to incline & dispose her and her Husband to come into or comply with such
measures as may have a proper tendency to promote her Spiritual & Eternal Good, & that of her family & Offspring . . . .
 6 My children John and his wife, Stephen with our Interpreter Mr Dodge are come hither Our Company & Cares increase. . . . .I had a sad Discourse with my Sister & her Husband and find they are not at all dispos'd to come & settle in ye Country I am at a great loss to know what course to take what measures to go into. . . .
 . . .
 9 Hot, and we are fatigued & full of Company—at night my wife poorly
 1 0 This morning my poor sister and company left us I think I have used ye best arguments I could to persuade her to tarry and to come and dwell with us but at present they have been ineffectual I must leave ye matter wth God—this I desire to do. N. B. Y when I took leave of my Sister and her daughter in the parlour they both shed tears and seemed affected Oh that God w^d touch their hearts and encline them to turn to their Friends, and to embrace ye religion of Jesus Christ."
In Stephen Williams's Diary, there is no record of any visit of Eunice to Deerfield. She came and went by way of Westfield, escorted back and forth from Albany, except on her last visit, by Stephen's son John. Her father died in Deerfield a year before her first visit to New England, and the surviving members of her family lived elsewhere. There was nothing to take her to Deerfield, except a natural desire to see the place of her birth. That she never forgot it is proved by the following:

PREFATORY REMARKS TO A SERMON PREACHED BY REV. JOHN TAYLOR AT THE FIRST CHURCH IN DEERFIELD, AUG. 27, 1837. *ON* **THE OCCASION OF A VISIT TO THAT TOWN BY THE CANADIAN DESCENDANTS OF EUNICE WILLIAMS.**

"On the 22nd. of last month, our village was visited by two or three families of Indians amounting in all to twenty-three of various ages calling themselves by the name of Williams on the ground of being descendants of Eunice The eldest of the party, a woman stating her age to be eighty years claimed to be the grand-daughter of Eunice adding that She perfectly remembered her grandmother. . . . .. During their short stay, a little more than a week, they encamped in the vicinity of the village, employing their time not otherwise occupied, in making baskets. They visited the graves of their ancestors, Rev. Mr Williams and wife, and attended

divine service on Sunday in an orderly and reverent manner. They refused to receive company on the Sabbath, and at all times, and in all respects seemed disposed to conduct themselves decently and inoffensively. During their Stay with us,. . . . . .. their encampment was frequented by great numbers of persons, almost denying them time to take their ordinary meals, but affording them as if to make amends for such inconvenience and privation, a ready sale for their fabrics. On the first of September they decamped and commenced their homeward progress towards Canada."

The visit of these Indians to Deerfield, seems to corroborate the Longmeadow evidence of Eunice's love for New England. The possibility that the old squaw was a granddaughter of Eunice is refuted, however, by what we now know of her posterity, Thomas Tehorakwaneken being her only grandchild. This old woman may have been one of Catharine's adopted daughters,—or one of the children of Louis Satagaienton, the husband of Eunice's daughter Mary, —by his second marriage.

D.ENSIGN JOHN SHELDON.

On his return from captivity, Rev. John Williams did not go back immediately to Deerfield, being naturally doubtful whether to settle there again. By the advice of the Elders in Boston, he yielded at last to Mr. Sheldon's entreaties in behalf of the Deerfield people and decided to cast in his lot with them. While in Boston he was the recipient of much kind attention.

His eldest son Eleazer, being away at school, had escaped the calamity at Deerfield and "by the help of divers charitable people especially in Boston," entered Harvard College in 1705, and was a Freshman there at the time of his father's return; and "living in the chamber over me," says Thomas Prince, then a Sophomore, "I fell into an intimate acquaintance with him." Just a week after his arrival, Mr. Williams delivered the Thursday lecture in Boston, and the two lads walked in from Cambridge together by way of Brighton, seven miles, if we may credit the ancient milestone still standing in Cambridge, to hear the lecture: "I, with many others went down," says Prince, "and in an auditory exceedingly crowded and affected, I heard the sermon."

On the 7th Samuel Sewall "invited the Governor to dine at Holmes's"; Mr. Williams and Mr. Sheldon were among the guests. Mr. Williams's sermon and the Deerfield captivities made a profound impression on Thomas Prince. In 1757 he writes:

"From the instance of this one town only, we may learn what number of the present people in Canada are the children of this province, or descended from them—which in case the sovereign GOD should ever lead a victorious army of ours into Canada, will clearly justify us to the world, if we should bring every child and descendant of New England, yea, of all the British Colonies, away."

E.MY HUNT FOR THE CAPTIVES.

Among other very rare books in the library of the "Pocumtuck Valley Memorial Association," at Deerfield, (a monument to the devotion and labor of the Hon. George Sheldon,) is one entitled in part, "Good Fetched out of Evil, in three Short Essays."

No perfect copy of this book is known; that at Deerfield is perhaps the most perfect. With other treasures, it contains the following poem written by Mary French, daughter of Dea. Thomas French :

"The Singular Circumstances of the little *Authoress,* will make Atonement for it, if we now add a Poem, Written by a Captive Damsel, about Sixteen or Seventeen years of Age; who being afraid that her Younger Sister, at a Distance from her would be led away by the Popish Delusions, addressed her in these Lines: "

> Dear Sister, JESUS does you call
> To Walk on in His Ways.
> I pray, make no Delay at all,
>   Now in your Youthful Dayes.
>
> O Turn to Him, who has you made,
> While in your Tender years:
> For as the Withering Grass we fade,
>   which never more appears.
>
> But if that God should you afford
> a longer Life to Live,
> Remember that unto the Lord
>   the Praises you do give.
>
> We still are called to Begin
> while we are in our *Youth.*
> For to depart from ways of Sin,
>   and Serve the Lord in Truth.
>
> Tis not *To Morrow,* Christ doth Say
> that we shall Mercy find;
> Oh, then while it is call'd, To Day,
>   your Great Creator Mind.

We are not certain in this World
We have an Hour to Spend;
But suddenly we may be hurl'd
where time shall have an End.

How soon may this sad News be told,
we no Assurance have;
In Winding Sheets our Corpse be roll'd
and we laid in the Grave.

But still our Souls must Live for aye
in Endless Bliss or Wo,
If Unprepared at the Day,

we down to Hell do go.

The Officer, as Christ hath said,
Shall us in Prison bind,
Until the last Farthing be paid,
we there must be Confin'd.

Since we so oft of this do hear,
Our Teachers have us told,
We shall without excuse appear.
If we to Sin are bold.

To dare the pow'r of Hell and Death!
yea, and of God most High! Oh!
Let us, while we have our Breath
Prostrate before Him ly.

And let us Wisdom now desire
before our glass is run;
For Understanding Let's Enquire
while Shining is our Sun.

All Wisdoms ways are Pleasantness.
and all its Pathes are Peace.
Those that Gods Throne aright address.
their Joy shall never Cease.

Set not your Heart on fading Toyes,

but still Gods Grace implore;
At His Right Hand are Endless Joyes
and Pleasure's ever more.

That Earthly Things are fading flow'rs
We by Experience see;
And of our Years and Days and Hours
we as uncertain be.

Of all Degrees, and Every Age,
among the Dead we find;
Many there fell by bloody rage,
When we were left behind.

Let us be Silent then this day
under our Smarting Rod.
Let us with Patience Meekly say,
It is the Will of God.

Of Friends and Parents, wee're bereav'd,
Distress't, and Left alone;
Lord, We thy Spirit oft have griev'd;
  And now as Doves we moan.

For any Worthiness of ours
No mercy ask we can;
But still God hath laid Helps and Pow'rs
  upon the Son of Man.

Now when the *Sabbath* doth begin
with sorrow we do say,
Oh! That we were God's House within,
  To Keep His Holy Day!

For God hath in His Anger hot
Out of His Sanctuary
Us banished far, that we hear not
  its Pleasant Melody.

The Temple Songs from us are gone,
to Sighs they turned be;
Ensnar'd we are, and there is none
  on Earth to set us free.

It is the mighty Hand of God
from which no man can fly.
Wee're under both His grievous Rod
  and His all-seeing Eye.

Dear Sister, for your sake now I
these Verses Written have.
Bear them upon your Memory,
  as going to the Grave.

Dear Sister, Bear me in your Mind;
Learn these few Lines by heart;
Alas, an aking Heart I find,
  Since we're so long to part.

But to the Care of God on high
Our cause we will commend,
For your Soul-sake these Lines now I
  Your Loving Sister send.

MARY FRENCH.

December 23, 1703. [5 ?]

F.

THANKFUL STEBBINS.

This copy of the baptismal record of Thankful Stebbins is given as a good example of the old-time records in Canadian parishes:

"Ce 23 dauvrile de lannee 1707 ie certifie f pierre dublaron faisans les fonctions dedans la paroiffe de chambly avoire fupplees aux cérémonie du facremens de baptefme a louife thereffe ftebene angloiffe de nation et baptisée en Angleterre, fon parrain et fa marine ont efté mre hertelle de chambly et mâde de perygny commandante du fort de chambly en foy de quoy jay figner"

Made in the USA
Lexington, KY
13 August 2016